Bodies of Evidence

Bodies of Evidence

Women, Society, and Detective Fiction in 1990s Japan

Amanda C. Seaman

University of Hawai'i Press
Honolulu

Library of Congress Cataloging-in-Publication Data

Seaman, Amanda C.

Bodies of evidence : women, society, and detective fiction in 1990s
Japan / Amanda C. Seaman.

p. cm.

Includes bibliographical references and index.

ISBN 0-8248-2736-8 (hardcover : alk. paper)—ISBN 0-8248-2806-2
(pbk. : alk. paper)

1. Detective and mystery stories, Japanese—History and criticism.
2. Japanese fiction—Women authors—History and criticism.
I. Title.

PL740.65.D45S43 2004

895.6'30872099287—dc22

2003022767

University of Hawai'i Press books are printed on
acid-free paper and meet the guidelines for permanence
and durability of the Council on Library Resources.

Designed by Janette Thompson, Jansom

Printed by The Maple-Vail Book Manufacturing Group

The commissaris picked up the paperback. "Translated. It's good. The Mexican background makes it even more interesting. Well written too. Would you like to read it in Spanish? Ignacio says there is a Spanish bookstore here. Maybe he can get you a copy."

De Gier sounded tired. "I don't read mysteries."

"Snob." The commissaris raised a correcting finger. "You're missing out on exercises in morality, the tension between libido and superego, the search for essential values—if any, of course—comparisons in relativity, the different, often conflicting, mores of sociologically separated groups, psychological insights, animal studies and tribal customs, the concept of the police as a uniformed mafia, the use of magic in crime."

—Janwillem van de Wetering, *The Hollow-Eyed Angel*

Contents

Acknowledgments

This book, which began life as a dissertation at the University of Chicago, has been fostered by the contributions and interest of many people. Norma Field, who first introduced me to the world of Japanese women's detective fiction when she gave me a copy of *Kasha,* encouraged my work on an emphatically nontraditional topic throughout my graduate career and after, while Bill Sibley has been an invaluable resource both personally and academically. My research and writing would not have been possible without financial support in the form of a Monbusho Scholarship from the Japanese Ministry of Education, a dissertation fellowship from the University of Chicago Center for East Asian Studies, and a Walter Craigie Research Fellowship from Randolph-Macon College. In Tokyo, I have benefited from the aid, generosity, and friendship of many—in particular, Professor Igarashi Akio of Rikkyo University, my mentor and sponsor; Narita Akemi; Professor Tachi Kaoru of Ochanomizu Women's University; Kim Soon Ah; Sato Shinichiro and Kobayashi Kazuko of Shinchosha, who provided invaluable insights into the Japanese literary market and the world of Japanese publishing; and Miyabe Miyuki and Matsuo Yumi, who made time in their busy schedules to discuss their work with me. At the University of Hawai'i Press, I would like to thank Pamela Kelley, who has enthusiastically supported this project from the beginning, Jennifer Harada, and Bojana Ristich for her meticulous editing.

Closer to home, I am grateful to the many colleagues who have supported me intellectually as well as emotionally, including (but not limited to) Sarah Frederick, Laura Holliday, Miho Matsugu, Eileen Mikals-Adachi, Katherine Sharnoff, Melissa Wender, Tom Porter, and especially Rebecca Copeland, who has been a generous, enthusiastic, and constructive advocate for this book and for the study of Japanese women's detective fiction more generally. Finally, I would like to thank Sean Gilsdorf, my husband, whose editing and comments made this book better and whose boundless love has sustained me throughout, and my son Benjamin, who knows the value of a good hug.

CHAPTER 1

Introduction

In 1992, Miyabe Miyuki's *Kasha* (Cart of fire, translated into English as *All She Was Worth*) was the most anticipated novel of the season. This prizewinning detective novel solidified Miyabe's reputation as one of Japan's top mystery writers, made it to the top of almost every "best mystery" list, and was even lauded as one of the "best novels of postwar Japan" by an eminent social critic.[1] *Kasha* was more than just a good story about a missing woman and her mysterious identity; it was an examination of pressing social issues gripping Japan: personal bankruptcy, the deleterious effects of rampant consumerism, and the crises arising from the largely unregulated and highly speculative consumer credit industry, which had helped to finance the go-go economy known popularly as "the bubble." In addition to its role as a social barometer, *Kasha* also represented a watershed moment in the history of Japanese women's detective (or *misuterii*) fiction, providing the impetus for a new wave of women mystery writers in the 1990s that dwarfed the earlier, limited female presence in the field. Inspired by both Miyabe's success and the increasing number of Western mysteries in translation, women began writing mysteries of all types, leading to the appearance (in 1997) of a two-volume anthology of short stories by women writers, *Aka no misuterii* (Red mystery) and *Shiro no misuterii* (White mystery), which made it very clear that women's detective fiction was more than a simple fad.[2]

The "boom" in women mystery writers has echoed far longer than many anticipated, owing not simply to the entertainment provided by female authors or to the savvy of their publishers, but also to the way in which these authors have used the narrative and conceptual resources of the detective genre to depict and critique contemporary Japanese society, especially the situation of women within it—a combination of storytelling and social awareness found not only in *Kasha,* but in many other works as well. In the following chapters, therefore, I focus upon the way in which five contemporary writers—Miyabe Miyuki, Nonami Asa, Shibata Yoshiki, Kirino Natsuo, and Matsuo Yumi—critically engage with a variety of social issues and con-

1

cerns: consumerism and the crisis of identity, discrimination and workplace harassment, sexual harassment and sexual violence, and the role of motherhood in contemporary Japan. In turn, I interrogate the structures and conventions of detective fiction that allow these writers to produce a different kind of social critique from that found in other forms of literature. Detective fiction is well suited to this type of critique since the genre has long provided a forum for reflection on and critique of modern urban life. Such a sociocultural analysis of women's detective fiction, I argue, provides us with a wealth of information about the "real world" of contemporary Japan, not in some essential or objective sense, but rather by revealing how a Japanese author imagines her own society to be—particular the kinds of problems besetting that society. This study thus explores the worlds that these authors construct in their novels and examines how these worlds intersect with other political, cultural, and economic discourses and with the lived experiences of contemporary Japanese women.

Japanese Detective Fiction: A Brief History

Detective fiction has a long and somewhat complicated history in Japan. Like many other Western imports, it has been both celebrated and dismissed on account of its foreign pedigree. Yet as with other "modern" literary genres in Japan (most notably the *shōsetsu*, or novel), the success of detective fiction was part of the broader social and cultural changes brought about by the Meiji Restoration. Detective fiction and its protagonist presented a new type of literature, stories (as Edgar Allen Poe called them) of "ratiocination," in which the detective works alone in the familiar world of city streets and alleyways, investigating disorder (crime) and restoring affairs to their "proper" disposition. Detective fiction thus was intimately bound up with the new social phenomena of urbanization and modernization, with their uncomfortable juxtapositions of old and new, urban and rural, wealth and poverty, and community and isolation. As critics have long noted, detective fiction in Europe and America was intimately linked to the urban environment and reflected both the terrors and the pleasures offered by newly industrialized cities like New York or Paris.[3] As an urban genre, therefore, detective fiction had a special appeal in the Meiji (1868–1912) and Taisho (1912–1926) eras in Tokyo, which was witnessing unprecedented changes not only in its economy, but in the details of everyday life as well.

At another level, detective fiction's success in Japan can be seen as part of the more general influx of Western ideas and texts in the late nineteenth and early twentieth centuries.[4] The individual most commonly accepted as the first Japanese detective writer, journalist Kuroiwa Ruikō (1862–1913), was part of the burgeoning literary market of the late Meiji era (ca. 1905–1912), one marked by growing numbers of newspapers, newspaper readers, and authors eager to provide a largely urban audience with a wide range of literature, including translations and adaptations of Western works (some of them bordering on plagiarism), as well as original stories and essays.[5] While in the beginning Ruikō simply translated foreign detective fiction, he often found that he had to adapt stories such as Émile Gaboriau's *L'Affaire Lerouge* for his Japanese audience, reworking the plot and changing the names and places to ones with which his readers would be familiar.[6] In the course of adapting and changing mysteries written by others, Ruikō began to create his own, producing a substantial oeuvre in addition to his better-known translations. His *"Muzan"* (In cold blood) is the earliest example of a Japanese mystery story, written in the form of a classic whodunit.[7]

Ruikō and the others who followed him at the end of the Meiji and the beginning of the Taisho eras concentrated on following the tenets of detective fiction established by Western authors like Edgar Allan Poe, Arthur Conan Doyle, Anna Katharine Green, and Austin Freeman.[8] These writers of classical Anglo-American detective fiction emphasized puzzles that could only be solved rationally and logically (e.g., the "locked room") and rules of fair play. The more clever and diabolically twisted these *torikku* (tricks) were, the more highly regarded the work. Indeed, the cultural critic Hirabayashi Hatsunosuke argued that detective fiction could exist only in a culture capable of logical thought:

> In order for detective fiction to develop, it is necessary to have a settled society. Without a settled social environment, there can be no detective fiction. In a broader sense, these social circumstances point to the development of scientific enlightenment, of the intellect, and of the analytic and logical mind. Specifically, when the criminal and the investigative method become scientific, the investigation of the crime and the subsequent trial are founded on valid physical evidence, and conviction is based upon written laws, this demonstrates the maintenance of national order.[9]

Hirabayashi's insistence upon modern scientific rationality as a prerequisite for detective fiction echoes the views of Western critics and writers and points to the deep way in which Japanese detective fiction was (from its earliest days) implicated in wider processes of cultural assimilation and modernization. As Karatani Kōjin and others have shown, however, these processes were far more complex than simple narratives of "modernization" or "Westernization" would suggest.[10] Part of detective fiction's success was also due to its resonance with earlier texts and traditions, such as Kuei Wan-Jung's *Tang yin bi shi* (known in Japanese as the *Tōinhiji*), a Chinese collection of criminal cases originally meant as a training manual for legal officials.[11]

Likewise, while Ruikō began his career translating Western mystery stories, other authors drew upon the elements of mystery, horror, and suspense found in Ueda Akinari's (1734–1809) famous collection of ghost stories, *Ugetsu monogatari*, and combined them with insights gleaned from more modern psychological research on obsession, fetishism, and sadomasochism.[12] Tanizaki Junichiro, who became famous later in life for his more "literary" treatments of these topics, began his career writing short stories like "Himitsu" (The secret, 1911) and "Yanagi-yu no jiken" (The incident at the Willow Bathhouse, 1918), which combine mystery, exoticism, and a heavy dose of eroticism.[13] These qualities of Tanizaki's work, as well as his creative use of writers like Baudelaire, Conan Doyle, and Poe, would have a profound impact not only on the noted mystery writer Yokomizo Seishi, but also on the most famous Japanese author of detective fiction—Edogawa Rampo.

Edogawa Rampo was the pen name of Hirai Taro (1894–1965), who was to change both the artistic conception of detective fiction in Japan and the manner in which it was produced.[14] Rampo is the defining figure of Japanese detective fiction because of his unique ability to combine the suspense story tradition of the Edo period with the scientific methods and logical devices of the Western detective story. This stylistic and technical blending of old and new, Japan and the West, was mirrored in the way that Rampo depicted the changing face of Tokyo in his stories, encouraging his readers to recognize the familiar traces of premodern Edo as well as the innovations and novelties introduced by modern technology and social reform. Many of Rampo's works feature themes that revolve around voyeurism, false or multiple identities, dismemberment, sadomasochism, doll-like people, and human-seeming dolls.[15] Yet in other works he is a sharp critic of the inevitable changes brought on by the modernizing city.

After graduating from Waseda University, Rampo bounced from job to job (including working for a trading company and selling soba noodles from a pushcart) before launching his literary career in 1923 with the publication of "Ni-sen dōka" (The two-sen copper coin).[16] This short story, which incorporates tricks about cryptography in its plot, won a prize offered by the youth-oriented journal *Shinseinen* (New youth), which went on to publish many of Rampo's stories in the ensuing years. Before 1920, most mysteries were published either serially in mainstream magazines or newspapers or as stand-alone novels. With the introduction of a magazine devoted to literature aimed at a young, primarily male audience, however, the mystery field enjoyed rapid growth—a surge in popularity that made Rampo's career possible. *Shinseinen* capitalized on the growing middle-class reading public, who had both leisure time to read and the money to buy books and magazines.

While there had been other magazines devoted to detective fiction, they were short-lived, and it was only with the appearance of *Shinseinen* that a forum was created for both Western translations and original detective stories.[17] Most of Japan's early detective fiction authors got their start by publishing in *Shinseinen* because of the increasing demand for new material. *Shinseinen* thus was responsible for popularizing and exploiting the mass market appeal for detective and adventure fiction by creating an audience who would continue to consume it.[18]

As a popular genre, moreover, detective fiction provided an outlet for aspiring women writers. Hiratsuka Raichō (1896–1971), who was best known for her editorship of the early feminist journal *Seitō* (Bluestocking), was one of the first to translate Edgar Allen Poe's "The Man in the Crowd."[19] Likewise, Hirabayashi Taiko (1905–1972), a left-wing author, wrote detective fiction not only for pleasure, but also for money. Her stories, "Supai jiken" (The spy incident) and "Irezumi jiken no shinsō" (The truth about the tattoo affair), were standard, puzzle-oriented detective fiction,[20] but the money that she earned allowed her to continue with her other writing.[21] Moreover, while some authors, such as Ogura Teruko and Ichijō Eiko, published their detective fiction in the pages of *Shinseinen*,[22] many others contributed to a series of spinoff magazines dedicated to female readers and featuring true-life accounts of women detectives, as well as mystery stories targeted at girls. In particular, the women's magazine *Shufu no tomo* (The housewife's friend) published serialized mysteries and mystery reviews.[23] These mysteries were different from those appearing in *Shinseinen* in that they often featured romantic themes or domestic entanglements.

Likewise, women's magazines such as *Fujin* (Lady), as well as *Shufu no tomo*, published true-life accounts of women who had taken jobs as detectives, and these contained an element of social criticism as well.[24] In the April 1924 issue of *Shufu no tomo*, under the heading "Shukugyō fujin no yorokobi wa nani ka?" (What makes career women happy?), was a story by Sugiyama Tamae. Supposedly the tale of a young woman's rise from foundling origins to a career as a detective, Sugiyama's account is quite critical of the social mores of her heroine's employers as the young woman is sent undercover in a wealthy household and comments upon the social classes and their foibles in Osaka at the end of the Taisho period.[25]

The growth of detective fiction, whether written by women or men, was abruptly halted during the Pacific War. In 1941, detective fiction of Anglo-American origin was banned in Japan, and writers of detective fiction turned their attention to either adventure fiction or spy fiction.[26] Even this outlet was curtailed, however, as a chronic shortage of paper effectively put an end to much of the publication of mass entertainment magazines. By the end of the war, *Shinseinen* was on its last legs and ceased publishing in 1950. In its place arose a new magazine—*Hōseki* (The jewel)—that took over as the main forum for detective fiction in Japan. More important for the renewed success of Japanese detective fiction were the efforts of Edogawa Rampo, who now turned much of his attention from the production of detective fiction to its promotion in Japan and overseas, as well as to numerous critical essays on the history and development of detective fiction in Japan and the West. In 1955, the Edogawa Prize was created through the joint efforts of Rampo and the Kodansha publishing company, which in subsequent decades became one of Japan's biggest publishers of mysteries, both foreign and domestic. Finally, the publication in 1956 of a collection of Edogawa Rampo's stories in English, as well as an issue of the *Ellery Queen Mystery Magazine* dedicated to his work, firmly established his reputation worldwide as the progenitor of detective fiction in Japan.[27]

Postwar Detective Fiction and the Place of Social Critique

Despite Rampo's stature, it is the work of another writer that has had the greatest influence upon the women writers of the late twentieth century: Matsumoto Seichō (1909–1992). Matsumoto, while perhaps most famous for his detective fiction, was also a cultural critic and activist. Born to a poor family in Fukuoka, he never completed high school and had to support himself with a variety of different jobs, beginning his writing career by producing advertising copy for the *Asahi shinbun*. Matsumoto's early literary works were not popular fiction but rather more serious "pure" literature, and in 1953 he received the Akutagawa Prize for best work of serious fiction for his novel *Aru Kokura nikki den* (One account of the Kokura diary), which told the story of author Mori Ogai's missing diary.[28] Not long after, Matsumoto switched to detective fiction, winning the Association of Mystery Writers Prize for "Kao" (The face), the story of a man who murders his mistress and whose guilt drives him to reveal his crime.[29] After his successful debut, Matsumoto continued to publish a series of detective novels, almost every one of them a best-seller. In fact, Matsumoto's popularity started a previously unheard-of boom in sales of detective fiction in Japan, to the point that critics of the genre refer to the "pre-" and "post-Matsumoto" eras.[30] When he was not writing detective fiction, Matsumoto was a social critic, writing extensively about true-life crime and other political and historical events, such as the impact of the American occupation on Japan.[31]

Matsumoto's socially conscious writing was notable for the way in which it deliberately exploited the historical and political possibilities of detective fiction. With its emphasis on the minutiae of daily life (clues from which the detective derives his solution) and its attention to "real-life" social problems (corruption, sexual scandals, financial misdeeds, etc.), detective fiction has reflected more immediately than other literary genres the fears and fantasies of the modern, urban bourgeoisie. Furthermore, as John Cawelti has argued, while detective fiction is often dismissed from critical study because of its formulaic nature, it is that very feature that makes it such a good vehicle for the expression of cultural complexities in an accessible format. In contrast to mimetic literature, which shows the reader the world as she knows it, formulaic literature allows for a balance between reality and the characteristics of an escapist imaginative experience. Thus, the reader can consider new and existing social issues in a safe and carefully controlled forum and resolve any tensions and ambiguities arising from them in a non-threatening manner.[32] For Cawelti, genre novels provide a "controlled space" that allows for the exploration of alternative perceptions and constructions, a space in which cultural fears and public concerns can be investigated by a wide readership. This suggests, according to Priscilla Walton, that "formula narratives have the ability to assist in the process of shifting ideological norms on a broad scale."[33] Ultimately, then, "formulaic evolution and change are one process by which new interests and values can be assimilated into conventional patterns of imaginative expression."[34]

Thus, detective fiction serves a dual role: first, it allows for interpretations in the text of certain issues, and second, it presents those issues to a larger audience, providing a forum to consider possibly alternative viewpoints. As Margaret Crawford has noted, this can be seen most distinctly in the way in which detective fiction represents urban life and urban problems, providing a discourse about the city that parallels but exists apart from that generated by academic urban studies. Due to its "historical link[s] with both urban reality and urban imagination," therefore, detective fiction's "continuing evolution . . . offers rich possibilities for rethinking the connections between subjectivity, interpretation, and urban space."[35]

This social, interpretive aspect of detective fiction is evident in the work of Edogawa Rampo. As Matsuyama Iwao has shown, Rampo's sensory evocation of the city in his stories revealed the depth to which everyday life was changing as a result of the rapid social and technological transformation of Tokyo in the 1920s. Rampo's 1926 story, "Yaneura no sanposha," commonly translated as "The Stroller in the Attic," relates the murder of an apartment dweller by his neighbor, who is driven to the crime by the former's loud snoring seeping through the paper-thin walls.[36] Such seemingly small details do not simply illustrate changes in living circumstances resulting from rapid urbanization; they also anticipate the sympathy (or at least comprehension) of readers who themselves had experienced a loss of privacy or felt trapped by the close proximity of strangers around them.

Rampo's willingness at times to directly address socially controversial issues likewise revealed his ability to move beyond the tricks of the trade current at the time, and it drew the attention of increasingly active government censors in the early Showa era (1926–1989). Thus his 1929 story, "Imomushi" (The caterpillar), which described a grievously wounded soldier's homecoming, was refused by the journal *Kaizō* because of its antiwar message. Although the story was later published in *Shinseinen* in heavily censored form, it was not allowed to be reprinted until after the war.[37] More generally, Rampo's fascination with deviance and the margins of society took on political overtones as the military government of the 1930s and 1940s took an increasingly dim view not simply of "foreign" literature, but also of what it perceived to be threats to Japanese stability and values.

Despite these early efforts, however, Rampo's detective fiction tended in the main to adhere to the conventions of what Japanese critics call *"honkaku-ha,"* or standard, detective fiction, albeit with a greater emphasis upon the exotic and the erotic.[38] Indeed, after the war Rampo disavowed any political goals in "Imomushi," arguing that he had been interested in the more universal aspects of the soldier's situation rather than in criticizing war or the government.[39] While this may reflect Rampo's own political retrenchment during the war years, it also points to the intrinsically ambivalent nature of detective fiction as a forum for social observation.[40] Despite changes in the genre—such as the development of the hard-boiled detective novel, which brought with it a shift from the deductive reasoning favored by earlier writers to the inductive-style logic characteristic of the post–World War II period—many of the basic components of detective fiction have remained largely unchanged.[41]

These components, in turn, are at their root conservative. Part of this conservatism is due to the very structure of the detective novel's plot, which moves inexorably from stasis to disruption to settlement in an attempt to impose order on the chaos of the city and its inhabitants. More important, within the context of the narrative, no matter what problems come to light (such as bankruptcy, incest, or fraud), they can be resolved only within the parameters of the preexisting social structure. Indeed, according to Franco Moretti, the detective novel is antinovelistic because "the aim of the narration is no longer the character's development into autonomy, or a change from the initial situation, or the presentation of plot as a conflict and an evolutionary spiral, [an] image of a developing world that is difficult to draw to a close." Instead, "the individual initiates the narration not because he lives—but because he dies."[42] Social inequities, the plights of individuals, or personal rationales for wrongdoing thus are eclipsed by the restoration of law and order. This characteristic is enhanced by the figure of the detective himself, a voyeuristic figure for whom seeing is often the same as doing. In the hard-boiled tradition in particular, it is the detective's ability to stay *un*committed and *un*involved, his ironic detachment, that allows him to do his (and by extension society's) job correctly.[43] Thus, while the detective novel may reflect the anxieties of society, it is also a site where the appeasement of those fears is structurally inscribed.[44] The problems that the detective novel features are resolved by the end of the text, with the guilty punished and justice prevailing.

While part of this tradition in a number of ways, Matsumoto Seichō nevertheless strove to take a more active position on the problems facing postwar Japanese society. His reinterpretation of the meaning and function of detective fiction led to the development of an entirely new subgenre, called *"shakai-ha"* (the social school) by publishers and critics. Unlike the dominant subgenre of *honkaku-ha*, which is characterized by entertaining puzzles and plot twists, *shakai-ha* is intensely realistic in its approach, with extensive attention to the characters' psychological motives and to social problems. Matsumoto's best-known detective fiction was set in the high-growth era of the late 1950s and 1960s, as Japan transformed itself after the devastation and privations of war. As was the case with Rampo, Matsumoto's works reveal the changes taking place in everyday life and how these changes—increased corporate corruption, urban sprawl, and alienation, to name a few—affect the characters in the novels. In contrast to traditional detective fiction, however, in which social problems are presented as either insoluble "facts of life" or details necessary for the creation of a "reality effect," Matsumoto brought social change and injustice into focus as intrinsic elements of the plot, causes for crime rather than simply its context.

Rather than relying on plot twists to propel the story forward, Matsumoto focuses on describing the motives of the characters and how the ordinary person can be driven to commit crimes normally outside his or her ken. In his best-known work, *Ten to sen* (Points and lines, 1958), he constructs a plot that centers on murders committed in order to cover up collusion between a high-level government official and a businessman.[45] Matsumoto's novel thus draws the reader's attention to the darker side of Japan's much lauded high economic growth, pointing out its personal, social, and environmental costs in a way that anticipated investigative journalism on similar themes in the 1960s.[46] The crimes Matsumoto describes, moreover, are not only the result of individual perpetrators, but also of the flawed or inequitable social structures to which those individuals belong.

Despite Matsumoto's success and popularity, the *shakai-ha* fiction that he pioneered has had relatively few adherents. Most contemporary detective fiction writers, while paying homage to Matsumoto, consider themselves to fall within the *honkaku* tradition. Much of this is due to the overtly political nature of Matsumoto's writings, and its left-leaning politics. While Rampo wished to remain outwardly apolitical, Matsumoto's political views colored both his fiction and its critical reception.[47] Coming of age at a time of great labor unrest, Matsumoto belonged to a proletarian reading group at the Yawata Steel Mill and was a reader of both *Bungei sensen* and *Senki,* the two prewar proletarian journals. Although Matsumoto did not identify himself as a proletarian writer and insisted that his works simply revealed his concern for the everyday citizen, his political background, as well as the explicitly critical stance of his detective fiction, has led critics to consider his works as more than merely entertainment literature, a judgment that carries both positive and negative connotations.

The ambivalent status of Matsumoto's work, in fact, called into question the place of detective fiction within the Japanese literary hierarchy, which has continued to be dominated by the distinction between *"junbungaku"* and *"taishūbungaku"* (pure and mass or popular literature).[48] While literary critics tend to agree upon the superiority of *junbungaku,* they are far less clear about what it actually constitutes.[49] Until Matsumoto, however, detective fiction's place within the dominant binary was clear. As a formulaic genre—particularly one that had been imported from the West—and as a form of literature that appealed to large numbers of readers, it was quite clearly *taishūbungaku.*

In 1961, this categorization was challenged in essays by two leading literary critics, Hirano Ken and Itō Sei. Hirano's essay, which came in the middle of a long serial discussion of the status of *junbungaku,* dealt with the origins of *junbungaku* and its relationship to proletarian literature. While Hirano dismissed attempts to recategorize detective fiction, he did concede that *junbungaku* and proletarian literature shared the same origins.[50] Itō replied that the realism identified by so many critics as a benchmark of *junbungaku* was equally present in Matsumoto's work.[51] In a subsequent essay, moreover, Itō argued that particular works of detective fiction shared some of the qualities of "pure" literature, notably those by Minakami Tsutomu, whose first-person narrative struck him as similar to that employed by the *watakushi shosetsu* ("I" novel). In turn, he noted that Matsumoto's fiction, like that of the proletarian writers, "successfully describes the incomplete capitalist society of the Showa era."[52] Itō went on to suggest that detective fiction, particularly that narrated in the first person or treating social issues, should be considered as "in-between literature" *(chūsetsu bungaku)*[53]—not quite pure literature but sharing some of the same ideals. Itō called detective fiction "social novels" and suggested that other examples of genre fiction should not be lumped together because they treated problems in different ways.[54] Because of Matsumoto's focus upon politics, moreover, Itō concluded that his works could be considered as *junbungaku.*[55]

To be sure, Hirano and Itō's inclusion of detective fiction within their discussions of *junbungaku* and *taishūbungaku* had little lasting effect upon detective fiction's status within the *bundan*, the Japanese literary community.[56] Their explicit focus upon Matsumoto's link to the proletarian movement and the political content of his writing meant that the decline of *shakai-ha* fiction of political activism in the mid-1960s removed the only "authorized" form of detective fiction from view. At the same time, their debate underscored the particular strengths of detective fiction as a potentially critical yet entertaining genre. Unlike proletarian literature, which "spreads a political ideology running counter to the hegemony of the capitalistic, monarchic ideology already in place," detective fiction amuses at the same time as it edifies (albeit in a far less didactic manner).[57] In turn, Hirano's reflections on the nature of "pure" literature—and in particular its "anxiety to portray the world realistically . . . yet maintain a detached attitude toward common society"[58]—revealed the degree to which *taishūbungaku*, and particularly detective fiction of a more "standard" cast, could fulfill many of the same functions.

Women's Detective Fiction: The "Boom"

It is no accident that Hirano's investigations into the nature of *junbungaku* came in the early 1960s, amid an onslaught of American television and other products. As Matthew Strecher has pointed out, attempts to redefine *junbungaku* have coincided with periods in which Japan was most open to outside influences—notably in the 1920s and 1930s and again in the late 1950s and early 1960s, but also in the late 1980s and 1990s.[59] In each instance, the Japanese literary guild feels threatened by the encroachments of popular literature and thus attempts to protect itself by reasserting the boundaries between the "pure" and the "popular." This sense of crisis has been exacerbated in recent years not only by the proliferation of mass artistic media, but also by a general feeling that *junbungaku* is out of touch with the reading public. Indeed, despite the recent burst of writers from the periphery of Japanese society receiving the Akutagawa Prize (such as Zainichi [Koreans resident in Japan] or Okinawans), there generally has not been much interest in these authors or their stories. This attitude can be seen both in the mainstream press and among figures in the literary establishment. Novelist and Nobel laureate Oe Kenzaburo has complained that *junbungaku* is now either so ephemeral or so universal in its concerns that it no longer tries to reflect what is happening in Japan itself,[60] while an article in the mass market magazine *Aera* declares that Japanese literary traditions have become stagnant, preventing "serious" authors from responding creatively to a rapidly changing society.[61]

This situation of literary ferment and crisis, however, has also opened the door to new authors and new approaches. In particular, Sato Shinichiro, an editor at the major publishing house Shinchosha, has suggested that genre literature, particularly that written by women, is filling the void left by the lack of interesting examples of *junbungaku*.[62] Leading this trend has been a new breed of young female detective writers, whose works combine not only the *honkaku-ha* and *shakai-ha* traditions of detective fiction, but also other literary genres as part of a new sensibility about, and new sensitivity to, women's roles within contemporary Japanese society.[63]

The genre in which these women work has been described by Kasai Kiyoshi as *shinhonkaku-ha,* a hybrid form that blends the entertaining plot twists and narrative devices of traditional Japanese detective fiction with the social critique characteristic of Matsumoto and the *shakai-ha* tradition.[64] This cross-fertilization represents a response to the women's detective fiction that developed in the postwar period. Initially, the creation of the magazine *Hōseki* and its increasing demand for detective fiction of all types led to the appearance of a number of female authors, but they received little recognition until 1957, when Niki Etsuko received the prestigious Edogawa Prize for her novel *Neko ga shitte ita* (The cat knew it).[65] Niki, who was followed as an Edogawa winner by Shijō Ayako in 1959 and Tōgawa Masako in 1962, was notable not only for her commercial success, but also for the social criticism in her works, which led to her recognition alongside Matsumoto as an instrumental figure in the rise of "social" detective fiction.[66] In the mid-1960s, however, the number of women writers declined, as many married or moved on to other genres.[67] The 1970s and 1980s were dominated by two female mystery writers, Natsuki Shizuko and Yamamura Misa, whose popular novels, often featuring young, unmarried heroines who found love at the end of each story, spawned a number of imitators and became representative of women's mystery writing. Rather than the social criticism of *shakai-ha* detective fiction, these women relied on clever plot twists and colorful locales to distinguish their books, a style that quickly became threadbare through overuse and overexposure in the form of film and television adaptations.

The dominance of this brand of detective fiction began to give way in 1987, when the previously unknown Miyabe Miyuki won the Japan Mystery Writers Association Prize for her short story "Warera no rinjin wa hannin (Our neighbor is a criminal)."[68] Miyabe's career signaled the beginning of a "new wave" of women mystery writers that owed its impetus to a variety of factors. The most immediate of these was the phenomenon of writing schools, which arose as a response to the explosion of literary prizes (and cash awards) offered by publishers, individuals, and corporations in the 1980s. Since many of these awards were established in order to recruit new writers and since they recognized short fiction, the prerequisites were far less daunting than for more established awards such as the Akutagawa or Naoki Prizes.[69] The schools that serviced this industry attracted large numbers of women, many of them housewives hoping to begin freelance careers. This was true as well for the writing schools associated with major publishers, which operated as a type of "farm system"; indeed, the school operated by Kodansha counts Miyabe Miyuki as one of its alumnae.[70]

Furthermore, critic Yamamae Yuzuru has suggested that the "bubble" economy of the 1980s, which in many ways benefited male workers far more than their female counterparts, had the opposite effect for women writers of detective fiction. This was so for two reasons. For one thing, female authors had more opportunities to publish their work due to the simple fact that men were fully occupied with the demands of a red-hot economy.[71] For another, the economic boom meant that more women were joining the workforce, leading not only to an increased readership for women's fiction, but also an increasing interest in a genre that (as will be seen in chapter 3) has much to say about the effects of work upon women and their relationships.

Finally, the boom in women's detective fiction was linked to a corresponding boom in the United States and the United Kingdom. From the early 1980s onward, with the work of Marcia Mueller, Sara Paretsky, Liza Cody, and Sue Grafton, who all created independent female private eyes in the hard-boiled tradition, women's detective fiction of all types became extremely popular in the United States. Japanese publishers capitalized on this phenomenon and marketed translations of these authors under the title "4-F" (the protagonist, the author, the translator, and the reader all being females). These translations proved to be exceedingly popular and had at least some influence upon all of the authors discussed in this study. For example, Sengai Akiyuki has suggested that Anglo-American women's detective fiction has compelled Japanese authors to create characters with a strong sense of individuality and a greater interest in taking on personal problems. Of particular interest for Japanese female detectives, says Sengai, are the problems of love and sex and how to resolve them.[72]

Yet while the influence of writers like Paretsky and Patricia Cornwell on Japanese women writers is undeniable, critics also have noted differences between the American and Japanese writers. While some issues (love and work) are discussed in a similar fashion, the emphasis on others, such as identity and community, reflects the particular nature of women's lives in Japan. This adaptability, in fact, indicates one of the strengths of detective (and other genre) fiction, which allows for similarities due to its formulaic plot structure, as well as for heterogeneities because of the need to tell a variety of different stories within the same framework.

Each of these elements—professional, economic, and literary—can be seen in the careers of the women who make up the contemporary "boom" generation. In the pages that follow, I discuss these writers within three distinct "waves." The first is epitomized by Miyabe and Takamura Kaoru, who received extensive attention both because they were women writing in what had been commonly considered a man's genre and because they were amateurs with surprising talent. By the time the second wave of women writers began to be published, the fact that they were women no longer was sufficient to attract interest, allowing them to build their reputation solely on the quality of their work. The third wave of women writers is marked not only by its size, but also by the increasing diversity of literary forms that its members bring to their work.

It is important to note that while detective fiction has always been considered entertainment fiction for the masses, there is elitism even within the genre. The numerous awards for detective fiction in Japan lead to the understanding that evaluative judgments have been institutionalized to determine what is "good." Thus some writers of detective fiction have won prizes and critical acclaim and some have not. The writers I consider here have been consistently rated the best in their field, regardless of their sex, and there are many female detective fiction writers who have not managed to attain a similar level of achievement.

Takamura and Miyabe: The Royalty of Mystery Writing

The first two authors of the Heisei era (1989–) "boom" were Takamura Kaoru and Miyabe Miyuki. Because they were the first two women to achieve financial and critical success with their work, they received the lion's share of media attention. Despite their differences (or perhaps because of them), they were often interviewed together, particularly in the early years of the boom (1992–1994), and their status as unmarried women and former office workers who became writers made them good interview subjects. After 1994, because of the influx of other women writers, Takamura and Miyabe did not receive as much individual attention. By this point, however, both were established writers, and their nonmystery writing was often seen in journals and newspapers.

In the early stages of the boom, it was clearly the gender of the authors, the strength of their personalities, and the quality of their work that piqued the media's curiosity and kept these authors in the spotlight.[73] Takamura, the older writer, became known as the "Queen of Mysteries," with the slightly younger Miyabe her princess.[74] This relationship continued to hold true until Takamura left the field of mystery writing in 1997. A graduate of International Christian University, Takamura (b. 1953) is the most respected among the women writers in the recent boom, but that respect also has served to isolate her from her peers. Certainly she is one of the better educated of the writers in this study (only Shibata, Kirino, and Matsuo completed their university studies) and the most socially active in her critical writings; nevertheless, she is not included in the *White Mystery* anthology and is only briefly mentioned by mystery critics. This isolation is due in part to the subject matter of her novels; despite the genre in which she writes, she aims at making her readers "struggle for their pleasure."[75] Her novels are dense ruminations on financial crime and international espionage that feature flawed and psychologically damaged characters. She also says she does not intend to write a mystery when she writes; rather, she feels that her work is *"futsū no shōsetsu"* (a regular novel).[76]

Takamura's attitude toward her writing also differs from that of other writers because she feels that she has a moral obligation *(gimu)* to her readers to explore deeper philosophical issues within the context of her fiction. Like Matsumoto Seichō, Takamura has taken on contemporary social issues such as nuclear power and terrorism in her novels, themes that reappear in her newspaper and magazine editorials.[77] This serious outlook is reflected in her personal lifestyle; by all accounts, she leads a workaholic, quasi-monastic existence, eschewing movies and nonnews television programs. More strik-

Miyabe Miyuki (Shinchosha Publishing Company)

ingly, Takamura strives, either consciously or unconsciously, not to be a *joryū* or *josei sakka* (lady novelist). Disavowing any ability to understand women, particularly when it comes to murder, she thinks that men's motives for killing are easier to comprehend and populates her novels with male characters.[78] Recently, Takamura has professed her disaffection with the genre and what she considers to be its limitations, and after the publication of her two-volume fictionalization of the Morinaga-Glico incident of 1984 (*Reidi jokaa* [The lady joker], 1997) she publicly gave up detective fiction in order to concentrate more fully on "serious" literature.[79]

In contrast to Takamura's brooding intellectualism, Miyabe Miyuki (b. 1960) insists on emphasizing the entertaining aspects of her work, despite the often weighty issues she takes on. Her output is prodigious: since the appearance of her first novel, she has published (as of this writing) over thirty full-length novels and collections of short stories and has had several long-running serials in such newspapers as the *Asahi shinbun*. She also has won numerous awards for her work, including the Yamamoto Prize, the Japan Mystery Writers Association Prize, and the Yoshikawa Prize, and in 1998 Miyabe was finally awarded the Naoki Prize, Japan's most prestigious award for popular literature, for her novel *Riyū* (The reason). In addition, while heralded as one of Japan's best mystery writers, Miyabe also has published a number of historical novels *(jidai shōsetsu)* to similar acclaim.

As one of the first women writers of the Japanese mystery boom, Miyabe has received substantial attention from the press—in particular after the publication of *Kasha* in 1992. Initially she was interviewed with and compared to Takamura Kaoru, but Takamura soon separated herself from Miyabe after quitting the mystery writing business. Miyabe has remained in the public eye because she is such a compelling and accessible figure. Her image is always that of a demure young woman, well-dressed and artfully accessorized, and many of her interviews are given in *kenjōgo*, the humble language of polite young women *(ojosama)*. Unlike other literary figures in Japan, Miyabe has not espoused any causes (such as speaking out on terrorism or the plight of the aged), but she occasionally writes essays on her and her family's memories of old Tokyo or the joys of traditional hot springs. These themes of memory and of the *shitamachi*, or working-class area of Tokyo, which has long been home to the city's craftspeople and petty merchants, recur in her fictional works.

In many of Miyabe's earlier interviews (1992–1994), she identifies herself as an "Edokko," a child of the old city of Tokyo, Edo. Her family has lived in Kōtō-ku, in the traditional *shitamachi*, for four generations. After graduating from Sumidagawa High School, she trained as a shorthand typist before working in a law office for several years. She began studying at Kodansha's

"Famous School" for writers, where she wrote her first novel. Unmarried, Miyabe continues to live at home with her parents, although she has an office near her house where she does much of her writing. Intensely involved in her career, Miyabe has never traveled outside of Japan and prefers to do much of her research in the local libraries near her house. Even within the city of Tokyo, Miyabe rarely strays across the Sumida River, limiting her trips to the Ginza.[80] She sees Tokyo as both a "mirage" and a frightening place that has changed significantly since she was young.[81] Yet despite this identification with Tokyo's more traditional side, Miyabe does not harbor an antitechnological bias. The characters in her books take technology for granted, and Miyabe herself does all of her writing on word processors. Her interest in technology extends to the foreign media, such as international cable news. While her books are riddled with references to Western popular culture (movies and songs), her fictional Japan is devoid of foreigners and foreign companies and products.

Miyabe's skill as a storyteller, her demure and ladylike demeanor, and her facility with both detective and historical fiction make her a popular writer among all members of the Japanese reading public. Yet despite the seemingly socially conscious aspects of her work, there is a darker, more conservative message underlying her novels, which advocate a return to the simpler past as a way to stem the tide of consumerism, as well as to recover Japan's "traditional" essence.

The Second Wave: Nonami Asa

While Takamura Kaoru and Miyabe Miyuki were the first women to write mysteries in the hard-boiled tradition, their novels rarely discussed women and never had a woman as the detective. In contrast, the women who make up the second wave of detective writers have begun to create detectives who reflect the desires and concerns of modern Japanese women. Foremost among these second-wave authors is Nonami Asa, who has been hailed by critics as the successor to Miyabe Miyuki and Takamura Kaoru. While Nonami has written in a variety of genres, she is most celebrated for her mystery and suspense novels.[82] Born in the same year as Miyabe (1960), she followed a similarly circuitous route to mystery writing. After dropping out of Waseda University, she worked a number of part-time and short-term jobs before enrolling in a school specializing in writing for television and movies. This phase of her career did not last long, and she turned her sights to mystery writing. Her first novel, *Kōfuku na chōshoku* (A happy breakfast), won the First Japanese Mystery and Suspense Award in 1988. Temporarily paralyzed by her sudden success, she was unable to produce anything for a number of years, until she eased herself back by writing short stories.[83] Despite debuting at the same time as Miyabe, due to this hiatus in her writing career,

Nonami Asa (Shinchosha
Publishing Company)

Nonami did not become well known to the mystery world until the release
of *Kogoeru kiba* (Frozen fangs) in 1996.

After the initial boom in women's mystery writing, the Japanese press has
not been as doting toward women authors, with much less coverage of their
works in the mainstream popular press. Nonami, however, has received substantial attention, in part because she was awarded the Naoki Prize, and in
part because of her unique, motorcycle-riding police detective heroine. Unlike
Miyabe, who presents an unrelentingly cheerful face to the media, Nonami
has a darker edge and is much more willing to discuss the misfortunes and set-
backs that she has suffered. This difference between the two authors manifests
itself in the way that each chooses to critique society. While both draw on
their personal experiences to form their plots, Miyabe's nostalgic social critique is lighter in tone and less personal than the almost brutal depiction of
male/female relations that Nonami provides. Yet Nonami's work, although
frank, is not uniformly negative, as there are hints of progress in gender relations in her treatment of the topics of women and work.

The Third Wave: Shibata Yoshiki and Kirino Natsuo

Shibata Yoshiki appeared on the mystery writing scene out of relative obscu-
rity in 1995, when her first novel in the Riko series, *Riko–Viinasu no eien*
(Riko–Forever Venus), received the Yokomizo Seishi Award for mysteries.[84]

Unlike Nonami and Miyabe, Shibata (b. 1959) graduated from Aoyama Gakuin University and worked in clothing and medical companies before moving to Kyoto. After the birth of her children, she began writing novels.[85] As with Nonami, Shibata's series features a police detective, Murakami Riko, who is a member of the sex crimes division in the Shinjuku precinct. Riko's success at her job exacts a toll on her, however, as her messy personal life threatens her professional accomplishments.

Kirino Natsuo is the other major figure in the third wave of women mystery writers. Older than Miyabe and Nonami, Kirino (b. 1951) graduated from Seikei University in Tokyo and worked in marketing. Like Nonami Asa, she attended a "scenario writing school" in order to learn how to write fiction.[86] After she married and had children, she wanted to start working again, so she began writing fiction, spurred on by her desire to win one of the prizes offered by the Sanrio Publishing Company to new writers of romance novels.[87] In 1984, she won the Sanrio Romance Prize for her novel *Ai no yukikata* (The method of love), and she wrote two other romances before turning to young adult fiction and adventure novels under the pen name Noharano Emi.[88] In addition to young adult fiction, Kirino also has written scenarios for women's comic books.

Kirino's prize-winning mystery debut, *Kao ni furikakaru ame* (Her face, veiled in rain, 1993), began the Miro series. It was followed a year later by

Shibata Yoshiki (Shinchosha Publishing Company)

Kirino Natsuo (Shinchosha
Publishing Company)

the second novel in the series, *Tenshi ni misuterareta yoru* (Night abandoned by angels). Both books reflect Kirino's interest in foreign detective fiction, in particular the new, hard-boiled brand.[89] In addition to her Miro series, which includes a story about Miro's detective father, Kirino has written a mystery set in the world of women's professional wrestling, which has become increasingly popular in Japan.[90] Her 1997 novel *Out*, the story of an ordinary group of housewives who dismember and dispose of a friend's murdered husband, drew substantial media attention and intrigued readers with the idea that a forty-year-old woman would have the passion to conceive and carry out such a crime.[91] Kirino addressed this issue in a long article in a leading women's magazine, in which she discussed how friendship among women in their later years develops into a deeper intimacy.[92] Kirino was awarded the 1999 Naoki Prize for her novel *Yawaraka na hoho* (Soft cheeks), another mystery involving the disappearance of a little girl. In 2003, after her success with *Out*, she revived the Miro series with the novel *Dark*.

The appearance of this third wave has gone unnoticed in the Japanese press, apart from accounts of individual prizes. While Miyabe and Takamura are still receiving media attention for their literary accomplishments and are sought for their opinions on current events, the latest wave of writers has entered onto the scene with little fanfare. These women, largely college educated, have benefited from the increased interest in detective fiction and the overabundance of prizes that exist to recognize new mystery talent. Many of them have come to prominence only through the receipt of such awards, while others have turned to mystery writing from other genres, such as romance and science fiction. At the same time, however, this critical mass of women writers (including Imamura Aya and Wakatake Nanami) guarantees that all types of women's stories make it into print. While individual novels by women continue to capture the media's fancy, the bulk of women's mysteries have become part of the literary mainstream, where they are noticed for their plots and characterizations rather than simply for their female authorship. Often, the appearance of a new female writer passes unnoticed, except in an anthology of other women writers.

Matsuo Yumi

While Matsuo Yumi chronologically belongs to the second wave of writers, her unusual brand of satire and her roots in science fiction place her in a separate category. She was born in Ishikawa Prefecture in 1960 and graduated from Ochanomizu Women's University with a degree in English literature. Matsuo's first publication, *Ijigen kafe terasu* (Coffee house, "another dimension," 1989), was followed by *Burakku enjeru* (Black angel, 1994). She was known primarily as a science fiction writer until she went in a new direction in 1994 with *Baruun Taun no satsujin* (Murder in Balloon Town), which was

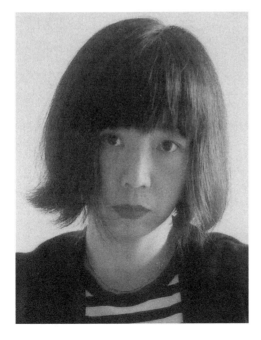

Matsuo Yumi (courtesy of the author)

billed as a "science fiction mystery."[93] After *Baruun Taun no satsujin*, she continued to write science fiction with *Pipinera* (Pippinella, 1996), *Makkusu Mausu to nakamatachi* (Max Mouse and his friends, 1997), and *Runako no kichin* (Runako's kitchen, 1998). Her other work, *Jendaa-jo no toriko* (The prisoner of gender, 1996), is a meditation on gender and what would happen if gender differences were eliminated. Unlike the other authors treated in this study, Matsuo has not yet achieved the same level of visibility in Japan, due both to her being firmly rooted in the science fiction camp and to the tongue-in-cheek treatment of her subject matter.

Gender and Genre: A Point of Departure

As the preceding survey has made clear, just as Matsumoto changed the landscape of detective fiction writing in the 1960s and 1970s, the writers of the "boom" in women's writing have continued to use detective fiction's critical potential to discuss social changes and problems that concern them. More than merely changing the degree to which social and political issues are presented, however, women's detective fiction results in changes to the genre itself. These changes have been the focus of increasing critical scrutiny over the last twenty years, most notably in the United States and England.[94] In particular, the appearance in the 1980s of the new female hard-boiled detective (epitomized by Sara Paretsky's V. I. Warshawski and Sue Grafton's Kinsey Millhone) has spurred a reexamination of the relationship between gender and genre. Scholars have been divided over whether a purportedly masculine genre can be changed by the addition of women. Some argue that generic conventions override the shift in gender and insist that despite independent heroines and plots focused on women's concerns, detective fiction's inherent emphasis on violence does not accommodate women.[95] Sally Munt takes this argument one step further, suggesting that women's detective fiction can only be a parody because of the immutability of the genre's demands. The only way to avoid this, Munt suggests, is through the use of the lesbian detective, whose sexual freedom from the dominant mode of heterosexuality allows her truly to occupy the position of ironic loner demanded by detective fiction (hard-boiled in particular).[96]

Other critics, however, have insisted that the addition of women to the genre, as writers and as protagonists, changes the form of detective fiction profoundly. In fact, Maureen Reddy argues that women's detective fiction has become an entirely new genre that provides a means by which to criticize the masculine elements of detective fiction itself.[97] I think that the answer lies somewhere between these two positions. Munt is correct when she says that female detectives still have to operate under the same patriarchal state responsible for their oppression. Nonetheless, women authors have found ways to question the status quo through the genre without having to change its structures. Thus, as Priscilla Walton and Manina Jones have observed, women writing mysteries "use an established popular formula in order to investigate not just a particular crime but the more general offenses in which the patriarchal power structure of contemporary society itself is potentially incriminated. They use the popular novel as a lens through which to filter cultural issues and problems which might be negotiated (if not solved) as part of the narrative of investigation."[98]

Undeniably, the most significant effect of gender shifts upon detective fiction occurs when women become the detectives. Women's relationship to detective fiction has been changing, following the progress that women have made in society. Thus, while women have been both producers and heroines of detective fiction since its inception, early female detectives were closely circumscribed by their (and their authors') social conditions. These early women detectives were forced by financial hardship to take up detection since "detecting" was not something that respectable women did seriously.[99] Even in the nineteenth century, an age when female social mobility had increased, women still were not supposed to leave the home and circulate unattended. Any woman who did so was likely to be seen as a prostitute since her appearance alone in public meant that she was like many of the goods available in the shop windows: she was for sale.[100] Thus, in a genre that made its home in the city streets, respectable women tended to be an occasional presence at best, often rendered invisible within the male-dominated urban landscape. As Rosalyn Deutsche has pointed out, this remained true in the hard-boiled detective fiction that had its start in 1920s and 1930s America.[101] The by-now familiar world of the hard-boiled male detective leaves little room for women, either as characters or as readers. In the words of one critic, the female consumer of hard-boiled fiction must engage in "a kind of mental transvestitism to take pleasure in it."[102] Likewise, women are almost excluded from the public spaces of the city in early hard-boiled detective novels. This absence, however, "links the dangers of sexual liaison with the dangers of the city" since women are essentialized into the purest of stereotypes, "rendered erotically lethal, vilified, and defeated."[103] Women, in other words, are seen as potentially dangerous, and the plots of these novels revolve around the subjugation of female agency and desire. Thus, the uncharacteristic freedom of movement and action enjoyed by the *femme fatale* is contained and constrained in some way, ultimately rendering the threat she poses to men as empty.

Given these conditions, one of the most notable developments in Anglo-American as well as Japanese detective fiction of the last twenty years has been the introduction of women into the hard-boiled detective novel as detectives rather than as sounding boards or stereotypical sex objects. This change, however, has brought contradictions with it. When Sara Paretsky, who is famous for creating one of the first truly hard-boiled female detectives in V. I. Warshawski, started to conceive her series of novels, she attempted to change the gender of the detective without changing any of the genre's conventions. This resulted in an unintentional parody since "the hard-boiled convention of female sexuality as dangerous and even evil conflicts with the heroic status of the detective."[104] The author thus must walk a fine line if she wants her detective to conform to the conventions of hard-boiled detective fiction but also break its gender codes. Ultimately Paretsky created a detective whom she describes as "someone . . . like me and my friends"[105]—that is, "self-reliant and independent, the prototype of a feminist ideal."[106] As can be seen from the wide range of women's detective fiction, "professional activities are no longer privileged: any woman can assume the role of detective; any social position, from welfare mother to First Lady, can constitute a vantage point from which to solve crimes and to interpret the city and the world. . . . Their lives demonstrate the fluid boundaries between public and private and a far more complex subjectivity than that of, say, Philip Marlowe."[107]

Margaret Crawford's observation above suggests the degree to which changes in the gender of the detective have required adjustments to other conventions as well. Specifically, critics have suggested that a woman detective's system of relationships, her gaze, and her use of knowledge differ from those of the male detective. Unlike the archetypical male detective who wanders the streets alone, the female detective is no longer a solitary figure but one with a network of relationships. While these may not be kinship ties in the strict sense, they often are modeled on the extended family, creating a quasi-affinal cohort that frees the woman detective from the patriarchal relationship of the family structure and provides her with close, emotional relationships of mutual aid and respect.[108]

In turn, when the female detective narrates her story, this regendering of the authorial voice alters the authorial gaze as well. This mitigates some of the voyeuristic quality of detective fiction, where women long have been the objects of the detective's gaze, turning what was woman-as-object into woman-as-subject. In particular, when the gaze of the female detective is turned toward violence against women and pornography, the reader is allowed—or even forced—to take a woman's point of view on topics that intimately concern women but that are often treated quite differently (or overlooked) by the mainstream media. This feminization of the gaze and the use of first-person narrative also make the character seem more "real" to her readers, an effect enhanced by depicting her everyday existence, the minutiae of life essential to the success of any form of realist literature. While the detective story is not an autobiography, it does use some of that genre's techniques, with the result that the first-person detective novel is "predicated on the complex relationship of identification, analogy, and even contradiction among author, fictional character, and reader."[109] This personal perspective, finally, aids in making the detective the authority who has the power and the knowledge to solve the mystery.

A third major change that occurs when the genre is regendered affects the structure and nature of knowledge. Traditionally, the core of the detective story has been the detective's quest for clues to solve the mystery, which translates into a search for knowledge and information. The goal of the detective is to narrow down a multiplicity of suspects, clues, and motives into the one "true" solution. When it is a female detective who is engaged in this enterprise, however, the knowledge is often "subjective, involved, [and] empathic," rather than the "objective, distanced knowledge which is the masculine epistemological ideal."[110] Often such knowledge leaves the detective torn between the need to seek justice from a paternalistic state and her desire to understand the circumstances in which the crime may have been committed—a dilemma rarely faced by the male (and particularly the male hard-boiled) detective.

To what degree do these seemingly programmatic claims about gender and genre reflect the writing—and realities—of Japanese women? As the following chapters attempt to show, contemporary women writers of detective fiction in Japan have used the sociocritical potential of detective fiction, its genre conventions, and its traditions in ways that both diverge from those of their Anglo-American counterparts and parallel them. While the writers of the "boom" are indebted in a number of ways to English and particularly American hard–boiled authors like Paretsky and Grafton, they have also created stories and characters that bear little resemblance to theirs. Miyabe Miyuki, for instance, completely eschews the female detective and creates women characters who are closer to the traditional model of the *femme fatale*. Likewise, Kirino and Shibata's independent protagonists enjoy none of the close relationships celebrated by Sabine Vanacker and others, but instead are loners in a world of *male* communities. Furthermore, the writers I will examine cross the political spectrum, ranging from the conservative Miyabe to the avowedly feminist Matsuo. What this means, in the end, is that while the critical work of Western scholars can provide valuable tools for analyzing (women's) detective fiction, it cannot replace close analysis of Japanese writers and their social milieu. And, as I will demonstrate, the differences that such an analysis reveals have much to tell us not only about popular fiction in Japan, but also about the experiences, perceptions, and ideals of Japanese women at the end of the twentieth century.

CHAPTER 2

A Home of One's Own

Identity, Community, and Nostalgia in
Miyabe Miyuki's *All She Was Worth*

You and me, we've been in this business for a long time. Long enough
to pick up some preconceptions. When a woman commits a crime,
there must be a man mixed up somewhere. Left to their own devices,
women don't have much criminal impulse. They do it for the man,
right? Women's crimes are crimes of passion.... But lately, things
have changed. No, not even lately.

—Miyabe Miyuki, *All She Was Worth*

Miyabe Miyuki is perhaps the best known and most popular female mystery
writer in Japan today, an author whose works (unlike those of the other writers considered in subsequent chapters) do not feature a female detective. As I
will demonstrate in the following pages, this writer, who explicitly avoids using
women as her main characters, ends up creating a nuanced if problematic
vision of their place within modern Japanese society—a vision substantially at
odds with that of some of Miyabe's well-known literary contemporaries.

Billing herself as an "entertainment writer," Miyabe insists that she is not
limited by genre and prefers to mix and match them, citing Stephen King as
the deepest and most abiding influence on her work.[1] In interviews Miyabe
downplays the more serious thematic elements of her writing. Refusing to
credit her success to feminism or to the social importance of the themes
about which she writes, Miyabe continuously stresses the lighter aspects of
her work, noting that she writes the final scene first and then fits the plot
around the visual image that she has created.[2] Thus, she tells how she
thought of the scene in *All She Was Worth* in which the criminal is caught
and then worked the plot around this image.[3] Yet this reliance on the entertaining aspect of her work is deceptive, as her interviews reveal (for example)

that she worked as a legal assistant in a law firm that specialized in handling personal bankruptcies, the key element in the plot of *All She Was Worth*.[4]

Miyabe's deprecation of the serious elements in her work also is reflected by the type of mystery that she writes. As we have seen, genre distinctions in Japan extend from the deep division between "pure" and "popular" literature to the variations within each genre. As noted in chapter 1, within detective fiction, authors and publishers distinguish between *honkaku-ha* and *shakai-ha* literature, the former focusing on the resolution of puzzles and tricks and the latter locating the root of a crime in social problems.[5] Within her works, and especially in *All She Was Worth*, Miyabe chooses to emphasize devices, despite the obvious social message in the pages of her novel. Although Miyabe wants readers to focus on the twists and turns of the plot, however, the social message is the key to Miyabe's broader view of contemporary Japanese society, and it is what makes the novel so intriguing.

All She Was Worth is generally considered to be Miyabe's best novel, both stylistically and thematically.[6] Written in 1992, it is her best-selling and most popular novel to date, a nominee for numerous awards, and the winner of the Yamamoto Prize. The only one of Miyabe's works to be translated into English as well as French, *All She Was Worth* was included in a recent list of best postwar novels.[7] While Miyabe's other works revolve around themes of memory (in particular memories of the war) and the influence of the media, *All She Was Worth* deals most explicitly with a social problem, personal bankruptcy.[8] Indeed, rather than remaining a mere backdrop for the action of the novel, bankruptcy becomes the motivating factor for the female protagonists and their deeds, and Miyabe's detailed examination of it ultimately demonstrates not only the dimensions of the problem per se, but also that personal bankruptcy itself can be the result of much deeper social ills.

Set in post–bubble economy Japan, the novel begins with the disappearance of the beautiful Sekine Shoko. Her fiancé, the successful young banker Kurisaka Kazuya, enlists the aid of his aunt's husband, Honma Shunsuke, to find her. As his marriage to Shoko approached, Kurisaka had suggested that she apply for a credit card with his bank. Shoko's request was denied, however, because it was discovered that she had declared personal bankruptcy several years before. Soon after, Shoko disappeared without a trace. As Honma, a member of the Tokyo Metropolitan Police on leave due to injury in the line of duty, searches throughout Tokyo, he discovers that the Shoko for whom he is looking is not the woman she seemed to be. As it turns out, Kurisaka's Shoko had assumed the identity of the real Sekine Shoko, a bar hostess from Utsunomiya who had been struggling with her finances. By means of a Polaroid photograph and a number of other clues, Honma eventually tracks down the real identity of the fake Shoko: Shinjo

Kyoko, a woman so determined to hide her own identity that she has killed to obtain another.

Kyoko herself is a victim of financial disaster, brought about when her family defaulted on a loan they had taken out to purchase a home. Hounded perpetually by the *yakuza* (Japanese mafia) sent to collect the debt, Kyoko decided that the only way she could escape was to assume a new identity. She devised a scheme to locate her victims through the market research data of a mail order lingerie company for which she worked, focusing on young women who had few or no living family members. In this way, Kyoko selected Shoko, but ironically Kyoko was unaware of Shoko's financial problems, because of which she had to begin her search anew. At the end of the novel, Honma finds Kyoko before she is able to kill again and assume another new identity.

Two structural features make Miyabe's novel especially suited to the examination of the social problems that she sees as the most pressing in contemporary society. The first is that the central mystery in *All She Was Worth* is solved within the first sixty pages, leaving the rest of the novel free for an exploration of the character's motivations. As R. Gordon Kelly suggests, all detective fiction is both a "whodunnit" and a "whydunnit" since "however perfunctorily works of detective fiction explicate motive, (it is) the psychological rationale underlying the act that brings the case into being. As works of detective fiction have become more 'novelistic' the emphasis on motive has become more explicit."[9] This is particularly true of *All She Was Worth*. With the bulk of the novel dedicated to exploring the motives of Kyoko and Shoko, Miyabe is able to explore the contours of contemporary Japan in greater detail than do most other works of fiction.

The second feature concerns the way in which the story is told. Although narrated from Honma's point of view, the novel contains little dialogue in which the characters discuss the issues raised in the plot. Instead, each conversation is crafted in order to advance the author's underlying message. Thus, characters appear and deliver monologues, interrupted only by questions from the other characters meant to enhance the point of the lecture. In the best example of this approach, an entire chapter is devoted to a lecture by Mizoguchi, a bankruptcy lawyer who aided Shoko; he tells Honma about the credit system, the practice of unregulated loans, and how easy it is to fall victim to them. This didactic chapter serves to educate the reader about the perils of unregulated credit card use and to reinforce the author's message that personal bankruptcy is not a moral failing, contrary to Honma's erroneous assumption at the beginning of the novel.

While reviewers of Miyabe's works tend to see *All She Was Worth* as a critique of consumer capitalism and the credit system in Japan, the issue of personal bankruptcy is tied to deeper issues—namely, the nostalgia that arises from the loss of a sense of place and the fragility of identity caused by that loss.[10] While the combination of nostalgia and identity is not new in literature, Miyabe's book is notable for its attention to consumerism and sense of place as competing bases for identity formation. In *All She Was Worth*, Miyabe has created a distinction between people who use place as a defining marker of identity and those who have lost their sense of place and substitute something else—in their case a desire for consumer goods—in order to make up for that loss. Thus, the characters in *All She Was Worth* fall into two major categories: those who belong to a "community" and those that do not. The community does not have to be defined by any particular physical space, but rather is inhabited by people who eschew the glittering world of late twentieth-century Japan and resist the temptation of the media and the advertising industry to buy into what I shall call "the Japanese Dream." What holds this community together are the "traditional" Japanese traits of self-denial, reliance on members of the community, and a belief that things will improve if people work hard.

The second group of people, those who have lost this community, are ultimately unhappy. Falling under the spell of the commodity, they reject their family or the community in favor of an individual identity created by the things that they are able to consume. Hit hardest by this desire for things are women who leave their families in order to establish such an identity. Even more intriguing, in Japan, where everyone describes him- or herself as "middle class," Miyabe paints a world where class differences play a significant role in the lifestyles, dreams, and aspirations of the various characters. Within the scheme of the novel, Miyabe firmly rejects the definition of identity as something that a person creates or chooses for him- or herself and stresses that a person's identity depends upon where he or she fits into society.

In the following pages, I examine the distinction that Miyabe creates between identity defined through place and identity defined through loss of that place, and the relationship between this dynamic and the phenomenon of nostalgia. I first consider how Miyabe has depicted place, in particular how she uses places in Tokyo as markers of identity. For some of her characters, neighborhoods serve as important parts of their identity, while for others the loss of geographical rootedness becomes the motivating factor for their actions. Next, I survey the role that consumption plays for those characters who have lost their sense of community and place. I then explore how the characters in *All She Was Worth* fall into these two identity categories, and the place of class, age, and gender in this process. In turn, I examine the role of nostalgia in Miyabe's novel and how place and identity become crucial for the discussion of a person's motivations. As a counterpoint to this discussion of place, consumption, and nostalgia, I conclude by considering another author, Yoshimoto Banana, who is of the same generation as Miyabe but comes from a very different background. Yoshimoto's *Kitchen* has been widely read both in Japan and overseas, and it offers an alternative treatment of these themes in Japanese literature at the end of the twentieth century.

Place

Miyabe's emphasis on place in *All She Was Worth* goes beyond the parameters of a regular detective story. As mentioned, detective fiction's descriptions of place become crucial elements of the narrative for heightening suspense and resolving the mystery; thus, one of Japan's most famous mystery writers, Matsumoto Seichō, exploits the geography of Japan via the minutiae of train schedules in his novel *Ten to sen*. Miyabe's treatment, however, exceeds this already well-defined emphasis on place. She regards it as specific, familiar, secure, and coherent, despite the fact that modern life has disrupted the formerly bounded nature of place. In the words of Gillian Rose, "senses of place develop from every aspect of an individual's life experience," and "pervade everyday life and experience."[11] The places Miyabe describes are more than a way to identify characters—they become a crucial component of those characters' identities. In *All She Was Worth*, identity becomes, as Rose suggests, "lived experiences and all the subjective feelings associated with everyday consciousness," but these experiences and feelings can be "embedded in wider sets of social relations."[12] As Jonathan Rutherford argues, "identity marks the conjunction of our past with the social, cultural, and economic relations we live within."[13] Thus, the places that Miyabe describes so carefully serve not only to tell the reader about where the novel is set, but also to indicate the characters' identity, providing a more detailed picture of those characters.

From the very beginning of the novel, Miyabe exploits detective fiction's reliance on realism in order to give her readers a rich sense of the places she describes. The details serve to acquaint readers with unfamiliar physical geographies, as well as the social nuances that they embody. When an author gives an address or describes a train journey, the reader is able to plot the character's movements on a map. Miyabe's reliance on this kind of realism is deliberate, serving to anchor the narrative in a specific time and place so that the social issues that she raises have particular historical relevance.[14] Places both in and outside of Tokyo are described with the same lavish detail: "Sekine Shoko's office was five minutes' walk from the West Exit of Shinjuku Station. The address proved to be a forlorn five-story building alongside the Koshu Expressway. Five of the six glass panels in the foyer window were stenciled with the names of companies. The last panel had no name on it, only a curtain" (50).[15] Similarly, a trip to Osaka is depicted with such realistic detail that one could use it as an itinerary: "Take the New Tokaido bullet train to Osaka. A five minute walk from New Osaka station puts you on Midosuji subway line, which cuts straight across the heart of the city, north to south. Twenty minutes of jostling brings you to Namba Station. Navigate the underground shopping arcade which is so big it would take a devoted shopper a couple of days to explore properly, then emerge into a jumble of small-time retailers and rental office buildings jammed up one against the other. Wedged in among them is a baseball stadium" (177).

Such detailed description extends to the neighborhoods inhabited by Miyabe's characters. Anyone at all familiar with Tokyo will know where Honma lives and sympathize with his commute from the center of Tokyo to the eastern edge of the city in Katsushika-ku on the packed Joban line train, with hordes of people pushing on and off at each stop. Looking at a map of Tokyo, one can find his housing complex *(danchi)*, one of the places where working-class people live. Honma, a policeman, is joined by his friend Ikari, who is self-employed, and they are surrounded by other families in which both parents work. Their working-class neighborhood is circumscribed by the kinds of employment and lifestyle of its inhabitants. Theirs is not the world of brand-name goods and foreign cars; rather, its inhabitants are focused on the needs and demands of everyday existence.

View of Sumida Ward in Tokyo. The taller buildings are the apartment complexes called *danchi*.

This working-class world is not simply reducible to the binary of center and periphery, a marginal area that becomes a site to evade dominant practices or engage in new identity politics.[16] Rather, it is the center of people's everyday lives, which display traditional Japanese values like thrift, self-denial, and saving. Although she does not explicitly mention class, Miyabe is keenly aware of the class differences among her characters, and class markers, such as they are, are visible in the novel. The most significant indication of class in Japan, in fact, is the geographical differentiation of both commercial and residential areas in the urban environment. The eastern area of Tokyo, or *shitamachi,* is the traditional home of the working class, while the "High City" *(Yamanote)* has always been home to the upper class, even in the premodern era.[17] This division between the western and the eastern sides of Tokyo has long been remarked upon in Japanese literature. The late critic Maeda Ai, for instance, discusses the author Tayama Katai's reasons for living in the more expensive High City area on the western side of Tokyo in the early twentieth century, tracing them to "the contrast between the stagnant but stable lives of the Low City dwellers, bogged down in their traditional communal customs, and the unstable but dazzlingly novel lifestyles that were emerging in the High City." In Tayama's words, "The High City is a giant whirlpool of lives led by men who have come from nowhere, lives fraught with unforeseeable difficulties, but surrounded by their cheerful wives and young families, full of great expectations for the future."[18]

Despite the passage of almost a century, the relationship between these two parts of Tokyo has not changed dramatically. What Tayama, who is known for his novel *Futon* (The quilt, 1907), sees as stagnation in the early part of the century, however, Miyabe values as stability at century's end. The difference between the two perspectives is indicative of the nostalgia that permeates Miyabe's work. What was once "fixed" and "outdated" in the Low City is now revalidated as "traditional" and "stable." In Japan, where foreign travel has become the rage, the *shitamachi* still is considered the embodiment of the "traditional" city. It is the home of the Tokyo-Edo Hakubutsukan (the Tokyo-Edo Museum), while Sensoji Temple (better known as the Asakusa Kannon) and its accompanying shopping streets are popular destinations for tourists, Japanese and foreign alike, in search of traditional Edo.[19] Miyabe is nostalgic for this world of communal customs and sets out to show that they have not withered away but rather are still vital, albeit changed. The nostalgia that Miyabe enunciates in her consideration of the Low City stems from a sense of change that she both mourns and tries to stop. Miyabe's nostalgia for place is that "sadness without an object" described by Susan Stewart, "a sadness which creates a longing that of necessity is inauthentic because it does not take part in lived experience." This nostalgia, furthermore, is always ideological, since "the past it seeks has never existed except as narrative, and hence, always absent, that past continually threatens to reproduce itself as a felt lack. Hostile to history and its invisible origins, and yet longing for an impossibly pure context of lived experience at a place of origin, nostalgia wears a distinctly utopian face, a face that turns toward a future-past, a past which has only ideological reality."[20]

These problems of history and the utopian quality of nostalgia are overlooked by Miyabe in her creation of the modern-day attributes of her community. In particular, stability is a major component of her conception of place. Once a place is stable, it is secure, and fear and uncertainty are left behind. It is clear that Miyabe sees Tokyo as a frightening place, and in both interviews and an essay in the *Asahi shinbun*, Miyabe has spoken about her inability to "see" or comprehend Tokyo *(miru koto ga dekinai)*. The image that Miyabe frequently employs is of Tokyo being a foreign country; to move there would be like "emigrating" *(imin suru)*. Miyabe thus makes a distinction between the center of Tokyo ("Tokyo") and her own neighborhood, which does not seem to be a part of "Tokyo." What she values is her hometown corner of the *shitamachi*. "Inner Tokyo is a simple place, unexciting, crammed full of people living a dull existence day after day. It is only that. The Tokyo in which I was born and raised is this boring kind of place."[21] Thus, the whirlpool of possibilities that Tayama describes is rejected in favor of the traditional communal spaces of the old city.

Yet despite Miyabe's affection for the *shitamachi*, she is not blind to its problems. Her protagonist, Honma Shunsuke (who often seems to be speaking in Miyabe's voice), was born in Tokyo, but his parents were from Tohoku, a rural area in northern Japan, and his wife was from Niigata on the Sea of Japan. Thus, he feels that despite the fact that he was born in Tokyo, he does not have a hometown:

> There was an indefinable gap between being in Tokyo and being a "Tokyoite." They say that "three generations make Tokyo home," but could a person ever feel a bloodline connection to the place? That was the real question. How could you really speak of "hometown Tokyo" or being "Tokyo born and bred"? Today's city was no place to put down roots. It was a barren field, soil that gave off no smell, unplowed and unwatered. Nothing grew in the big city. People there were tumbleweeds, living on the memory of roots put down somewhere else by their parents or their parents' parents. And those roots dry up and wither (129–130).

Above all, the city of Tokyo is a place that "assimilates" *(dōka sasete shimau)* everything. Thus, people who are able to keep their nonstandard accents even when they move to Tokyo are those who indicate that they have roots and remind the Tokyo-born Honma of his own rootlessness.

The antidote to this rootlessness is another integral part of Miyabe's concept of place: a sense of community. This community is based upon an everyday existence that is composed of "open and porous networks of social relations" and is situated in a place where identities are "constructed through the specificity of (people's) interactions with other places."[22] In Miyabe's world, people have put down roots in their *danchi* and have formed a community. Within this community, people know each other and look out for each other's needs and interests. It is a place where people of similar backgrounds and needs are quickly integrated into the group; those who are not are conspicuous. Miyabe does not locate the authentic community in the *furusato*,[23] nor does she seem to be saying (as does sociologist John Clammer) that what links the neighborhood together are networks of consumption or the *matsuri* (festivals) or local government (as do Theodore Bestor and Jennifer Robertson respectively).[24] Rather, for Miyabe the authentic neighborhood is the network of human relationships formed by people of similar social and class backgrounds who live and remain in one place.

What is intriguing about Miyabe's depiction of community is the almost complete absence of women. Honma, a widower, has a ten-year-old adopted son, Satoru, and must continue to work. He has hired his friend, Ikari, an out-of-work architect, to be their housekeeper and run the household. When Honma's job requires him to be away, he can always count on "Uncle Ikari" to be there. Ikari has the time because his wife, Hisae, is a successful interior designer and supports them. Apart from Hisae, however, women do not play an important part in this community. Yet Miyabe suggests that the community is not sustainable unless someone is willing to fill the traditional role of nurturer.[25]

Not only does this community provide Honma with assistance and companionship, but it also becomes a part of his identity. In *All She Was Worth*, identity becomes the crucial issue as Honma discovers that the person for whom he is looking has assumed another's persona. Tracking down the woman who he thinks is Sekine Shoko makes him reassess his idea of identity. For Honma, identity is predominantly a matter of the community to which one belongs and the role one plays within it, making it something based on one's relationships. In contrast, Miyabe paints Shoko and Kyoko as people who believe that identity is not fixed and that by creating an independent existence, they can become different people. In his pursuit of Kyoko's true identity, Honma is made to reconsider the difference between the outward, legal trappings of identity and the more internal, "affective" criteria that constitute it. As Honma knows, however, there is a legal document that serves to mark, and even define, a person's identity: the *koseki*, or family register. The *koseki*, located in a person's hometown, is a record of all the births, marriages, and

Danchi, or public housing complex, in Sumida Ward.

deaths that occur in a family; it thus literally is an official description of the patriarchal family and serves as a form of legal identification.[26] As Honma muses, "even now, when you get right down to it, you aren't your own person, you're just one new line entered into the record of an entire family" (62). In addition to the family register, each person is supposed to have a residence certificate that lists his/her current residence, as well as family information from the family register. To have an official identity in Japan, one needs to have both these documents; thus, when the character of Kyoko takes Shoko's identity, she goes so far as to create a new family register (with Shoko's data), listing herself as the head of the household.

Nevertheless, for people like Shoko and Kyoko, identity is located outside the register and the community and can be gained either by occupying a certain place or by owning certain things. The rootlessness of these characters is a result of the anomie occurring from "a lack of embeddedness in a coherent social and religious structure."[27] Thus, their separation from their families, either by force or by design, cuts them off from their roots, and they attempt to fill that void by reliance on consumer goods. Yet they are not immune to the idea that the acquisition of their own "place" is necessary for a sense of identity and happiness. The acquisition of such a place, whether it is a home or an apartment, signifies that they will be truly happy. Whatever their old identities may be, these can be replaced easily by the acquisition of things and a place of one's own.

The idea that identity is dependent on one's position in society and one's family was repugnant to Shoko, who believed that by moving away from her family and her hometown, she could recreate her identity and ultimately be happy as a new person. Shoko was from the small city of Utsunomiya, an hour from Tokyo on the *shinkansen* (bullet train).[28] Not satisfied with an identity rooted in her community, she attempted to create a "place" for herself by moving into an apartment in Tokyo and developing her "own" tastes with the guidance of women's magazines. When Honma, accompanied by Tamotsu, Shoko's childhood friend, goes to visit Shoko's friend in Tokyo, she tells them of Shoko's dreams: "Shoko always used to say she came to Tokyo only because she couldn't stand it out there in the boondocks any more . . . . Not a single good memory, that's what she said. It seemed like she always wanted to get away from her hometown and lead a totally different life. Guess she found out, though, it's not so easy. Can't change your life just like that" (215). Despite dreaming that a new place would completely change her, Shoko found that she was unable to transcend the realities of her situation. Limited by her background and appearance, she thus had to try to fulfill her desires in another way.

In the end, after Shoko is freed from her debts and inherits a small but significant sum of money, the desire to create a "place" for her family and put down roots overwhelms her previous need to be free of such constraints. Her parents, who both died before Shoko disappeared, were too poor to be able to afford a burial plot, so both her father's and mother's ashes were stored at an Utsunomiya temple. Shoko's last desire is to buy a plot for the Sekine family. It is on the tour to see the cemetery that Shoko meets Kyoko. Despite Shoko's attempts to flee her family and her old Utsunomiya identity, she ends up searching for a place where she and her parents could at last be reunited. This displacement of her need for her own home into the world of the dead is reminiscent of the *butsudan*, or Buddhist altar to the dead, which is found in the home of the head of the family. Having a *butsudan* is the traditional demonstration of filial piety, and for Shoko, a symbol of her return to the community of her family. Moreover, having a *butsudan* also requires a specific place in the home that Shoko lacks. Ultimately, Kyoko foils Shoko's final desire, and Shoko's dismembered body shows up at the edge of a cemetery in another prefecture.

Kyoko, on the other hand, is cognizant of the fact that place is important in the construction of identity. She, however, must change her identity to get the place that she wants. Capitalizing on the rootlessness of people like Shoko, who have severed their ties to their hometowns, Kyoko can use the outward legal trappings of identity in her quest to achieve her goal. As Honma begins to investigate the fake Sekine Shoko, he realizes that she is not what she seems. "The girl that Kazuya had gotten to know was someone she'd constructed, a person conjured out of thin air" (41). Attempting to hide her past forced her away from any place associated either with that past or with Shoko, making her even more rootless than any resident in Tokyo. Yet she continued in her pursuit of a new identity and hoped that through the conventions of marriage she would be able to gain a place, a home, for herself. Ironically, it is this very ambition that leads Honma to learn of Kyoko's true identity and to unravel the web that she had woven. After visiting her apartment with Kazuya, Honma finds nothing that tells who "Shoko" was, except one Polaroid picture of her standing in front of a model of a Swiss chalet. Honma traces the photo to a housing show in Osaka, and from there, by the type of uniform that "Shoko" was wearing, to her old company and her old identity. Yet it is this picture of a house without a foundation that epitomizes Kyoko's search for her own place. As her friend puts it, "someday she'd have a family and live in a place like this. That was her dream, and all the things she'd been through only made it all the more important for her. She was pretty determined" (260).

Another important aspect of Miyabe's novel is the role that class plays in identity. Shoko is clearly a member of the Japanese lower class, and her involvement in the "water trade" causes her to fall even lower in terms of class and status.[29] Kyoko, on the other hand, the daughter of a white-collar middle manager, retains the trappings of the middle class despite the troubles she has had. As John Clammer notes, "differentiation through acts of consumption has become a means of locating and distinguishing oneself in Japan,"[30] and thus social position is demonstrated through one's consumption patterns—a fact that holds true regardless of geographical location.

The class difference between the women is evident from the response that Honma receives when he shows Kyoko's picture to the people in Shoko's world. Kyoko, an attractive young woman with perfect teeth, does not look like a denizen of the bar hostess world and thus was conspicuous whenever she visited one of Shoko's haunts. Once Kyoko became Shoko, she transformed her into the kind of person that Shoko had always wanted to be. She moved from a run-down apartment in Kawaguchi in neighboring Saitama Prefecture, an hour by train from the city, to an immaculate one filled with a few quality pieces of furniture and ski equipment in the more upscale neighborhood of Honancho, a mere twenty minutes from the business hub of Shinjuku. Despite Kyoko's lack of education, once she entered her twenties she stayed in white-collar jobs, albeit low paying ones. Whatever pretensions to the middle class that Shoko had, her appearance and her habits clearly marked her to the people around her.[31] As her lawyer said, "her clothes, her make-up, everything still had 'bar' written all over" (49). It is this difference that allows Honma to discover Kyoko's "substitution" so quickly. In fact, Honma's first hint that the Shoko for whom he is looking is different is her teeth. The real Shoko had such crooked teeth that they were the only thing people remembered about her. Kyoko, however, had small, white, even teeth, a fact to which Miyabe refers several times throughout the novel.

In contrast to Shoko's troubles in refashioning herself and finding her own "place," the character of Ikumi demonstrates how "reverse migration" back to a community is possible. Ikumi is the wife of Tamotsu. Ikumi, like many other young women, came to Tokyo after graduating from high school in Utsunomiya. With more economic advantages than Shoko, she was able to attend a junior college and thus could find a better job and more financial and social security. Unlike Shoko, who has been stuck in a trading company on the eastern edge of Tokyo, Ikumi is a secretary in a company in the heart of Marunouchi, the financial district of Tokyo. When her brother is transferred from Utsunomiya, Ikumi quits her job and returns to the countryside to take care of her parents. One night, while walking home from the coffee shop by the station where she works, she witnesses the death of Shoko's mother, who falls down a steep flight of stairs. It is there that she meets Tamotsu, and they are married soon after. She has a son and is pregnant with another child and is less than happy about the prospect of her husband running off to Tokyo to help in the search for Shoko.

Yet it is Ikumi who, having done the socially correct thing—given up her job and her life in Tokyo to take care of her parents—ultimately gets rewarded with what the other women in this novel so desperately seek: a home of her own. When Ikumi expresses her unhappiness about the Shoko search, Honma remarks, "When all this is over, I hope you'll make him buy you something really expensive," to which Ikumi responds, "He's going to build us a house. We've already got the land. I want to live in one of those split level homes" (167). Ikumi's dream is not free from consumer desires, but unlike the other women, she is patient enough to wait for the right time for the things that she wants. Content with the smaller things in life, she surrounds herself with her family and occasionally indulges in small luxuries such as pretty lingerie. "Ikumi hardly ever gets to buy any new clothes, but she says she doesn't mind as long as she feels pretty underneath," her husband explains (208). For the larger things in life, what further separates Ikumi from the other women is that her husband is going about obtaining them in a more traditional way that will not bankrupt his family.

Described as "thoroughly ordinary, nothing special to look at, [somone who] probably hadn't gotten particularly high grades in school, but . . . was one smart woman [who] kept her eyes open," (160) Ikumi succeeds through the very means disdained by (or denied to) Shoko, and her place within her family and her community is secure. Miyabe, who metes out punishment to her characters for their flaws, rewards Ikumi for returning to the *inaka* (countryside) and her family and for putting her personal desires aside. She alone among her contemporaries is satisfied with who she is, and she is the only person who acquires what the others long for—a house.

Miyabe's portrayal of women in her novel is notable, for although the search for one woman is the catalyst for the action, it is the parallel lives of the missing woman and the one whose identity she usurped that dominate the narrative, creating a more complex story than the plotline of a simple "whodunnit." Although the male detective has the central active role in *All She Was Worth*, it is the desires and the motives of the female characters that make the novel more than just a didactic detective story about the perils of personal bankruptcy. The first half of the novel is dedicated to Shoko, chronicling her life and her descent into bankruptcy, while the second half explores Kyoko's history and motivations for the crime that she commits. The other female characters, coworkers and friends of the two women, serve to provide more information about Kyoko and Shoko.

The character of Ikumi plays a different role in the novel since Ikumi is the only woman to talk about something other than the missing Shoko. Her function is to provide a counterpoint to the other women, to demonstrate how a woman who has resisted the lure of luxury looks at herself and others. Like most of the speech in the novel, Ikumi's views are presented in monologue form, a technique that Miyabe favors when she has important, didactic information to convey or a point to make. Tired of living in Tokyo and working for a company that puts a premium on the age of its female employees rather than their abilities, Ikumi welcomes the opportunity to return home and take care of her parents. This decision is reinforced when an old friend calls her from Tokyo, "feeling left out and at the bottom of the heap. So she thought I'd left the company, not to get married or study abroad or anything, but only to go crawling back to the sticks. I *had* to be more miserable than her. At least she was living in the big city. So she called" (159). Ikumi has sympathy for this former friend, who feels so wretched that she seeks out someone more unhappy than herself for consolation, but she is frustrated by Tamotsu and Honma's inability to understand why her former friend is so discontented.

Ikumi's comments on how women are treated in Japanese companies, and Shoko's desire to break away from the stifling network of social relationships in which she is ensnared, suggest why women succumb to the pitfalls of consumption. Despite the traditional-minded Ikumi's embrace of the domestic life, Miyabe seems to suggest that it is not the only way for women to be happy. This is emphasized by the successful women in the novel outside of the domestic sphere: Ikari's wife, Hisae, who runs her own interior design firm; Honma's physical therapist; and Shoko's landlady, Konno Nobuko, who owns and manages several buildings. The key to building a community is not that women play traditional roles, but that despite working they maintain their community ties. If a woman does not maintain these connections, then she fills the void with material goods and overseas trips. Consumption becomes a way to satisfy the desires bred by a lack of fulfilling work.

Miyabe's treatment of women is directly related to a basic feature of her fiction—namely, her emphasis upon male characters. As noted, Miyabe's works are largely lacking in female protagonists, and the female characters she does create tend to be the victims or the perpetrators of the crimes that the detectives seek to solve. *All She Was Worth* is no exception, although the treatment of Shoko, Kyoko, and, to a lesser extent, Ikumi is richer and more psychologically detailed than in Miyabe's other novels. The portrait that Miyabe paints of her male characters thus is simultaneously liberating and troubling—liberating because there have not been many depictions of a community of men who live together and share in the housework, and troubling because of the absence of women and the possibility that they could be a part of this community.[32]

Just as the depiction of women has been influenced by class, the same is true for the men in Miyabe's book. First, there is the trio of well-bred, well-educated young men attached to Kyoko, about whom Honma has ambivalent feelings. All three are described as "self-assured, with above-average ability, but, somewhere deep inside, the boy-next-door's need to rebel against his upbringing . . . [but] not by anything so obvious as delinquency or openly taking on his parents" (233). Significantly, the narrator says that these men are unable to deviate from the path that their parents mapped out for them and also are unable to treat their parents as equals, regardless of how high they rise in the world. Thus, they are susceptible to Kyoko's charms and see a liaison with her as a way to strike out on their own path.

In contrast to these blandly uninteresting young men is the group that helps Honma with his investigation. His old friend from the police force, Funaki, provides him with the official records to which he otherwise has no access. Ikari, on the other hand, essentially serves as Honma's "wife" since he takes care of his house and his son while Honma is at work. The three of them are joined by Tamotsu, Shoko's friend from Utsunomiya, who is on leave from his father's garage. As Ikari cooks up meal after meal, they talk over the various angles of the crime and test out different hypotheses on each other. These men are united by a camaraderie born of shared socioeconomic status (Funaki and Honma are policemen, Ikari cleans houses as his job, and all are from a working-class background) and shared space (Honma and Ikari live in the same building). It is clear that the core members of this group both antedate and will outlive this particular investigation.

Furthermore, while Miyabe has taken changes in society into consideration (such as women working outside the home), her community of men still retains the characteristics of a family unit. It is a very supportive group in which everyone fills a role that the family once occupied. When Tamotsu comes to join them in the investigation, he quickly adapts to the community and assumes some of the duties of the family, such as looking after Satoru while Honma is away. Another thing that distinguishes the men in the novel from the women is their friendship with one another and their willingness to draw new people into their community. When Tamotsu arrives in Tokyo, he books himself into a hotel, but soon Honma insists that he stay with them. In contrast, the women lead extremely solitary lives, characterized by few friends who do not know them very well.

Another hallmark of Miyabe's oeuvre is her focus upon the relationship between young boys and older men, a relationship that sometimes is familial (such as that between a grandfather and grandson in *Sabishii karyūdo* [The lonely hunter]), and sometimes is between neighbors (e.g., the young boy who adopts an older lonely artist in *Tokyo shitamachi satsujin bōshōku* [Murders in downtown Tokyo]).[33] Such relationships serve a dual purpose. First, they situate the themes of the novel in other, simpler terms. Second, they suggest that among the younger generation of Japanese, there are those who are not prey to the social problems that afflict the majority. That these relationships occur between males is also no accident since much of Japanese society is structured around the dominant gender ideology of "women inside, men outside" that, although not borne out by facts, is supported by the government and numerous public opinion polls.[34]

In *All She Was Worth,* the relationship between Satoru and the men in his community serves a similar purpose, showing how the community of men operates on a daily basis, locating the individual's place in relation to the community, and teaching how one should react to people who transgress against the community. These issues are epitomized by a particular incident involving Honma's son. Satoru and his friend Katsu have adopted a stray dog, although pets are not allowed in the *danchi*. When the novel opens, the dog has disappeared, drawing Ikari and Funaki into the hunt for the animal. Despite a long search, the dog is never found. One day, Satoru comes home in tears because a classmate has bragged that he killed the dog and threw his body in the trash. Satoru and Katsu are inconsolable and report that the classmate told them, "If you don't like it then go buy yourself a real house." Honma ponders this and responds that since the classmate's parents have a house, "(this) is why he can have a dog. But let a poorer family keep a pet, never. Must be some complex he's got" (213).

The children do not understand the anger felt by Honma and Ikari, nor their pity for the bully. It is left to Tamotsu to articulate this anger. When he puts a little funeral together for the dog, he makes the connection between how the dog died and how Shoko probably met her end. Afterward, as Satoru and Honma talk, they realize that the classmate was denied a dog by his parents when they moved into their new house. Having one's own house, in other words, does not necessarily bring a person happiness. Thus, the discussion that Honma and Satoru have about the dog's death and how to deal with the classmate becomes a morality lesson on how to deal with people who taunt others for their professions and lack of possessions. At the end of their conversation, Honma explains to Satoru why he is looking for Kyoko: "This woman, she had reasons. . . . She didn't do terrible things to other people just because bad things had happened to her. She *wanted* to do the bad things" (256). Kyoko's deeds, because they grew out of her desperation to have a house and not merely from her need to hide from her pursuers, are worse in Honma's eyes than the classmate's murder of the dog. Using the dog's death, he is able to explain to Satoru the different motives for murder and why Kyoko's actions seem particularly heinous to him.

Consumption

Throughout *All She Was Worth,* Honma's search for Shoko and later his attempt to understand Kyoko teach him how little he knows about women. Widowed after several years of marriage, he has little understanding of them and the crimes they commit. During the course of the investigation, Honma is reminded of one of his early cases, which involved a female shoplifter who stole clothes from the best boutiques but only wore them at home. "Clothes, watches and other accessories—posing like a model in a fashion magazine. Just for the mirror" (8). This memory comes back to him at the beginning of the novel, when he is in agony from his knee injury but refuses to sit on the train. He compares his refusal, even though no one is watching and no one cares, to the actions of the woman who shoplifts. While Miyabe does not offer any further comment, Honma's interpretation suggests an incomplete grasp of the situation. Honma believes that possession was the young shoplifter's aim, but the clothing was not stolen to be worn; rather, it was intended to fulfill the shoplifter's desire to have the things that fit her desired identity—an aspiration that he cannot begin to fathom.

Honma's study of Kyoko makes him better able to understand female behavior and thus solve a case for his friend Funaki. When the wealthy husband of a younger woman is murdered, the police have no motive and no firm suspects other than a friend of the young widow. Before the death of her husband the woman is seen sneaking out of the house in business wear, but no evidence of any lover is found. Honma deduces that the woman had her husband killed because he denied her the opportunity to work after marriage. Once Honma's suspicion is confirmed, he realizes that "all this had occurred to him thanks to 'Shoko Sekine': women don't always commit crimes of passion" (123). He realizes that this woman killed not out of love, but out of ambition and a desire to succeed on her own. Ultimately, Honma is enlightened by this case: he learns how women have changed and that Shinjo Kyoko is a new kind of woman. "She's like a wall covered with paper in a bright floral pattern: underneath it, reinforced concrete. Impenetrable, as solid as they come. An iron will to survive. *For herself and no one else.* That was her. A woman who ten years ago scarcely existed in Japan" (124, italics mine).

Honma's general misapprehension of women's motives, I would suggest, is not simply a fictional representation of male chauvinism; rather, it stems from Miyabe's own misunderstanding of contemporary women. While she grasps many of the frustrations that women feel in relation to their jobs and lack of prospects—an awareness demonstrated by her sympathetic depictions of Ikumi and Shoko—she too cannot comprehend a character like Kyoko. While the passage quoted above seems to describe Japanese women throughout history since the "iron will to survive" displayed by Kyoko is one example of the "endurance" *(gaman)* valorized in Japanese culture, what baffles Miyabe and separates Kyoko from the other female characters is that she wants to survive "for herself and no one else." This personal ambition to the point of isolation and fierce independence runs counter to the idea of community that Miyabe advocates. Unlike women in the past, whose iron will is used to ensure the survival of their families, often to their own detriment, Kyoko's survival instinct is for herself alone.[35] The other women in *All She Was Worth*, Shoko and Ikumi, eventually end up returning to a community, but Kyoko's solo run would have continued unchecked had Honma not unraveled her web of deception.

The twists and turns of his investigation gradually educate Honma about the problems and the power of consumerism. In the beginning of the novel, he is puzzled by the young female shoplifter, but as he continues his investigation, he starts to understand the influence that consumerism exerts on all the characters, particularly Shoko and Kyoko. For example, when Honma meets Shoko's former roommate, Tomie, he is treated to her interpretation of why Shoko fell into debt: "Also there weren't so many different places to pour money into. No expensive makeovers, no cosmetic surgery, no glossy magazines showing every product ever made. . . . Everything's easy now. All the dreams that money can buy. Those that have, spend it, and those that don't, borrow their pocket money and wind up like Shoko" (217). Tomie, who also is working as a bar hostess to pay off her debts, is aware of the temptations that consumption presents and is sympathetic to Shoko's desires. Her observations about how young Japanese women are now spending their money is also a reflection of their desires and dreams.

What the characters in this novel want, especially Kyoko and Shoko, is not merely consumer goods, but, more important, space in which to enjoy them. This need reflects the way in which marketers have targeted specific items toward the Japanese consumer based upon class, age, and gender. The "Japanese Dream" has come a long way since the first "three C's" of the mid-1960s—the car, the cooler (air conditioner), and the color television.[36] The new Japanese Dream is to have one's own space. Shoko wanted a Tokyo apartment, and Kyoko, a house; Shoko wanted a grave site, while Kyoko wanted the space that a new identity would provide her. Counter to this is the ideal community created by Honma and Ikari, who have no desire for "things" and are more interested in maintaining relationships with each other, even to the point of adopting a stray dog.

Consumption is a complex network that links together desire, the body, and identity in postmodern capitalist society with more general "concerns with material culture, the organization of the everyday life world, the presentation of the self and the micro-economics of households, whether comprised of families or of individuals."[37] The culture of consumption has flourished in Japan for many centuries, and in particular in the last third of the twentieth century, due in part to the country's stable political situation and the fact that Japan has had to spend very little of its GNP for defense.[38] In the 1980s in particular, the Japanese economy expanded very rapidly and because of its economic success, the basic needs of most citizens were satisfied. As Marilyn Ivy puts it, "since everyone has the same basic array of consumer goods already that array signifies the individual's specific desires."[39] These desires are focused upon identity formation—namely, the desire to become a particular kind of person through the consumption of certain material goods and the desire to create a self that is an autonomous being "rather than a plaything of history or of social forces beyond the control of the individual."[40]

Manufacturers searching for new markets have turned from the fulfillment of needs to stimulating people's desires for luxury goods. Coupled with diversification in marketing and an increase in the number of venues in which to market, the late twentieth century has witnessed a shift away from the boom in sales of objects to short-lived fads. Thus, "to stimulate consumer demand, producers have been compelled to appeal to (and create) highly targeted, diversified, and nuanced types of consumer desire."[41] In particular, women in Japan (and elsewhere) have long been the targets of marketers for many kinds of goods. The rise of the popular press in the form of magazines has contributed to this process by organizing the goods that are available into trends and lifestyles in order to facilitate easier consumption.[42] These modes of disseminating information about commodities and creating a sense of desire leave the consumer deluged by information on what to buy in what season. Moreover, desire has been stratified to the point that there are magazines targeted to different age groups, as well as magazines that serve as buying guides for a particular brand of luxury goods.[43]

In 1992, when Miyabe wrote *All She Was Worth*, the Japanese economy was just starting its downturn, and the social relevance of her plot was not as obvious as it is now. After the burst of the economic bubble in the late 1980s, there was an increase in the number of personal bankruptcies in Japan, brought on by the ease with which consumer credit was available and by unregulated interest rates in the unsecured loan sector. Japanese consumers started to fall into debt at an ever-increasing rate. Yet the end of the bubble economy did not put an end to consumption, as an increasing flow of consumer goods became available and necessary. Just one indication of how desirable consumer goods have become is the *enjo kōsai* (or compensated dating) phenomenon that arose in Japan in 1996.[44] Stimulating this demand for luxury foreign goods was the strong yen, which hit an all-time high against the dollar in April 1995. This made foreign travel more accessible to the average office employee, a possibility driven home by relentless advertising promising the instant gratification that Miyabe decries.[45] This trend of the high yen, however, was not to continue, and the dollar gradually regained some of its strength as the Japanese economy weakened.

Despite consumption's power, Miyabe is not criticizing it per se in *All She Was Worth*. Instead, she is criticizing both the fallacy that consumption alone can create an identity and the desire for instant gratification of one's material desires prevalent in Japanese culture in the 1980s and 1990s. The desire to have things, and have them *now*, leads to the results that Miyabe sees as problematic: "Judging from the photos in the newspaper inserts, mail-order catalogs, and TV commercials for the big department stores, there seemed to be no end to the nice things on the market these days. And to look was to want, preferably right there, on the spot. Producing a card at the cash register and signing the little receipt would be an easy habit to fall into. . . . There was nothing to tell a person when to put on the brakes" (139). The desire to create a certain lifestyle that led Shoko to leave her hometown and become grist for a large company in Tokyo is the same desire that causes people to abandon their roots. While this rural-to-urban migration is not new, I believe what Miyabe is criticizing is that Shoko does it to satisfy her own desires rather than out of any economic necessity.[46] What Miyabe finds disturbing, in other words, is not simply the disorienting effects of the market system, which requires workers to relocate in order to find and keep steady jobs, but also Shoko's efforts to construct a self that exists apart from the larger social fabric of the community.

Again, Shoko's friend talks about Shoko's reasons for coming to Tokyo— the search for the good life that she was unable to have in Utsunomiya: "For her, the good life isn't anything she's going to get by plugging away at it. She wants it, she's just going to have to go after it, *some* way. Back in the old days, used to be you either worked your way up or put up with what you had. . . . Not anymore though. Now nobody wants to work at their dreams. But nobody's willing to give them up, either. For Shoko, it was money for shopping, courtesy of the credit card companies" (216). These comments echo Miyabe's own views on consumption, expressed in interviews, and reveal Miyabe's belief that desires are not achieved instantaneously, rather, they are satisfied through hard work and planning.[47]

The desire that accompanies consumption is not just a matter of wanting a thing; rather, it involves levels of imagination, symbolism, and materiality that also have emotional, even erotic, components.[48] All of these are present in the desire that grips Miyabe's characters. Certainly for Kyoko, they have such an intense hold that she is driven to murder to achieve her heart's desire. Shoko's descent into credit hell was due to all these things. Honma and his friends have nothing but pity for Shoko, a creature that slipped through the cracks, cherished only by her childhood friend and overshadowed in death by the woman who stole her identity. What ultimately elevates Shoko from being a silly, impoverished bar hostess is her final desire to buy a "place" where she and her parents can rest together.

Home, Community, Nostalgia

In her book *Fast Cars, Clean Bodies*, Kristin Ross examines the modernization of France in the era following World War II and provides a cogent description of how the identity of the French family became centered around the house and away from the workplace. In particular, in her discussion of cleanliness in relation to the home, Ross looks at how privatization, or the shift from identification with a public space to a private one, turns people away from political socialization and toward their homes, where they attempt to find a way to anchor themselves. The accompanying shift leads to a decline or decomposition of identities based on work, in which a person's whole being was connected to the place where he or she worked. What remains, then, when this identity is stripped away, is an identity based on the home. Citing Henri Lefebvre, she suggests that "everyday life, private or 'reprivatized' life and family life" is linked with the identity of the home dweller and with the practices connected with "the sole remaining value, *the private value par excellence, that of consumption.*"[49] Consumption and identity with the home and the family thus become central to the identity of the French in the postwar era. As Ross puts it, "to be 'at home' . . . is to have an identity, one based on security and permanence," in which privatization, or "losing oneself in the repetitions and routine of 'keeping house,' meant an increasing density in individual use of commodities and a notable impoverishment of interpersonal relations."[50]

Ross' observations on the shift to the home as site of identity and its connection with consumption in postwar France give us a useful perspective on the role that the house plays in the imagination of Japan in the late twentieth century.[51] Shoko and Kyoko yearn for this kind of identity, centered around one's own home, and for the actual space of the home, although a family does not necessarily figure into the equation. Their desires are reflected in the words of philosopher Gaston Bachelard: "Our house is our corner of the world. As has often been said, it is our first universe, a real cosmos in every sense of the word. . . . The house is one of the greatest powers of integration for the thoughts, memories and dreams of mankind. . . . Without it, man would be a dispersed being."[52] Unlike the women, Honma and his community stand opposed to the process of privatization described by Ross and Bachelard. There is a different sense of place among the two groups of people in *All She Was Worth:* Honma and his friends conceive of place in terms of social relations and are, in Doreen Massey's term, "unbounded," whereas the others see place as private, epitomized by the home and the individuation that goes along with it.[53] It is perhaps no coincidence that the names of the characters reflect this spatial divide. The characters in Honma's name mean "true space" or "original space," while Shinjo Kyoko's family name means "new castle." Thus, different attitudes toward place are indicated even at the level of personal names.

The search for private space in order to create new identities also limited the young women's interactions with other people. Indeed, in tracing Shoko's past, Honma is able to glean significant information about who she was and what she did from only one friend. Within a new private space, the women believed that they would be able to start again, to create new identities, and (in Kyoko's case) to literally become a new person. For them, the home is a place where personal growth and development occur, rather than a place where there are possibilities for new social relations. While Ross' description of the privatization of the home and the postwar modernization that took place in France can be applied to modern Japanese home ownership, Honma's communal existence, which harkens back to the premodern way of life in the countryside and the cities, is incompatible with the lifestyle to which Kyoko and Shoko aspire. His identity is very much tied into a larger place, the neighborhood where he lives, and it runs counter to the emphasis on consumption that home ownership seems to entail. The privatization of daily life, then, produces a loss of the sense of neighborhood and community and reveals just how fragile one's identity is when severed from that place.

What Miyabe is expressing in the world of *All She Was Worth,* in fact, is a nostalgia for an authentic Tokyo (or perhaps Edo)—a romanticized vision of a precapitalist communal world where people knew themselves and their "place" and were content with that place. It is a world that Miyabe believes she continues to inhabit, a place that she describes in her books, where everyday life follows the rhythms of an earlier age and where the community is the focus of a person's life. It is a place where everyone knows everyone, a world that is effaced when people move. Honma laments this change when he talks about hometowns, accents, and the way in which Tokyo assimilates everything and everyone. Yet what Honma has done is to create a version of this *furusato* communalism in his Tokyo *danchi*, suggesting that it is not the place itself that is necessary for identity formation but the people and social relations in it. It is ironic that this vision is achievable only because Ikari has a nonstandard career and Honma is on leave from his job. This world in other words, is possible only because there are people who do not work in routinized jobs that keep them away from the home. In order to maintain this kind of community, there always must be people who are willing and able to stay at home and take care of the needs of others.

While this wistful contemplation of the passing of a gentler way of life is not new in Japanese literature (the works of Nagai Kafu come to mind), its presence in detective fiction, a genre seemingly inextricably linked to the modern urban setting, at first appears misplaced. Yet Miyabe's articulation of problems brought on by encroaching urban standardization echoes themes found in Agatha Christie and the subgenre of the "cozy" detective novel. In many of Christie's stories set in the interwar period, the action takes place in the hermetic world of the country estate rather than in London, a shift in location that occurs because rapid urbanization and the breakdown of class and gender divisions in the city become too much.[54] Despite removal from the city, murder still happens. Christie's novels and the continuing subgenre of cozy detective novels, in which nostalgia for a lost way of life based on traditional gender, age, and class roles form the backdrop, offer a poignant tribute to a way of life that is gradually disappearing. Miyabe continues this tradition and, in the case of *All She Was Worth*, makes it a thematic center-piece of the novel.

In Miyabe's nostalgic view of Honma's neighborhood, she is also creating a place that fights the creeping homogenization of neighborhoods and the countryside. Tokyo is a place that is constantly being rebuilt, as the vestiges of older neighborhoods are buried under the weight of individual houses and high-rise apartment buildings. Moreover, Miyabe is quite clearly depicting a neighborhood that is not filled with the white-collar middle class. Her Tokyo, the Tokyo east of the Sumida River, is populated with various groups that still hold on to older ways of life, and the characters that populate her novel are representatives of these groups, whose differences are neither judged nor rejected. Overall, then, her characters and her Tokyo resist the standardization of the *sarariiman*, white-collar workers, and office lady or O.L. types who permeate much of the popular media representations found in Japanese television programs, romance novels, or even other detective novels. Yet Miyabe's vision of the community, in which class differences have not been effaced by the increasing affluence of the Japanese population in general, is due in large part to the author's turning a blind eye to the realities of the Japanese economy, where "mass consumption is now entrenched as a dominating principle of everyday life," and everyday life is bound up with economics.[55] Miyabe's novel thus can be seen as a form of resistance to the routinization of consumption in everyday life, a call for a return to the more "authentic" rhythms of life surrounding the communities.

Miyabe, however, is not nostalgic for a return to the *furusato* so vividly described by Marilyn Ivy. In her *Discourses of the Vanishing*, Ivy argues that *furusato* "resides in the memory, but is linked to tangible reminders of the past; when the material, palpable reminders of one's childhood home no longer exist, then the furusato is in danger of vanishing. Since the majority of Japanese until the postwar period had rural roots, furusato strongly connoted the rural countryside while the urban landscape implied its loss."[56] In *All She Was Worth*, however, such a hometown, a place where authentic Japan resides, is unattainable for the characters. Despite Honma's plaintive search for the accents of the countryside, he is fully aware that he himself is from Tokyo and has no roots in the northern country from which his parents emigrated. Moreover, with a dead wife and an adopted child, such connections become even more tenuous. Honma realizes that it is not one's place, either rural or urban, that becomes important for one's identity but the family. Yet Honma's notion of family is not limited to the natal family but includes the constructed family that arises from one's personal associations and affinities. A person's community, then, becomes the site where identity is rooted through processes such as the creation of fictive kinship ties, rather than the rootless consumerization of identity that infects the other characters.

The themes that Miyabe highlights in *All She Was Worth* are also foregrounded in other works by contemporary Japanese authors. In particular, the emphasis on consumption and personal identity that she finds so appalling and yet so pervasive in *All She Was Worth* is central to two earlier novels, Tanaka Yasuo's *Nantonaku, kurisutaru (Somehow, crystal,* 1980) and Yoshimoto Banana's *Kitchen* (1988). This common interest aside, however, these three works frame consumption in very different ways—framings that allow us to discern the very different aesthetic, social, and political values espoused by each author.

Despite the thin plotline of *Somehow, Crystal,* the book has received attention due to its connection of personal identity with the consumption of luxury goods. Resembling in no small part contemporary American movies with their prominent "product placements," the work includes footnotes in which the author tells his readers where the featured items are to be purchased. In her essay, "Somehow: The Postmodern as Atmosphere," Norma Field first discusses critic Eto Jun's appreciation of the novel for providing commercial information that "reach(es) beyond regional and generational subculture." Field's interpretation of Eto is much more interesting, however, because she places his praise in the context that the book's wide availability causes it to "become an agent for the preservation and the promotion of Japanese community."[57]

Field's reading of the characters in the novel demonstrates the connection between the consumption of goods (i.e., brand-name luxury goods) and national identity, a connection stated by one of the characters: "I guess in the end you have to say that we have no resistance to brand names. Our generation. Maybe it is not our generation, maybe it's all Japanese."[58]

The pervasiveness of this connection between brand-name goods and identity can be seen in Masao Miyoshi's epilogue to *Offcenter*, in which a pointed critique of Yoshimoto Banana is followed by an attack on critic Baba Keiichi, who, in an article in *Chūō kōron*, described his 1990 novel, *Leica of Love and Sadness*, as one meant to "help Japanese shed their provincialism at this moment of internationalization," although one wonders if he was being serious or not. Baba "laments the insular boorishness of his countrymen who have not yet acquired the cosmopolitan taste for elegance. He finds that the top-ranking brand-name goods that the Japanese love to talk about in daily life are not sufficiently introduced into their fictional world."[59] What galls Miyoshi the most is that Baba's essay demonstrates not a whit of self-irony, but what I find fascinating is Baba's belief, whether serious or not, that a discussion of brand-name consumption is required in literature.[60]

Yoshimoto Banana's novel *Kitchen* takes Baba's message to heart, as the pages of her story are filled with the consumption of expensive items. *Kitchen* is the story of a young woman named Mikage, orphaned at a young age and then left all alone when her grandmother dies. After her grandmother's death, she goes to live with her classmate Yūichi and his mother, Eriko, a transsexual who used to be Yūichi's father. Yūichi's world is different and yet very similar to the one Mikage left. In this world, a seemingly unending flow of items shows up, and the items are exclaimed about; then, a few pages later, another set of items appears without any particular reason. When Yūichi comes home with a word processor, Mikage reflects that "these people had a taste for buying new things that verged on the unhealthy. And I mean big purchases. Mainly electronic stuff."[61] Again, several pages later, Eriko returns home with a brand new juicer, as well as a gift for Mikage. She is overjoyed to be included in the gift giving and her previous disapproval disappears.

This parade of goods serves as a prop in the formation of a "home" for the orphaned Mikage. The creation of a home becomes tantamount for the characters in Yoshimoto's works, as they yearn for the home and the families that they never had—a yearning that becomes the root of the nostalgia that they feel. Always in the back of the characters' minds is the feeling that this home could never exist. The trope of family appears in many of Yoshimoto's earlier works, but as John Whittier Treat has pointed out, she describes the nuclear family in terms that are not always positive.[62] It is the family based on affinity that seems more real for the characters. As Mikage says about her own natal family, "When my grandmother died the other day, I was taken by surprise. My family had steadily decreased one by one as the years went by, but when it suddenly dawned on me that I was all alone, everything before my eyes seemed false."[63] She is swept into Yūichi's family and apartment, which act as a locus for all her fantasies about families and home life.

Mikage spends her time throughout the narrative fantasizing about a place where she feels at home, a place replete with light, space, and consumer goods. Over and over she dreams of kitchens, and these dreams fill her with a sense of longing. It is this longing, this desire for things that she has lost and perhaps things she may have in the future, that makes Yoshimoto's discussion of nostalgia a counterpoint to that of Miyabe. Indeed, as Treat suggests, Yoshimoto's characters, in *Kitchen* as well as in others of her works, are longing for a family and a kind of life that they may never have known. It is the image of the nuclear family that is at the base of their longings, but they have never known one, so the family that they construct in its place approximates the contemporary Japanese family. While on the surface Yoshimoto's and Miyabe's stories seem to be connected by their support of the constructed family, the overriding desire in *Kitchen* for the nuclear family (albeit one without its patriarchal father), a desire that "lacks a determined past to validate it," separates Yoshimoto's story from Miyabe's.[64] The former's nostalgia is a "desire for desire," in which the narcissistic aspirations of the characters combine to produce an emptiness but with no potential to satisfy their desires or attain the yearned-for object.[65]

All She Was Worth acts as a countermeasure to this depiction of identity as defined by consumer goods and of the home as a place for the nuclear family surrounded by goods. Miyabe rejects the notion that identity can be based on the acquisition of consumer goods by showing the reader how difficult this kind of identity is to attain and how it does not lead to happiness once it is achieved. Moreover, the quality of nostalgia in *All She Was Worth* also is different from that of *Kitchen*. Whereas Yoshimoto's characters' memories are divorced from any possible experience they might have had, Miyabe's characters demonstrate that what they yearn for is not irretrievably lost but can be recreated elsewhere. The past can be the future for the characters in Miyabe's story. While Kyoko and Shoko are lost to these possibilities, Tamotsu and Ikumi are still involved in their communities, so the potential for the maintenance of the communal Japanese lifestyle remains.

Miyabe's novel, furthermore, does not simply accept the dominant order of things. Honma and his friends live a lifestyle different from that of many people in Tokyo who are not *danchi* dwellers, so they are surprised by how rootless and alienated from one another people of Kyoko and Shoko's generation appear to be. Thus, by creating a detective with a different attitude toward prevailing beliefs, Miyabe makes him not one who upholds the status quo, but a voice from the margins of society. Miyabe's notion of margins is not political in that her characters are neither repressed by society nor politically disenfranchised; rather, their very existence is at odds with the rest of society because of their lifestyle.[66] These characters have no concept that they are speaking from the margins because they have little idea how society has changed around them. Unlike the other inhabitants of Tokyo, who are caught in the cycle of work and consumption, these voices from the margins express ideas that were the hallmark of traditional Japanese culture. Honma's marginality itself, in other words, is presented as a core Japanese value, while the cultural status quo is revealed to be a source of anxiety and danger to those in the novel.

The tone and style of *All She Was Worth* reinforce the author's views. Both the carefully depicted places and the conversations of the characters lend this novel a cinematographic style that is reminiscent of Stephen King's work and serve to present the author's views seamlessly, without any forum for dissent. Moreover, Kyoko and Shoko, whose lives and life choices directly contradict Miyabe's vision of identity and community, are denied a chance to speak for themselves. They thus become object lessons rather than active agents, relegated to a passive role as narrated rather than narrating subjects. Unfortunately, this seamlessness leads to a sense that the characters are more flat and two-dimensional than the situations in which the author places them. The interesting and seemingly liberatory details of the characters' lives (the adopted son, the widower, the male housekeeper) are negated by the rather traditionally conservative message that the author is conveying.

Miyabe wishes to emphasize that Sekine Shoko's problems are not due to a moral defect, as Honma originally assumes, but to her having been cut off from her community and identity. Here guilt is not a matter of one's individual failings but those of an entire institutional system, one responsible for the destruction of Kyoko and Shoko's lives. Yet, as Franco Moretti proposes in "Clues," "detective fiction exists expressly to dispel the doubt that guilt might be impersonal, and therefore collective and social."[67] Thus, the crime must be one committed by an individual and not one for which society is responsible. We can see this play out in *All She Was Worth* as two women pursue two different paths to resolve their financial problems. Miyabe easily excuses Shoko's bankruptcy as having its origin in society, but she cannot forgive Kyoko's killing of two people in order to hide her bankrupt status. Although Honma initially finds himself caught in Kyoko's web of vulnerability, both Tamotsu's desire to find his lost friend and the incident of the dead dog remind him that Kyoko's actions are wrong. Thus, he is unwilling to blame society for Shoko's murder, although a number of people lay the blame for Shoko's financial problems on society and the financial and advertising systems.

Miyabe's conception of identity as determined by one's place in the community is also rather limiting. Just as one cannot fully be described by the items that one consumes, one cannot be described solely by the place that one inhabits. This limiting definition shares some of the same flaws that the *koseki* has as an external measure of identity. Too often it has been used to prevent members of minorities, such as the *burakumin* (Japan's outcast group) or Zainichi Koreans, from joining the mainstream. Moreover, the *koseki* long served to restrict the status of women; wives often had to wait for legal and symbolic inclusion in their husbands' families, leaving them for a time legally nonexistent, while divorcées would find themselves literally erased from their husbands' families, stigmatizing them and often their offspring.[68] Thus, whereas Tamotsu is able to fit into Honma's community right away, Honma's late wife's cousin Kurisaka Kazuya (whose missing fiancée Shoko started the whole search), is treated as an outsider the whole time. Clearly, he would never fit into the community because of his disregard for his family and interest in money, and no attempt is made to include him. In addition, this community appears to be closed to women, and there seems to be little alternative for them. Nowhere is there a place for women in Miyabe's communal world—even the pregnant Ikumi remains outside this group of men. Furthermore, there does not seem to be an option for women to form a community of their own.

It is Miyabe's creation of community (the focal point for Honma and his friends), the nostalgia that Honma feels for this community, and his anxiety over its loss that are the most disturbing elements in the novel. Miyabe's world of communal living, which harkens back to the late Meiji and early Showa visions of the *shitamachi,* is one of stability and security, where the influx of new ideas and items can be curtailed. Miyabe's nostalgia for this world and her stubborn desire to recover the lost past thus lead her to create a superficially attractive yet unattainable view of community. As John Clammer says of this kind of nostalgia, "While it can be a retreat from the present, (this sense of longing) also contains utopian themes, and so, like all utopias, represents an implicit critique of the present."[69] The present that Miyabe is critiquing is the one on the other side of the Sumida River, the "foreign" Tokyo that she mentions in her *Asahi shinbun* essay. Not only does nostalgia have a utopian aspect, but it also, as I mentioned above, seeks to suppress the origins of what is lost, resulting in an effacement of the problems that arise from the communal lifestyle that Miyabe so valorizes.

There is an oppressive side to Miyabe's communalism that also is connected to the closed aspect of the *shitamachi* attitude toward the rest of the world. The security and stability that are so important for her characters come at a price. Despite the *shitamachi*'s long, historic connection to the Yoshiwara pleasure quarters and the contemporary transient neighborhood of San'ya, where the day laborers live, Miyabe excludes them from her fiction. The marginal, sexual world of the pleasure quarters, which exist now in the form of hostess clubs, are not a part of Miyabe's "authentic" Tokyo, while San'ya receives only the briefest mention. Edward Fowler's portrait of San'ya, the transient neighborhood surrounded by the *shitamachi*, details the suspicion with which the people of the surrounding area view the day laborers. One of Fowler's informants, who has run for the Tokyo Assembly and lost, shrugs off his loss as a result of "the mistrust that Shitamachi residents have for outsiders, especially one without family."[70] Notably, it is to San'ya that Kyoko's father flees after the breakup of their family. The price that one pays for stability, therefore, is relinquishing the ability to act outside of the norms of society; it calls to mind the wartime neighborhood associations that patrolled the streets and became the enforcers of government edicts about the rules of everyday life.[71]

Miyabe's notion of identity, which is closely linked to a place, also has larger implications in the light of rapid globalization. Today, with the rise of multinational companies and the sense that the world is shrinking, the image of Japan as a monoethnic society also is changing. Both David Harvey and Doreen Massey point out that societies have a tendency to cling to a sense of place in reaction to increased internationalization. As Massey notes, "when time-space compression is seen as disorientating, and as threatening to fracture personal identities (as well as those of place) then a recourse to place as a source of authenticity and stability may be one of those responses."[72]

Seen in this light, Miyabe's vision of a community-oriented world intimately linked to one's place in society is both comforting and compensatory. Miyabe herself has made it a crusade to ensure that this world is not lost, speaking from her secure position as a best-selling author. Both her popular detective novels and historical fiction reinforce the idea that a person's place in Japanese society is crucial to being Japanese. Yet as redevelopment continues unabated, stealing more and more land from Miyabe's *shitamachi*, her work has begun to take on notes of defiance and despair. In her 1997 Naoki Prize–winning novel *Riyū* (The reason), she chronicles the gradual breakdown of the "old neighborhood" under pressure from the hypermodern world across the river, epitomized by a luxury high-rise built near Kita-Senju station in the northern *shitamachi*.[73] This high-rise is the perfect place for a murder because it is cut off from the rest of the neighborhood, and thus the lives of its inhabitants go unremarked. In *The Reason*, therefore, the separation between the good and bad parts of Tokyo asserted in *All She Was Worth* has been breeched, allowing the "High City" to contaminate the "Low City" physically (in the form of high-rise construction) as well as morally (through the pernicious influence of the new residents and the consumer ethos that they embrace).[74]

In the face of such challenges, Miyabe has sought solace not from the too modern world around her, but from the world of the past, a response epitomized by her 1998 travelogue (and first piece of nonfiction) *Heisei okachi nikki* (The Heisei traveler's diary), a collection of essays based on her "magical history tour of Japan."[75] In the preface, she explains that *toho* were lower-ranking samurai of the Edo period who did not have the privilege of riding a horse. Miyabe wants readers to walk and find Edo on foot. From the *toho*'s perspective, therefore, Miyabe takes the reader on a journey to the site of famous Japanese stories, most notably *Chushingura*.[76] The book is filled with maps and pictures of the fresh-faced Miyabe, clad in historically evocative yet ladylike garb, looking like a pilgrim on a tour to resurrect a lost Japan. As she describes several of Japan's famous historical moments as ones in which Japan's noble ambitions were crushed by the status quo, Miyabe combines a celebration of Japan's most splendid isolationist period of history, the places where this period's perhaps most enduringly popular mythic narrative unfolded, and her engagingly simple style to create a work that reinforces the image of Japan as a stable, and stabilizing, community. While *The Reason* represents a lament at the passing of the *shitamachi* and its way of life, therefore, *The Heisei Traveler's Diary* is a defiant attempt to rescue the small but resilient moments of Japanese history, and by extension to reclaim what Miyabe considers the "real" Japan.

CHAPTER 3

Office(r) Ladies

Police Work as Women's Work

"There's no doubt that the male police officers can only see me as a woman. Rather than being their partner, I'll always be someone of a different sex, and ultimately a different kind of animal." For better or worse, that was what Takako learned when she became a police officer. We're not people: in the end, we're just men and women.

—Nonami Asa, *Frozen Fangs*

For women writers attempting to create a strong and believable female detective, the combustible issues of sex and gender loom large. The author must address a number of difficult questions in her attempt to situate her character in a setting that resonates with how readers perceive the world to be. How, for instance, does a woman's presence in the workplace affect the men around her, who have spent years steeling themselves from the horrors with which they deal on a daily basis? How does a female character deal with the often sordid world of crime, in which women too often are the victims? Failing to consider such questions and to answer them can result in a protagonist who is either unrealistic or simply unbelievable. This and the following chapter thus examine the tropes of sex and violence in Japanese women's detective fiction, focusing first upon the portrayal of sexual harassment and sexual violence in the workplace and then analyzing more explicit treatments of the relationship among sex, violence, and female experience.

Although women have been involved in Japanese law enforcement for many years, it is only in the last few decades that they have begun to play a more active role as officers and, more recently, detectives. This brave new world of female police work was depicted in stark terms by Nonami Asa, whose 1996 novel, *Frozen Fangs,* was awarded the 115th Naoki Prize. Although Nonami was not the first woman to create a female detective as her heroine, her novel was unique in its in-depth treatment of the day-to-day struggles of a woman trying to make it as a member of the Tokyo Metropolitan Police. In *Frozen Fangs*, a straightforward mystery plot serves as the backdrop for a careful and often critical analysis of a woman police officer's relationship with her partner, her peers, and her family. Unlike the utopian picture of an all-male community that Miyabe paints in *All She Was Worth*, Nonami's view of women in society is bleaker. Her depiction of how women function in the public world of the workplace and how their jobs structure their relationships, both professional and personal, suggests that despite the gains that women have made in police work (as elsewhere), they have had to pay a heavy price. The problems that Nonami's character faces are not unique to her work, however; they arise as well in the novels of Shibata Yoshiki, featuring the female police detective Murakami Riko. Despite a professional history marred by harassment, Riko has persisted in her work and has adopted an interesting strategy for dealing with the problems that arise.

That Nonami and Shibata chose to create heroines who work as police detectives was no accident. Their depiction of women detectives was bound to resonate in 1990s Japan with its steadily increasing female workforce, a resonance amplified by the medium of detective fiction. In particular, the genre of the police procedural, which is a story about how a job is performed, provides both authors with a way to discuss women at work that is not intrinsic to other types of literature and becomes a valuable representation, or figuration, of the place and possibilities of women in contemporary Japan.

Unlike the private detective, who not only operates independently, letting the circumstances of each case determine the course of the investigation, but also is free to select which cases to solve, the police detective is tied to the bureaucracy and hierarchy of a public office. This very public and male-dominated world, in which these authors' heroines must flourish, is quite similar to the professional sphere of Japanese business. Both Nonami and Shibata are veterans of this sphere, having worked in a variety of different careers before turning to writing. Their explorations of the problems women face in a traditionally male world—such as sexual harassment, unsatisfactory personal lives, and doubts over professional competence—offer a more personalized glimpse into the conditions of women in the workplace. By couching women's work experience in the ultramasculine world of the police, the authors are able to depict the external and internal pressures on these women in an unrelentingly realistic manner. Moreover, this fictional setting allows them to explore not only the negative aspects of working in a nontraditional profession, but also the rewards that such work might provide.

The presence or absence of women in the Japanese workplace has been studied by scholars in Japan and elsewhere for decades, but these accounts have consisted of either social-scientific studies of the workplace or anecdotal evidence provided by individual women. The social imaginary of women's work has not been explored as has that of men, as in the genre of the "business novel" (or *keizai shōsetsu*), treated by Tamae Prindle's *Made in Japan and Other Japanese "Business Novels."*[1] While representations of working male identity exist in the realm of popular culture, women rarely appear beyond the subordinate positions of secretary or sex object. The advent in Japan of detective fiction featuring women detectives, particularly the police procedural, therefore provides a valuable representation of women's experience in the workplace. The detective novel that features a woman as the protagonist is a novel about woman as worker and about how women see the overwhelmingly male-dominated workplace in Japan and envision their place in it.

Women, Work, and the Police Procedural

In the larger realm of detective fiction, novels featuring police detectives, called police procedurals *(keisatsu shōsetsu),* differ greatly from those that feature private detectives, despite the fact that the two subgenres evolved together. Unlike the private detective, who is a loner and belongs to no group, the police detective is a servant of the state and is expected to uphold its rules. Moreover, the police detective cannot reject the demands of the patriarchal state but must support its authority. As Kathleen Gregory Klein puts it, "Police are bound by bureaucracy, hierarchies and politics. Historically they are paid by a system which inhibits individual action and decisions; they are assigned to cases, bound to standard investigative behavior, and responsible for the state's vision of justice."[2]

Despite these strictures on the police detective, in the course of the police procedural's literary history, authors have sought alternatives to the image of the police detective as a simple cog in the machinery of the state. The alternatives themselves reveal cultural differences and values. The American police detective, for instance, often finds himself at odds with the dictates of his higher-ups, so he strikes out on his own as a renegade cop to find the killer. Often he discovers that his bosses are corrupt, and in the process of solving the crime, he ferrets out the corruption, giving the police department a chance to start afresh. Yet while the plots of all detective fiction are necessarily embedded in a political or social context, the police procedural and private detective fiction share the belief that guilt is individual. Thus, during an investigation, the police must identify specific individuals and hold them responsible for specific crimes rather than questioning society's culpability.[3] Robert P. Winston and Nancy C. Mellerski, in their investigation of the police procedural in Europe, state that the genre's predominance there reflects the way that European society has developed:

The rise in the police procedural . . . suggests a response to the technological penetration and increased bureaucratic complexity of post-industrial
society which operates by proposing a squad of individualized detectives,
each possessing certain crucial skills which enable them to work collectively
to investigate the same systemic evil that the hard-boiled detective nostalgi-
cally confronted alone. Thus, the formula of the police procedural reacts to
the new socioeconomic reality by requiring a corporate detective, a squad
sufficiently diverse to cope with the complexities of a world controlled by
corporate powers.[4]

Women police detectives have been present in detective fiction for as long
as their private counterparts, if in name only. Kathleen Gregory Klein identifies two British policewomen—the first in an 1864 novel, *The Female
Detective,* and the second in 1884—as the first fictional examples of women
police.[5] Despite their early arrival on the literary scene, however, female
police soon disappeared in favor of their private counterparts and remained
in the minority, and the female professional detective followed quickly on the
heels of the policewoman. For the next century, women protagonists in detective fiction were largely private investigators, and significant differences
arose between public and private detectives, leading to certain persistent
characteristics in detective fiction featuring women. These include utopian
models of female agency, the exploitation of the transgression of social mores
by the deployment of disruptive humor and parody, and the feminization of
male authority.[6] These characteristics, which are ubiquitous in women's
detective fiction, are absent from the police procedural, which is anchored by
the realistic hierarchies and patriarchal authority of the state. Rather than
transgressing social mores through humor and parody, the female police
detective is by her very existence "transgressive."

It is not because of the writer's explicit interest in women's work experience that the police procedural becomes a vehicle for such treatment, however, but because the conventions of the genre lead to an overstatement of
gender differences. This genre, more specifically, shows how the situation of
women police officers can be read as symptomatic of the problems women
face more generally in the workplace. Thus, the police procedural becomes a
compelling site at which to locate a narrative about women's entry into a
previously all-male arena. Because the purpose of the police procedural is to
describe how the police solve a crime, the subgenre of the police procedural
is deeply concerned with the mechanics of the workplace and the details of
job performance. The workplace, moreover, is not merely the police station
but the neighborhoods and the streets, making the entire city the domain of
men who are responsible for its maintenance and regulation. The protagonist

of the police procedural is not the police hero, but someone involved in the routine of police investigation, often working on more than one case at once, as part of a team that shares both work and credit.[7]

Another characteristic of detective fiction that contributes to this portrayal of women in the workplace is its mimetic quality. In general, detective fiction is seen as reflecting the society to which it is addressed, and in so doing, it is a strand of "realistic" literature—that is, works that represent life and the social world as it is for the reader.[8] Raymond Chandler, the famous creator of the private detective Philip Marlowe, thus insisted that realism was the most important part of a detective story, which must be "realistic in character, setting, and atmosphere . . . about real people in a real world."[9] In this sense, not only the introduction of women to the police force in the police procedural, but also their reception by their fictional colleagues and communities must reflect the social Zeitgeist in which the novels are produced.

The appearance of the female police detective thus can be seen as a straightforward register of changes in women's positions in society, reflecting "the mechanics of women's entry not just into the workplace but into the professional managerial positions that became available to them during the 1980s."[10] As Walton and Jones have suggested, crime fiction is most likely to reflect social change in the occupational category of the police, and the casting of a policewoman as the main character has a twofold effect. First it represents the possibility of women's integration into mainstream society in equal relationship to men (the goal of liberal feminists); second is "the disruption of the perceived social harmony within law enforcement agencies themselves."[11] Thus, the police procedural is able to depict how police departments (and the society that they represent) try to resist women's participation and women's concerns.

Walton and Jones also point out that in the United States, the police procedural was the forerunner to the female private detective novels and began to address anxieties of the women's movement in the 1960s and 1970s such as the place of women in the male-dominated workplace and problems of social justice—"justice both as it is administered *by* the law and as it is conducted *within* the law itself."[12] Yet while police procedurals featuring women detectives are not new in the Anglo-American context, they are comparatively few. Those written by women are even rarer, as women writers focus the bulk of their attention on the private detective. This is not to say that strong female police detectives do not exist, only that they are far fewer in number than their private counterparts. In 1999, of the detective novels in print in the United States and the United Kingdom, 39 percent feature a female private investigator, while only 17.5 percent of the police procedurals had a female protagonist.[13]

Outside of North America and the United Kingdom, the female police detective is an even rarer creature. Each of the major television networks in Japan has broadcast a program with some form of female police officer since the mid-1900s—for example, the 1997 series "Hamidasu deka" (Rebel cop) and an ongoing series of movies beginning in 1995 called "Obasan deka" (The auntie cop) featuring an older female police detective.[14] The female police officer, however, has rarely made the transition to literature; indeed, the first significant fictional treatment of the female police officer was in Nonami's *Frozen Fangs*. Miyabe Miyuki has suggested that literature (and here she uses the term *"bungaku"*) demands more realism than television; thus, until there are more women police officers, fictional women detectives will be few and far between.[15] Part of Miyabe's critique stems from the difference in style between her and the writers considered in this chapter since her social criticism contrasts with their highly individualistic and inward-looking view of society. As Nonami and Shibata's novels amply demonstrate, however, the presence of women in the police precinct is not unusual or unrealistic, given the inroads that women have made in other male-dominated fields (such as the Self-Defense Forces).[16]

Miyabe's gloomy assessment of the possibility for female police detectives notwithstanding, the relative absence of women in the Japanese police procedural bears questioning.[17] In general, I believe, as Walton and Jones have indicated about Anglo-American procedurals, the novels featured in this chapter depend upon social circumstances that are necessary for such literature to exist. In particular, there needs to be a significant and enduring number of professional women in areas that have traditionally been perceived as "male," so that it would not be inconceivable for a woman to be present in an analogous fictional environment. Due in no small part to the Equal Employment Opportunity Law of 1985 and to Japan's booming economy until 1992, record numbers of women entered all levels of the workforce. While the end of Japan's bubble economy slowed (and even reversed) this progress, women are still working in all sectors.

As a result of the economic circumstances, novels have appeared that are concerned with issues particular to women in the workplace. In these novels, the most striking feature is the detective's awareness and experience of sexual harassment. Unfortunately, the strides that women have made in the workplace have been accompanied by the dark shadow of sexual harassment, or *seku hara* as it is known in Japanese,[18] a problem that is insufficiently regulated or rarely addressed.[19] In a few landmark cases victims have brought suit against their abusers, but the majority of cases have not been pursued, and the benefit of the doubt goes to the harasser.[20] The concern in the police procedural, thus, is the absence of a forum to address these issues.

Without such a forum, where women can gain official or public recognition of their plight, the problem continues.

Sexual harassment, while a part of the Japanese workplace for many years, was long considered one of the "perks" of working, or an instance of personal misconduct, or the result of a communication gap between the sexes.[21] Sexual harassment as a concept did not enter the popular imagination or become a part of the vocabulary until the late 1980s. Once there, the term became exceedingly popular, but it was not seen as a serious problem, either by the media or by the public at large, until 1990, when a landmark court decision punished a company for supporting a hostile work environment. In 1999, the Labor Ministry amended the 1985 Equal Employment Opportunity Law in order to make firms liable in sexual harassment cases, replacing language that had merely encouraged firms to discourage harassment.[22] The amendment has spurred many women to take their harassers to court, yet the burden of proof in these cases still lies with the women, who also must face the challenges of the legal system, as well as a society that frowns on litigation to address wrongs.[23]

Otomichi Takako: Lone Wolf or Team Player?

The continuing problem of harassment, as well as more subtle but equally pernicious forms of prejudice directed against women in the workplace and conflicts between the demands of work and family, feature prominently in the first work discussed here, Nonami Asa's *Frozen Fangs*. Nonami's novel, followed by *Hana chiru goro no satsujin* (Murder when the petals scatter, 1999), *Kusari* (Chains, 2000), and *Miren* (Attachment, 2001), introduces a new detective, Otomichi Takako, and charts the obstacles that she faces as she attempts to navigate her way through a new work environment—not just the long hours that she must face, but also harassment and questions about her competence that are rarely spoken but nonetheless loom over her.[24] In fact, it is Takako's struggle to resist the mind-numbing pressure of the police force, its rules, and its culture (rather than the novel's rather flaccid storyline) that makes *Frozen Fangs* compelling, providing the reader with a fascinating study of character under pressure.

The novel begins "at sunset, as the north wind began to strengthen" (3), when a family-style restaurant off the brightly lit main street catches on fire.[25] One man is burned to death, incinerated by a device hidden in his belt buckle. Several days later, a businessman's mauled body is discovered miles away. Finally a newly married young woman is found in the snow, bitten to death. These cases, which have the police baffled, eventually draw all the members of the police force to the Tachikawa police station. Takako, a thirty-something police officer from the motor patrol division, is paired with

Takizawa Tamotsu, a veteran detective. Takako, who normally spends her day on motorcycle patrol, finds the adjustment to detective work challenging. Trailing along behind Takizawa, who she correctly perceives does not like her, she endures his criticisms silently since she has never learned how to curry favor in the male-dominated world of the police.

Despite her reticence, Takako turns out to be the one who breaks the case open. The solution to the mystery is not particularly complicated. A former police officer, Sasahara, whose family life has been torn apart by the drug addiction of his teenage daughter, has decided to seek revenge on the people responsible. The first victim ran the *terekura* (Japanese abbreviation for "telephone club") in which his daughter had participated, the second victim was a client of the *terekura,* and the third victim was a friend of his daughter's from the days when she lived on the streets.[26] Now, Sasahara's daughter, Emiko, is institutionalized, her brain wrecked by drugs and her body wasted by venereal disease, and her father has acquired a magnificent half-wolf dog, Hayate, to take care of her. The dog is devoted to Emiko but also has been trained to kill on command. After Sasahara's house has been burned by the last man he is trying to punish, Hayate escapes, and it is left to the police to capture him before he kills again. With Takako in pursuit on her motorcycle, Hayate runs along the expressways of nighttime Tokyo until he is cornered in a park and ultimately captured.

On the surface, Nonami's novel appears to be a straightforward police procedural, a bleak story peopled with bleak characters. What separates this novel from others, however—aside from the introduction of a female police detective—is its description of the thorny working relationship between its protagonists. Unlike many other works of detective fiction, where antagonisms among characters are played out in the open and affect the community as a whole, the tension between Takako and Takizawa is intensely personal and expressed in more subtle ways. Nonami focuses upon the characters' inner thoughts and emotions, an effect obtained by alternating the narrative voice between the protagonist and her partner. This shifting perspective allows *Frozen Fangs* to vividly depict the development of a working relationship between two people separated by age, experience, and gender, and the depiction is enhanced by the novel's clear-eyed presentation of each character's faults and failings, as well as their insulting thoughts about one another.

In the first chapter, the author's use of multiple points of view effectively introduces each of the characters, portraying them in environments where they are comfortable and in control. From the family restaurant the novel switches to Takako's apartment, small and cluttered, where she comes home after a long day of work. She watches the fire on the television news and notes that it falls in her office's jurisdiction. The action again switches, this time to Takizawa, one of the first officers to arrive at the scene of the restaurant fire. He is the one who controls the pace of the investigation at the beginning. Shivering in the biting wind, his leather coat thrown over his suit, Takizawa is aware that he is getting older and fatter. He and his colleagues, who are used to standing around crime scenes and waiting to do their jobs, joke about how high the building is and how often they eat at such out-of-the-way restaurants, indicating the amount of time that they spend away from home. Once the firefighters arrive, a body is found inside the burning building. Takizawa and the others ride to the police station with the body; while he is used to seeing dead and decaying bodies, the others are not. He assures a white-faced colleague that "you get used to it" (24). He returns to the scene with the other detectives, and they begin their investigation of the site, finding valuable clues amid the debris.

Although Nonami initially presents the two principle characters in places where they are comfortable and appear in control of their surroundings, she quickly throws them together in an antagonistic relationship where neither feels fully at ease. Nevertheless, the window she provides into their private thoughts and fears helps to make them more sympathetic and human and allows the reader to follow the slow process of growth that both undergo. At the beginning of the book, Takizawa is portrayed as the mature, worldly detective, but once he begins to work with Takako, his criticism of her shows his dark side. Without any access to Takako's thoughts, his impression is that she is an emotionless person just going through the motions of her job. By the middle of the novel, however, such stereotypes have been replaced with fuller, more compelling portraits of people attempting to traverse the difficult terrain of work and family. While in the beginning Takizawa heads the investigation and dictates its pace and parameters, Takako's discoveries—which turn out to require her specialized motorcycle skills—slowly tip the balance of the relationship in her favor. Thus, for Takizawa his relationship with Takako challenges his superiority in the field, while for Takako the stress of working a new job causes her home to become fraught with emotional booby traps and reminders of her failings—a mutual destabilization that reveals how the boundaries of male-female relationships are not fixed and are subject to reevaluation by the characters. This interaction between the two detectives also charts the process by which a younger woman earns the respect of her older, male partner. At first, their relationship is deeply sexualized, as even the insults that pass between them center on Takako's gendered body. It is not until Takako proves that she is able to efface her "femininity"—that is, to take his insults without becoming emotional or reporting them to the authorities, to learn how to pursue a hunch logically, and finally to ride a motorcycle through the streets of Tokyo—that he accepts her as a partner. Her situation, notably, is aided by the fact that she is unmarried and does not appear to have any personal relationships that would interfere with the time she devotes to her job.

Nonami's use of shifting perspective is also useful in revealing Takako's experience of work. The reader not only has an insight into what Takako endures as the lone woman on the investigation, but also is able to see the effect of her presence on a stereotypically crusty older detective. Confronted with a new partner that he must train, Takizawa makes no allowances for her lack of experience. He does not have much use for her police skills and criticizes her for not using the "female" skills of empathy and intuition. In fact, he is particularly harsh on her when she begins to develop her own leads. Takizawa's treatment thus stems not only from Takako's status as a newcomer, a novice among seasoned veterans, but also from the more general police force culture of misogyny and sexual harassment, in which female competence and professionalism are constantly challenged and the presence of women on the workforce is seen as an open invitation to abuse.

Such pressures, found whenever women enter a male-dominated work environment, are particularly acute in law enforcement, where group cohesion is necessary not only for effectiveness, but also for survival. Likewise, challenges to a woman's competence resonate strongly in detective fiction, where the ability to solve crimes is a protagonist's defining characteristic. In the contemporary women's detective fiction of Sara Paretsky or Sue Grafton, readers do not question the detective's ability to solve the case, but this was not always true. As Kathleen Gregory Klein points out, modeling the female protagonist on a male prototype establishes conditions for her failure as either an investigator or a woman—or both.[27] In these cases, the female detective would not be able to solve the case without assistance from a man, or she would be attacked, kidnapped, or injured and would need assistance to free herself. It is difficult for women to demonstrate that they are capable of handling an investigation because they are assumed to be neither authoritative nor equipped with the skills to perform an interrogation.[28]

Takako confronts these difficulties from the moment she is called to work on the murder task force. So many officers have reported for duty to the Tachikawa police station's "war room" that they are required to sign in, and when Takako does so, there is confusion about how to read the Chinese characters of her name. This misunderstanding, however, causes less of a stir than her entrance into the meeting room, where her presence is met with stares and muffled laughter.

> "Think nothing of it," said the chief, who was walking next to her. Takako glanced at him and replied, "I'm used to it."

A woman is unfit to be a police officer because people find fault with her, either regarding her as a curiosity or as a despicable creature. This is what Takako learned when she was transferred from the traffic patrol division to the detective division. Even though the chief had been kind to her just now, last year Takako couldn't hide her confusion and really felt like a woman more than usual.

Just because this one meeting upsets me doesn't mean that I can't do this, she thought (36).

Nonami's decision to focus intimately upon only a few protagonists has the effect of condensing the highly social and diffuse phenomena of misogyny and harassment into a single relationship—namely, that between Takako and Takizawa. Takizawa's initial harassment is centered on Takako's bodily appearance and serves as an attempt to defeminize her in front of the other male police officers.[29] After she introduces herself to Takizawa and hands him her business card, he simply mutters, *"Dekai, na,"* before sauntering off without looking at her card (46). *"Dekai"* (huge or hulking), while not pejorative per se, is clearly used here as an insult—a reference to Takako's body, which until now has not been described—and is meant to emphasize her difference from the stereotypically diminutive feminine form. As Nonami shifts perspective, however, it becomes clear that Takizawa's problems are more than skin deep:

Takizawa didn't dare speak to her, but he had his reasons. First, he didn't trust women. Women lie. They betray you. They're fickle. They're emotional. Takizawa's job was based on trust and teamwork. There was no reason to be partnered with someone like her. Second, he just wouldn't accept a female cop. This is man's work and a man's world. This job was intense and went hand in hand with danger. You only saw the dark side of human nature, which was stressful. . . . Third, it was a nuisance. With a man you didn't need a bathroom, but being with a woman meant that you had to stop at one. When you went home late at night, you had to worry about whether to let her walk alone, and you had to watch what you said and couldn't say what you felt. Fourth—well, this one really got under his skin. When Otomichi Takako appeared in the squad room, the other cops were excited. . . . She was a striking woman (60).

To be sure, Takako takes an equally dim view of her new partner, whom she sees as an "old fool" and whose personal appearance—"Oily, lumpy skin, teeth stained with tar . . . hooded eyes and rank smell" (48)—repulses her. In the beginning, however, Takako's feelings are kept private, in marked contrast to Takizawa's very open expressions of contempt. As they set about investigating the case, Takizawa's abuse shifts from Takako's appearance to the way that she does her job, continuing to focus nevertheless upon what he perceives to be her nonconformity with gender-appropriate behavior and attitudes:

> "Feel free to walk behind me, but don't give me that scowling, high-and-mighty face. It's bad enough as it is."
>
> Takako's face reddened immediately. She started to speak, but he wasn't finished.
>
> "Because you're a woman, you should use that sensitivity as a weapon. Smile. It's easier to get people's good will that way, rather than copping an ugly attitude. That's how you get good—listen to what people say. But you, you hate my kind, don't you? And when you hate a guy, you find it hard to listen to what he says."
>
> "That's not what I had in mind" (86).

Yet while Takizawa castigates Takako for not exploiting her "womanly" skills (such as intuition and compassion), he is even more critical of her failure to "toughen up" and live up to his masculine ideals of police work. When they interview one of the witnesses to the fire, Takako hangs back, inhibited by the pain that the injured witness is suffering. This apparent unwillingness to engage with the investigation irritates Takizawa, and he criticizes her for not attempting to talk to the witness: "You're not merely a decoration! Don't waste opportunities. . . . You'd better pray that you only get to interview men who love women and women who're afraid of men!" (63). Frustrated by her behavior and unable to understand its cause, Takizawa vows not to coddle her and angrily insists that she do the next round of interviews. Takako's calm acceptance of her partner's criticisms and her attempts to follow his advice and perform in a more "masculine" way do little to placate Takizawa, who is irritated by her failure to conform to his stereotypes and scornful of her efforts.

Takizawa's constant questioning of Takako's competence is exacerbated by her own sense of isolation, both within the workplace and in her private life. One characteristic of police fiction that reflects the reality of modern police work is the relative absence of women on the job. Since there are very few women in the police force in Japan with a rank sufficient to work on a murder investigation or in the major crimes division, it becomes next to impossible to have a veteran female police officer as a mentor; moreover, in the strictly hierarchical world of the police force, there are unwritten rules about fraternization between detectives and lower-ranking officers.[30] This can be seen in *Frozen Fangs*: although Takako is friendly with the members of the women's police corps, or *fujin keisatsukan,* they are uniformed officers and quite clearly segregated from her. As a result, the few women detectives tend to be isolated, separated from other women on the force, and denied the benefit of veterans' experiences.[31]

Nonami's bleak portrayal of Takako's work life is enhanced by the genre of the police procedural itself, in which the structured world of the job is presented as ordinary and life beyond it as unusual. This situation lends a character's private life a somewhat exotic tinge and makes events outside the realm of work take on a deeper significance than they would otherwise. When the gender of the protagonists is changed, women are placed in a double bind by the police procedural's inversion of work and home—that is, the things typically associated with being a woman (such as home, family, and children) become exoticized or (more often) marginalized. This leaves a female protagonist alienated from other women workers since they cannot accept her as part of their world. While the female private detective's actions are transgressive because her job takes her places where women are not traditionally supposed to go, such as the streets at night, the female police detective is transgressive due to her very presence in the male-dominated world of the police station.

Furthermore, while tensions arise from this transgression, they also are rooted in the very nature of the work regime, as Arlie Russell Hochschild has pointed out in *The Time Bind*.[32] Such tension, in other words, is endemic to society—as is made explicit in *Frozen Fangs*. Since Takako must spend so much time at work, all her effort is directed there, to the detriment of her personal life. For women police officers, as for women in other fields, the need to focus on work during work hours is not merely due to the demands of the workplace but to the unwritten rule that women must do so in order to prove that they are serious workers.[33] In Japan, women must assimilate to the male work regime, where family is subordinated to work, where the work group becomes a kind of alternative family unit—one whose existence, however, is founded on (female) domestic labor and maintenance—and where access to power and influence is deeply dependent upon involvement in social networks that are generally closed to women.[34]

Takako is no exception to this rule. During the course of the investigation, she becomes completely separated from her family and others as she spends long hours on the job. Single after a divorce that was finalized barely a year before the story begins, she buries her sorrow over a broken marriage in her work. Her family, however, is not that easy to escape. Her parents are not pleased by her job choice, and Takako avoids their complaints and exhortations to quit only by ignoring them as much as possible. Yet as the oldest of three daughters, she has family obligations, and her mother regularly leaves guilt-inducing messages on her answering machine.

The problems of her job and the pressures of her family come to a boiling point just as the case is reaching a critical stage. Takako's sister Tomoko, who is embroiled in a love affair with a married man, is using the pretext of staying with her sister to see her lover. Takako, who divorced her own husband due to his infidelity, refuses to assist her in any way. It is at this crucial point that Tomoko attempts suicide, prompting her mother to order her eldest daughter home to help out. Takako appeals to her father, who decides, "Things here are what they are. Your work is more important." He adds that "Since Yuko and I are here, you don't have to worry about Tomoko and your mother" (289). Takako promises to come home once there is a break in the case. Her mother, however, is not able to leave Takako alone, and she continues to harangue her, blaming her for not spending enough time with her sister. "Every day, every day, I don't know why you are so busy. If your work is such that you can't make your sister a priority, then you should quit. If you keep this job, then you will never be successfully married" (311).

The weighty demands of Takako's job are unrelieved by the family. In fact, the author makes it clear that the family is a source of problems and even misery for each character in the novel since men too are forced to subordinate family to work. When Takako picks up Takizawa late at night, she sees that his face is bruised and learns that his son has hit him. After his family's destruction, Sasahara, the master mind of the crime, goes down the road of revenge and to his own demise. He feels that his neglect of his family while he was a police officer led to his daughter's involvement in drugs and prostitution, prompting him to seek retribution.

With the family as a source of vexation for these characters, the home ceases to be a place to relax and escape from the problems of work. Published just four years after Miyabe's *All She Was Worth*, *Frozen Fangs* demonstrates the limitations of both Miyabe's idea of community and even the idea of home ownership that Miyabe's young female characters cherish. Miyabe saw home ownership as emblematic of a shift away from the community and from an identity based on one's place in that community toward a private place in which one's identity could be constructed. The young women in Miyabe's novel sought a place where they could replace identities through material and symbolic consumption and pursue the "Japanese Dream." For the characters in Nonami's novel, however, the house is a place of isolation and unresolved relationships. Rather than a site of comfort or community, for Takako the house is merely the repository for her belongings and a place to satisfy her bodily needs. She keeps her motorcycle there and comes home to eat and sleep alone. Her family can still inflict pain and guilt on her there by calling and visiting, so Takako is driven to spend more and more time away. In a significant parallel, Takizawa's home also becomes a dangerous place when he is beaten by his son; as a result, he spends even more of his time away from his family, either at work or fishing with his colleagues. For both characters, then, the home's association with the family is a source of discord and, in Takako's case, a constant reminder of her failed marriage. It becomes not a place for relationships but a place to hide from them (in Takako's case) or simply a place to hide *from* (for Takizawa).

In many ways, Nonami presents a more realistic view of how work affects the idea and reality of "community." Miyabe's vision of the community depends on someone being at home to maintain relationships, but Nonami shows that work in today's world makes this impossible. Takako is a lonely figure, estranged from both her family and her colleagues. Her isolation from colleagues in the police department means that she, like the young women in Miyabe's novel, is alone. Unable to join the community of police officers because of her sex, she does not find solace in a consumption-fueled drive for identity; instead, her whole life revolves around her job. In addition to living alone, Takako is also socially disconnected. In part, this is due to her busy lifestyle, but it also stems from the fact that she does not have any friendships with women—a situation that dates back to her time in college and at the academy and is reinforced by comments like "It's not men but women who are the enemy" (73).

Takako's commitment to her job does not initially translate into acceptance or even tolerance from the men with whom she works. Takizawa clearly does not see Takako as worthy of a personal relationship with him and thus does not spend any time outside of work with her. This reflects the reality in many modern police forces, where younger women learned police work from older male police officers, "many of whom resented having female partners; these male officers sometimes displayed their resentment by openly expressing doubts about women's proficiency in law enforcement."[35] With these avenues to inclusion closed to her, therefore, Takako is forced to prove herself in the only way that she can— by demonstrating her abilities in the face of opposition and ridicule. It is she who makes the connection between the victims' dog bites and the presence of the wolf dog, and she continues to push this line of inquiry despite Takizawa's jeers.

"You really think a wolf dog did this?" he asked.

"I think it would be a good angle to pursue."

"Then you're doing it yourself, because that's where I get off. It's a stupid idea." He lit another cigarette, a disgusted look on his face.

She turned to him and sighed. "Why?"

"I want to catch people. Dogs should be left to the Bureau of Health. Let someone else do that. . . ."

He blew cigarette smoke at Takako and gave her a scornful look. The cold winter wind swept the smoke away, and it never reached her face.

"With you as a partner, I'll never solve this case" (145).

Initially, Takako's attempts to pursue her theory are hindered both by her partner's hostility and by more generic discrimination against her as a female cop. When she goes to investigate the police dog kennels, the man in charge rebuffs her, and it is only when Takizawa steps in that they learn about the training of dogs. Over time, however, Takako's investigative interest in the case leads Takizawa to stop harassing her. As the case builds momentum, the number of times he is perturbed by her very existence decreases, and her persistence ultimately wins his respect, to the point that he publicly gives her credit for her hypothesis. He starts to let her do more of the work, such as note taking, and also begins to defuse critical comments directed at her by other men. In turn, being taken seriously gives Takako the courage to challenge Takizawa on smaller issues, such as how to get to a crime scene, and ultimately enables her to voice her opinions in the staff meetings.

Takako's intimate knowledge of Tokyo's highways and byways, gained through her work with the patrol corps, also is a crucial part of her job and helps to establish her competence as a homicide investigator. A telling instance of this newfound confidence comes when, in a striking break with their normal relationship, Takako corrects Takizawa on the best way to get to an appointment:

> After he confirmed the address and hung up the phone, he went over to Takako. He grabbed her arm as she was opening her mouth. "The station, the station," he said as he began to walk. From here in Ginza, would going to Shinjuku be faster? he thought. Son of a bitch, why do we have to take the train?
>
> "Takizawa?" Otomichi said.
>
> He felt his frustration grow and ran for the subway stairs as fast as he could, but she persisted. "Where are we going?"
>
> "Kawasaki in Tama Ward," he replied without turning around. "We'll take the Odakyu line from Shinjuku."
>
> "If we're going on the Odakyu line, then I think it's faster to change to the Chiyoda line at Omotesando. You can get to Omotesando on both the Ginza and Marunouchi lines."
>
> Takizawa, who had put his ticket in the turnstile for the Marunouchi line, didn't think and stretched out his arm. . . .
>
> "The Ginza line is this way."
>
> Otomichi's voice was calm. She started through the crowds fluidly and quietly like a fish, confident in her course. Takizawa hastily changed directions to follow her (169).

Later, after Takizawa becomes too drunk to drive, Takako takes them to another crime scene, despite his grumblings about women drivers.

Ultimately, Takako's midnight motorcycle ride through the streets of Tokyo in pursuit of the wolf dog Hayate most fully demonstrates her mastery of the urban environment and gains her the full respect of her partner. This episode marks not only the beginning of the end of Takako's isolation from Takizawa and the masculine world that he represents, but also the belated recognition of her own independence and power—a problematic juxtaposition embodied in Nonami's symbolic linking of Takako and the wolf dog. This mixed breed combines traits from its wild and domesticated parents, displaying fierce loyalty but also remaining highly independent and hard to train. Once his owner, Emiko, is killed, Hayate does not feel any tie to his old life and begins to roam aimlessly through the city. As the author makes clear, it is this same type of restlessness, independence, and (in the end) isolation that characterizes Takako, a connection recognized by her partner: "Takizawa, nodding silently, watched the figure of Takako with her jacket molded to her back. He continued to have the illusion that she and the wolf dog were two hearts beating as one as they ran, and he felt that there was something that bound them together. On the highway, the motorcycle and the wolf dog moved in unison, looking like they were enjoying the space of the road. They were not pursuer and pursued. He felt that they were both headed somewhere specific" (341–342).

Like the dog, Takako is a loner who does not belong to the pack because she too is neither one thing nor another. She is drawn to the dog from the beginning of the case and upon cornering him is captivated by his "majesty, dignity, and wisdom" (325). At the end of the chase, however, when she finally allows the animal handlers to capture him, she no longer identifies with the independent dog but with the collectivity of the police community. Her ride has demonstrated her mastery of the city streets to her partner and the other members of the police force, and Takizawa's acceptance of her as a partner is the reward. On a symbolic level, then, Takako's relationship with the wolf dog represents her maturation as a police officer, and the subjugation of the "wolf" part of Hayate, the loner, turning him into a "dog" in captivity, represents a similar shift in Takako. The transformation from "nature" (wolf) to "culture" (dog) is problematic, however, when extended to Takako—a binary, as Sherry Ortner has argued, commonly employed to express the distinction between women and men as one of hierarchical subordination.[36] Takako's personal development thus is subordinated to a structural one, a movement "up" from her position as police*woman* to *police*woman. Rather than changing the police with her femininity, she allows herself to be molded by the job, becoming more "masculine." Nevertheless, as the image of "taming" suggests, Takako is left in an awkward place at the end of the novel, "something intermediate between culture and nature, lower on the scale of transcendence than man."[37]

It is in Nonami's three subsequent novels, which chronicle Takako's development into an ace detective, that Takako's metaphorically ambivalent position is gradually resolved—a process highlighted by the author's "fictional *(kakū)* interview" of Takizawa at the end of the 1999 paperback edition of *Murder When the Petals Scatter.* This interview, conducted in a bar over drinks, shows Takizawa to be suspicious about women in general and Takako in particular. Nonami asks him to express his feelings about Takako, eliciting a stream of invective similar to that found in *Frozen Fangs,* in which Takizawa accuses Takako of being untrustworthy, emotionally distant, and unforgivably tall—"truly an unpleasant woman."[38] When prompted by Nonami, however, he admits that his partner is "a superior police officer" *(yūshū na keiji).*[39] The fact that Takizawa, who was initially unable to forgive Takako for being a woman, praises her without affixing "female" to her job title and describes her as his colleague *(senyū)* before disappearing into the crowded bar clearly is meant to represent not only a shift in Takizawa's attitudes, but also a call to rethink traditional beliefs about the relationship of gender to the workplace.[40]

Murakami Riko: Sex and the Workplace

While the harassment that Takako undergoes at the hands of her male superior causes her embarrassment and resentment, it is relatively benign in comparison to the relentless campaign that Shibata Yoshiki's heroine, Murakami Riko, faces in *Riko—Forever Venus.* The first novel in the Riko series acutely demonstrates the problems that authors have had placing women in the detective novel, and in particular reconciling the norms of the genre with the reality of women's position in society. Traditionally, the detective novel depicts a man who does not have a permanent sexual relationship or has a family from whom he is estranged—a hard-drinking womanizer. Shibata Yoshiki has created a heroine very much in the mold of the tough guy cop, an image that does not conform to that of stereotypical women in contemporary Japan, epitomized by the young female office lady or the well-manicured housewife. When the tough guy model is applied to women, there are dissonances in the text, manifested in the detective's behavior, that keep her from becoming a credible figure. Shibata's series thus is troubling because while it presents a strong woman who is no longer a novice detective, her professional abilities are often overshadowed by her image as a cigarette-smoking, bisexual, promiscuous loner.

The Riko series is narrated in the third person from Riko's point of view, and the reader is privy to her thoughts. Unlike Takako, who does not dwell on her past, for Riko the past is full of ghosts that continually need to be resurrected and reexamined. As the plot unfolds, Riko is plagued by memories of past harassment and pain, but she manages to suppress the traumatic experience that influenced her personal and professional life until she begins working with the man responsible for her anguish. The narrative is interrupted with stream-of-consciousness dreams, musings, and meditations. These thoughts serve as a window into Riko's inner life, revealing how her current situation triggers recollections of abuse and mistreatment.

The plot of *Riko—Forever Venus* comprises two different stories that often intertwine but are not joined at the end. The first is a tale of crime and its solution, while the second describes the tangled personal life of the heroine. The novel opens at the Sakuradamon headquarters of the Tokyo Metropolitan Police with Murakami Riko, a police detective. Riko, a member of the sex crimes division, receives permission to expand her precinct's investigation into a series of kidnappings and rapes of four young men. While the victims were in the kidnapper's custody, their rapes were videotaped and used to blackmail the victims and their families for millions of yen.

Unfortunately for Riko, she is assigned to work with Takasu Yoshihisa, to whom she had once been engaged and to whom she is currently not speaking. Takasu is just one person in Riko's constellation of lovers, past and present, who seem to have some relation to the plot. Her relationship with Takasu is the most troubling since he, along with two other police detectives, raped Riko, a crime that she has never reported. In addition to Takasu, there is her female lover, Tōyama Mari, from the patrol division; Ayukawa Shinji, her colleague at the Shinjuku precinct (where she is currently assigned); and Andō Akihiko, her former boss with whom she had an adulterous relationship several years before. When Riko becomes pregnant, she does not know which of these men is the father of her baby, but Andō eventually offers to marry her, an offer she accepts by the third novel.

In the midst of this personal turmoil, Riko begins her investigation into the crimes and discovers that all but one of the victims have either been murdered or committed suicide after their release. One night, after leaving a mysterious message on Riko's answering machine, Ayukawa is found dead of a drug overdose in his apartment. While working to discover Ayukawa's murderer, she learns that he had been at loggerheads with his former boss from the Ueno precinct, Mogi. As Riko begins to investigate Mogi, she discovers that Mari is Mogi's lover and accomplice in the kidnapping/rape scheme. Horrified by this discovery and the knowledge that Mari was involved in two murders and the kidnappings, Riko resolves to kill Mari and then herself, and during a period of intense love making, she gets Mari to confess. Riko's plan is thwarted by Mogi's arrival, and Mogi and Mari hold her as a hostage as they flee to the airport. They are apprehended, however, by Andō and his men, who kill Mogi and Mari in a burst of gunfire. In the end, Riko figures out that the common link among the victims was Mari, who had issued all of them traffic tickets while they were driving through Shinjuku.

Nonami's attempt to depict a woman with a stereotypically male attitude toward sex highlights the problems of personal life in women's detective fiction. As the defining space of home and family comes to be increasingly compromised, women—and their male coworkers—are forced to come up with codes of behavior and norms for the new realities of work and work space. Often, the presence of women in the workplace, combined with new and prevailing stereotypes about women, leads to an increased focus upon female sexuality, in particular how sexuality affects one as a working professional. While characters like Otomichi Takako have successfully suppressed their sexuality, Murakami Riko's sexual openness forces this issue to the fore, causing the novel's ostensible theme—the investigation and solution of crimes—to be almost entirely overshadowed by the character's sexuality and by problems arising from how her colleagues perceive her behavior.

These perceptions, and Riko's acute awareness of them, are made clear early in the novel, when Riko and Mari meet for a drink after work. As Riko describes the meeting at the Sakuradamon headquarters, some men in the bar persist in making sexual advances toward them, despite being rebuffed. When they realize that Mari and Riko are policewomen, however, the harassment changes to verbal abuse:

> "Hey, bitch cops!"
> When Mari heard this, she grew angry and took a swig of her drink. "Did you hear that? What's a 'bitch cop'? A bitch cop! Can you forgive them for saying something like that? Didn't you learn in elementary school not to insult someone's profession? Ignorant fool! People like you should be killed!"
> Riko laughed. "'Bitch cop'—isn't that cute? When you compare it to what I've been called . . . my colleagues have called me."
> They knew the law. Selling your body—even if you were actually giving it away for free—was a crime. Riko would never forget the feeling of humiliation. They treated her like a slut. They said it in so many words.[41]

As this brief exchange makes clear, the boundary between Riko's "private" and "professional" lives is tenuous at best. Sex and sexuality, as we come to find out, color nearly every one of her workplace interactions—not simply the crude misogyny of her barstool hecklers or the constant but low-level harassment experienced by most if not all female cops, but also much more pointed insults directed at her sexually open behavior and even physical assault of the most heinous kind.

The intimate link between Riko's sexual choices and the abuse to which she is subjected can be seen most clearly in the circumstances surrounding her relationship with Takasu. Riko's conflict with Takasu begins with a common instance of sex in the workplace—namely, Riko's adulterous affair with Andō, which ends badly when his mentally unbalanced wife finds out and, enraged, stabs Riko. The resulting turmoil alerts Takasu to the affair; rather than simply breaking off the engagement, he retaliates against Riko by raping her with two of his friends while they are all studying for the promotion examination. Afterward, she goes to the doctor, who wants her to report the incident. Riko realizes, however, that she cannot report the crime: given her reputation as a "loose woman," she would never be seen as a victim, and the resulting publicity would undoubtedly cost her her job:

> The doctor's words still reverberated in her ears.
> "There's no possibility of pregnancy, is there? If there were, then I think that we'd know within the next two weeks."
> When Riko turned her head to look at the doctor, he said, "You should go to the police as soon as possible. It is our duty to submit a report on the victim's behalf."
> Rape is not an offense subject to prosecution only on complaint. If the doctor filed a report, then the incident would be made public against her will. She took her badge from her jacket and laid it in front of the doctor. At that moment his startled face had almost a bemused look on it, but when he saw the determined look in Riko's eyes, he didn't ask any questions.
> "I see. In that case, here's the report" (150–151).

With the doctor's help, Riko is able to cover up the incident and keep her job, a decision that has the painful result of leaving her to share an office with Takasu until her transfer. When she is forced to work with him again, memories of the crime well up inside her, a trauma exacerbated by Takasu's refusal to leave the event in the past. He continues to refer to her private life when they are working together, insists on making insulting comments, and even urges her to forgive one of her assailants before the latter's wedding day.

In addition to this treatment at the hands of Takasu, Riko often is criticized by her other colleagues for not behaving in what they consider to be a feminine fashion. Much of this criticism focuses on her oft-discussed sex life, but she also is attacked for the way that she behaves when her partner (and lover) is murdered. When she is questioned about his death, the police officers shout, "Were you his lover or weren't you?" (185) and criticize her stoicism. It is not until she is alone with Andō that she is able to cry. This silence and stoicism is misinterpreted by her colleagues as indifference, and she is told that she is cold for not showing any emotion.

Riko's adulterous relationship with her boss hovers over the entire series like a malevolent spirit, haunting her every attempt to succeed. When she is promoted, it is said to be because she slept her way to the top: "If you looked at it one way, Riko slept with her boss several years ago and her boss' wife went nuts. After that, people said that Riko's promotion in the police force was due to her boss, and that he 'used women.' Takasu Yoshihisa, on the contrary, saw Riko as an evil woman who used her wiles to get what she wanted" (36). These rumors diminish somewhat after Riko's transfer to the Shinjuku precinct, but with the death of her colleague Ayukawa, they flare up again.

The harassment that Riko endures extends to her work in the field. During the course of her investigation, Riko goes undercover to pose as a potential victim for a subway pervert who has been attacking women on train platforms, in order to see if there is a link with her case. She is attacked by criminals, her gun is taken away from her, her clothes are torn off, and she is almost raped before managing to escape. Yet she refuses to take any time off to recover, continuing her pursuit of the men in order to prove that there is no difference between her and other policemen. This attack demonstrates that violence directed at the police takes the form of sexual violence in her case and suggests that the differentiation of female police officers extends to the kinds of threats they may face in the field.

Despite the claims of those around her, the endemic sexual harassment that Murakami Riko faces at work and in the field is not simply a result of her sexual choices, but rather of more general perceptions of women as potential sex objects. It is significant, I believe, that readers are never given a physical description of Riko. While much is done to Riko's body, there is never an account of what it looks like. I would argue that this is on purpose, to suggest that it does not matter whether or not Riko is attractive or whether she dresses in a sexually provocative manner; instead, she is harassed merely because she is female, coded as a sex object simply on account of her sex. For many men in the novel, Riko's contributions to the workplace are overshadowed by her body and the belief that her body is accessible to everyone. This perception is furthered by both her past and the fact that she is working in the sex crimes division of her precinct. Moreover, the fact that she has dated only members of her precinct since her affairs suggests that the line between Riko's personal and professional life has become blurred.

The focus on a woman's sexuality at the expense of her workplace performance is not unusual. It is reminiscent of earlier women's detective fiction (written by men) in the West that falls into the *Penthouse* mode of storytelling, using graphic sex scenes rather than the solution of the crime to propel the story.[42] Yet Shibata's novel does not simply rely upon this narrative method; rather, she suggests that Riko has picked up her methods of dealing with her love life from her male colleagues. As I will show in the next chapter, it is not until Riko starts a relationship with a woman that she reverts to the submissive, "feminine" role, allowing her lover to manipulate her both sexually and emotionally. Her affairs with men are included, therefore, to demonstrate that constant harassment has hardened her and made her more "masculine," as if the only way to avoid being troubled by such harsh treatment is to become more like her male colleagues. At the same time, Shibata takes pains to show that Riko is not entirely masculine since she, unlike her male colleagues, is susceptible to sexual violence in the field, and her rape and harassment make her more sensitive to others' pain. She thus is portrayed as a deeply contradictory character, hypermasculine in some ways and hyperfeminine in others—a portrayal that reflects, and is the logical product of, the hypersexualized police environment as imagined by Shibata.

In spite of her convoluted personal life (or perhaps because of it), Riko is quite good at her job. Unlike Takako, a rookie trying to understand her job and the culture that goes with it, Riko has been a police officer for a number of years. While she faces the same loneliness and alienation that affect Takako, Riko's experience frees her from an incessant questioning of her competence and makes her able to understand and engage in the subtle negotiations for attention and leads that go on between her colleagues and her superiors. She is aware of her abilities and in particular her talent at using her "trump card" (37) to get victims of sexual assault to testify against their attackers—that is, since she was also a victim of sexual violence, she understands their pain and their desire not to make such a crime public. Part of her confidence comes from the knowledge that she is a good police officer, and part from the approval of other officers.

Yet Riko is not immune to competition with the male members of the police force over who gets what lead, nor to the perception that she is there only to serve her male colleagues.[43] As she prepares for a meeting at police headquarters in the beginning of the novel, Riko frets that she might be asked to pour the tea, a task that she finds demeaning.[44] She does not enjoy fighting to get credit for following a lead; however, she finds herself succumbing to the pressure to compete for attention:

> Wasn't it almost a given that Andō gave Takasu a tip on that case?
>
> That's just unfair. It is just terrible to think that he carries his grudges to the office. It's just worthless vanity.
>
> But in the depths of her heart, Riko could not admit that she had a guilty conscience about Takasu (78).

Although she is not happy about competing for leads with the men, she does it anyway, and when Andō asks her if she wants to accompany him when he goes to interview a victim, Riko leaps at the chance. Nevertheless, her willingness to "play the game" with her male colleagues does not prevent her from being treated as "easy." One indication of this is her colleagues' frequent use of her personal name, "Riko," rather than the more professionally appropriate "Murakami." This makes her an easy target for harassment by her peers, eliminating the discursive distance provided by titles and family names and placing her in a linguistically (and by extension socially) subordinate position.[45]

Despite having more seniority and a greater degree of competence than Nonami's heroine, Riko still is pressured to quit her job. Unlike Takako's situation, however, where the impetus to resign comes from family members, Riko is advised to quit by other women, such as Mari and a bar hostess whom Riko is trying to help. Even after the birth of her son, Riko continues to juggle her responsibilities as a mother and a police officer in the face of opposition from her family. She is even willing to risk a fragile accord with her father, negotiated after Andō marries her, to continue her career. In the final novel of the series, *Diana's Daydream*, Riko promises Andō that she will quit after her unit solves the case on which is she working. She is horribly injured during this last case and realizes that she can be happy only when she is working. When she returns to work after being released from the hospital, she visits the criminal she has apprehended in prison and attempts to piece his story together. He stonewalls her, but she realizes that she will figure his story out.

> Riko waits.
>
> I will continue to wait. I will wait until Yamauchi opens his mouth. My heart beats faster, my ears perk up, and I will hear that voice. I have not started yet. I must begin.
>
> In a system where people judge people, you must do your job from the beginning—that's what a cop does. You listen carefully and seriously to the people around you. At least up to now.
>
> Why must Riko continue to be a police officer? Did she choose this? The answer is around her.
>
> I can listen to people. I must be able to. I don't have any other skills, I have no abilities, but I can listen. This is why I continue to be a cop.[46]

In the end, when Riko realizes that she has sacrificed her beauty and possibly even her relationship with her father, she concentrates on the task at hand: being a good police officer. Nevertheless, like Takako, she is aware of the difficulties of women on the police force. The inconveniences of being female in a job that demands constant attention and allows for no free time concern her, and Riko ponders the problems of having to live up to female social expectations in a physically and emotionally draining job:

"Eat quickly, you'll feel full." As Andō said this, he wolfed his food down. Riko was accustomed to eating quickly while she was at work; even so, it was hard keeping up with Andō. Try to eat and go to the bathroom as quickly as possible. Refrain from drinking any liquids on the way to work. Fixing your makeup is pretty much forbidden. Learn to put on lipstick without looking in a mirror. Choose stockings that don't run easily (80).

In addition to the physical problems that she has to endure, Riko also suffers from alienation. The biggest question on Riko's mind is not how she can manage to eat or even how to fit into the police world, but how, if she did fall in love, she would be able to balance her career and her ideal of what a relationship should be: "I was brought up to be with this person so that I can't do anything without thinking about him. I want to work, think, feel pain and succeed with this person" (129). This question in particular informs not only *Riko—Forever Venus,* but also its sequels, as Riko's professional maturation is accompanied by a constant struggle to meet the demands of her job, her relationship, and her young son.

Police Procedurals and the Plight of the Working Woman

As I have tried to show in this chapter, detective fiction—and in particular the police procedural—offers a critical site for the imaginary treatment (in the fullest sense of that word) of gender and work issues in Japanese society. Unique among other types of literature, both "pure" and popular, for its depiction of women and work, detective fiction allows the author the opportunity to address issues that affect working women in general. In the novels by Miyabe and Yoshimoto discussed above, work does not play an integral part in the female characters' lives; rather, it is simply the means to achieve their consumer desires. There is only one brief episode in Miyabe's *All She Was Worth* in which women's desire to work, and to have an identity based on that work, comes into play. Moreover, the male detectives in *All She Was Worth* investigating the murder of a woman's husband cannot fathom the female murderer's desire to identify herself apart from her relationship with a man. Police procedurals, however, offer a forum for women to talk to other women (and men) about issues in their daily working lives. These novels do not depict a fantastic place where women can gain revenge on the men who harass them; rather, they provide a more modest arena where the heroine can find professional satisfaction doing a job that she has selected. The problems she encounters, like the mystery itself, are resolved in the end due to her competence and perseverance.

With the creation of their female characters, Nonami and Shibata have produced novels that, as Walton and Jones put it, "exceed the technically oriented aspects of the police procedural formula in favor of developing female characters who tread the boundaries between the real and the fictional—as well as the conventionally masculine and feminine—realms."[47] Thus, at certain points both authors test the limits of the realism that detective fiction seems to require, a tactic that allows them to address the plight of women in the workplace in novel ways. Yet while this strategy is apparent in both novels, each author has pursued it in different ways with differing results.

At first glance, *Frozen Fangs* seems to be the more deeply rooted in reality. Nonami's depiction of women and the challenges they face in a traditionally male arena echo a situation common to many Japanese women who work in traditionally male professions. The low rank of the protagonist and the expectation that she will perform in the same way as a man, coupled with daily questioning of her competence by both her peers and the people that she is supposed to serve, sound eerily familiar. This novel presents Takako's experience straightforwardly, with all the resentments and hurts that accompany her working life, particularly her struggle with an older man set in his ways. It also reveals disagreements with her family that take a further emotional toll and shows how she must entirely suppress her sexuality in order to succeed in this world.

This unrelentingly realistic story, however, culminates in the transformative experience of Takako's midnight ride through the streets on her motorcycle. This episode, which ultimately wins her the respect of her partner and the other police detectives, also captured the imaginations of female readers. The image of a leather-clad woman on a motorcycle was a powerful one, played out in a series of advertisements by Suzuki that featured the author, Nonami Asa, talking about her own bikes.[48] These ads appeared on the Marunouchi subway line, which runs through the financial district and the Ginza, past the seat of the national government, before reaching Shinjuku, another business and shopping district. Thousands of women ride this train on their way to and from work, making the ads an effective way to capitalize on women's fantasies of escaping their humdrum existences. Moreover, Takako's pursuit of a wolf dog on her motorcycle presented an even more powerful image of woman as hunter, rather than as weak victim or hunted. This compensatory vision, in other words, acts as a palliative for the suffering to which the heroine is subjected by the male members of the police force.

Conversely, Shibata's *Riko—Forever Venus* would appear on the surface to present a more transgressive and exotic message. Unlike Takako, with her almost nunlike existence, Riko exhibits freewheeling attitudes toward sex and relationships whose primary literary function seems to be the titillation of readers. This element of Shibata's novel, however, contains both a liberatory message—a woman is free to carry on three affairs at one time—and a punitive one—sexual license leads to harassment by one's colleagues. Therefore, whereas Kathleen Gregory Klein suggests that such sexual escapades are offered as a kind of compensation for the creation of a strong female character,[49] it would seem that Shibata is using her character's exaggerated sexuality to demonstrate the extent of the harassment inherent in the male-dominated world and the problems a woman encounters when she attempts to follow that world's rules in toto. Responding to pervasive harassment by adopting many stereotypically masculine behaviors, such as hiding one's emotions and having a less romantic view of sexual intercourse, does not provide the relief that Riko desires. Rather, she is harshly criticized by her colleagues for attempting to act in a way inappropriate to her gender.

As noted, the appearance of such female police procedurals in 1990s Japan is no accident. Despite the downturn in the Japanese economy, ever-growing numbers of women are still participating in the workplace. Yet women's presence in the bastions of masculinity is still the exception rather than the rule, and they have not been entirely integrated into the workplace culture. Thus, Nonami and Shibata's heroines and their travails in the male-dominated world of work have an appeal for female readers, who are able to sympathize with their problems and revel in their escapes. In particular, the world of the police officer is not hospitable to women. The long hours on the job are shown to be not only detrimental to a woman's personal life, but also physically damaging to her health. Despite this, both Takako and Riko are shown to be good police officers, hard-working and dedicated. Takako is a novice detective, learning how to investigate crimes from her curmudgeonly superior. Riko, on the other hand, is given extraordinary latitude to demonstrate her initiative. While she is not a renegade and there is no instance of her clashing with authority, Riko nonetheless calmly goes her own way in the investigations. The determination that both these women show in light of the constant harassment they face is another compelling image for working women.[50]

Indeed, despite the challenges that Otomichi Takako and Murakami Riko face, there seem to be benefits that counterbalance harassment and physical hardships. In the police force, women who do not necessarily fit the stereotype of the "feminine" Japanese woman (such as Takako) are able to be physically active and participate in duties such as motorcycle riding on a daily basis, opportunities they would not have elsewhere. In the beginning Takako is ambivalent about police work outside of the motorcycle corps, but as the case unfolds and she develops a talent for investigation, she embraces it. For Riko, who entered the police force in an attempt to fulfill her father's expectations, police work provides an outlet for her sense of justice and compassion, as she draws upon her own experience as a rape victim in order to help others. For both women, therefore, the police force offers an opportunity to fulfill ambitions that would have gone unmet were they to pursue a more typical career trajectory.

Rather than merely portraying how women are treated in the workplace, then, these novels address the frustrations of Japanese women workers in a nondidactic and sympathetic fashion, showing readers two women able to succeed at difficult jobs and persevere through difficult circumstances. Yet while both works provide finely drawn pictures of what it is like to be a woman in the masculine world of the police, they remain problematic since in both, despite all the harassment, neither Takako nor Riko criticizes the institution of the police. Perhaps this is due to the dearth of women on the police force and their isolation from one another, leaving the female protagonists without a sympathetic ear for their criticisms or complaints. Another explanation is not that women are unable to complain, but that they may not find any reason to do so since the stakes are so low. It is only recently that "*seku hara*" has ceased to be merely a trendy catchphrase and has become an actionable offense.[51]

The problems facing these fictional Japanese policewomen, of course, are not unique to Japan. In Paula L. Woods' novel *Inner City Blues,* the heroine, a Los Angeles police officer, describes her difficulty in combating the harassment of a white male officer: "Women and minority officers knew that to protest the casual racism and sexism of our co-workers singled us out as difficult, opening the door to an even more rigorous dosage of fun and games at our expense. If you complained of racial or sexual harassment to the Internal Affairs Department, it would automatically trigger an investigation and no one would work with you. And without a partner you could trust at your back, your ass would be grass, left out to dry in the Santa Ana winds."[52]

The similarities between this account of an American woman police officer and those in the novels of Nonami and Shibata are striking, perhaps stemming from generally similar hierarchies and bureaucracies within Japanese and American police departments. Nonetheless, readers might perceive the situations differently. Although the treatment of women police officers in the Los Angeles police is appalling, it represents a "worst case scenario," found in bastions of masculinity such as the military and its civilian analog, the police. In Japan, on the other hand, the late and tentative arrival of women in the working world means that the workplace situations in general often bear a strong resemblance to those described by Nonami and Shibata. The fictional harassment of Takako and Riko is likely a familiar model for Japanese women, who can find a parallel in their own lives. While an American reader of Woods' novel is likely to react to the protagonist's harassment with outrage, the Japanese readers of Shibata's and Nonami's novels may regard it as all too familiar and something with which they can identify. Despite the recent success of some sexual harassment suits in Japan, it remains difficult to bring a case to trial, and no matter the outcome, the plaintiff usually finds it hard to remain in her profession.[53] Many women thus can sympathize with Takako and Riko's decision to accept harassment rather than give up careers for which they have sacrificed so much.

These dilemmas, moreover, are not just fictional since the attitudes toward work found in both novels stem from the authors' own life experiences. In particular, Nonami, herself a victim of sexual harassment, has spoken publicly about her experience, about her inability to complain out of fear for her professional and financial well-being, and about frustration resulting from this powerlessness—a frustration shared by many other Japanese women.[54] It is not hard to imagine how this kind of frustration, expressed in the pages of Nonami's novel, might resonate with female readers, and it may help to explain the ongoing popularity of Otomichi Takako (including three sequels and a television movie).

In turn, while these police procedurals show what happens when a woman enters the masculine world of the police, they underscore how the woman must change to accommodate the demands of the job, often to the detriment of her own health and welfare. This observation of women in the police is not limited to Japan, as Sandra Tomc observes that the stress in Anglo-American police procedurals on "corporate action over independent action and occupational over gender alliances seems to chronicle and champion women's entrenchment in corporate culture."[55] Both Takako and Riko make incredible sacrifices in order to belong to this male-dominated workplace and seem intent on proving their willingness not to make any changes to the system but to submit to its demands. The dire situation faced by all female members of the police force thus points out the larger problems of a workplace that is oppressive for all its (female) members.

CHAPTER 4

Sex and Violence
Is That a Gun in Your Pocket,
or Are You Just Happy to See Me?

"Why are you making that face?" Yashiro took a bottle of mineral water out of the fridge and handed it to me.
"Thanks." I took a drink from the bottle and then handed it to Yashiro.
"I'm leaving now—you wanna get together again?"
"So I'll be one of those disposable girls that you throw away after one use?"
"That would be boring."

—Kirino Natsuo, *Night Abandoned by Angels*

In 1993, Kirino Natsuo's first novel in the Murano Miro series, *Kao ni furikakaru ame*, won the Edogawa Rampo Prize for best mystery. The most notable feature of this novel and those that followed was their protagonist, the hard-boiled female private eye Murano Miro, a woman whose independence and toughness resemble those of her sister detectives across the Pacific.[1] The series, which describes Miro's transformation into a professional detective, was the first to feature a heroine who takes charge of her own relationships. In the debut novel, Miro's search through the gritty underside of Tokyo for a missing friend plunges her into the world of sadomasochism (S & M) and the adult video (AV) industry, a world defined by sex and violence.

Kirino's novel is more than merely titillating; rather, it indicates the troubling relationship among women, sex, and violence in Japanese popular culture, a relationship that is more starkly highlighted by the genre of detective fiction. Kirino's heroine, like Shibata's police detective Riko, attempts to negotiate an environment where violence colors her personal and professional relationships. In both series, the detectives are unmarried, older, independent women with active sexual lives. Yet both Murano Miro and Murakami Riko are aware that sex is more than merely pleasurable since the crimes they are investigating revolve around the destructive potential of sex when used as a weapon and the sexual exploitation of the innocent for profit. Indeed, Kirino's Miro series and Shibata's Riko series are striking for their frank and often graphic discussion of sexuality as it figures both in the personal and professional lives of the detectives and in the crimes they investigate.

Their novels stand apart from others featuring women detectives in the struggle of their protagonists to express their sexuality. In contrast to the female loners in Nonami's and Miyabe's work, or the young, unmarried heroines of earlier authors like Yamamura Misa and Natsuki Shizuko, Miro and Riko struggle with the problematic interconnection of sex and violence, reflecting the often ambivalent portrayal of women's sexuality in contemporary Japanese culture.[2] In some respects, Shibata's and Kirino's protagonists appear to be irresponsible hussies, sexually promiscuous women whose escapades either damage their careers or place them in harm's way; in other respects, they are presented as perversely titillating victims, subjected to voyeurism, sexual abuse, and psychological manipulation. In either case these two portrayals are linked by a vision of heterosexual relations as agonistic, dangerous, and potentially destructive or violent for women. To be sure, many of the lurid details can be attributed to the need to sell books, but the presence of sex and the way that it is depicted raise the troubling issue of the difficulties that single women have in asserting their sexual agency. This is particularly unsettling in women's detective fiction, which, at least in Anglo-America, has been seen as a place for the creation of a positive image of women, forcing us to confront some of the limitations inherent in changing the gender coordinates of the genre.

In this chapter, I examine the ways in which Kirino and Shibata explore the relationship between sex and violence and how their portrayals are made more complex by language and imagery from other media, the voyeuristic treatment of their female protagonists, and the protagonists' ambivalent relationship to sexual violence and violent sex. Finally, I discuss how detective fiction itself is implicated in the sex-violence relationship and hence how the narratives under discussion are linked at a deeper level to the practices and paradigms of pornography. As I show, Kirino and Shibata take two different approaches to the complex connection between sex and violence. Kirino's novels directly address this relationship in its most immediate and graphic manifestation by confronting pornography, while Shibata's novels use homoeroticism (and more particularly lesbianism) to suggest possible alternatives to (hetero)sexual violence and conflict. Despite their varied approaches, however, both authors come to similar conclusions about the nature and the potential of sexual relationships in the life of the single woman.

Sexuality and the Figure of the Detective

Rewriting the hard-boiled detective novel to incorporate a female detective requires not only a mere switching of pronouns, but also a reconfiguration of some of the basic characteristics of the archetypal figure of the detective. This has led to the suggestion that the female detective is fundamentally a parodic figure or (as Sally Munt argues) that placing a woman in the role of the detective creates a bifurcated text, progressive on its surface but conservative underneath.[3] That is, despite appearing to be an independent, self-reliant woman, the female detective remains defined by mainstream, bourgeois (and hence masculine) values.

Munt's critique notwithstanding, the change in the gender coordinates of the detective novel presents a challenge in the depiction of the detective's sexuality.[4] Sexuality, both its presence and its absence, is critical in the context of a detective novel. In general, interpersonal relationships in detective fiction are limited since the stereotypical detective is solitary and aloof. The best that a detective can hope for is a competent sidekick or, lacking that, a good secretary. Raymond Chandler's Philip Marlowe is an excellent example of a man who is alone and keeps it that way. One exception to the limited relationships rule is sexual relations, which provide the hard-boiled detective with a way to demonstrate his mastery of the world and, more particularly, of women. The symbolic linkage between women and worldliness is accompanied by another such linkage—between women and danger. This is most evident in the notorious hard-boiled convention of the *"femme fatale,"* the conniving, mocking, yet seductive woman who embodies the dangers, attractions, and moral ambivalence of the detective's world.

At one level, this problematic construction of female sexuality has haunted the transition from the gentlewoman detective to the hard-boiled female detective. As Kathleen Gregory Klein has noted about the early female hard-boiled detectives, "The most striking and reiterated change in the hard-boiled detective characters . . . is their acknowledged sexual activity; authors use this as a shorthand for worldly knowledge, cynicism and experience, as though ceasing to be a virgin were a woman's only initiation rite. Conversely, they often make sexual activity the women's only form of experience . . . even though men's sexual behavior in hard-boiled novels reinforces rather than replaces all other aspects of their work."[5] To be sure, this is less true of the hard-boiled detectives of Sara Paretsky and Sue Grafton, whose work lives (as well as personal experiences) are vital to their identity. Nonetheless, their sexual relationships mirror those of Philip Marlowe and Sam Spade, amounting essentially to "one–novel stands."

In another sense, however, the inclusion of women as protagonists in detective fiction has led to a different emphasis on sexuality within the genre.

Changing the gender of the genre results in differences in language and the way that the detective behaves. No longer is the detective a loner who walks the mean streets; instead, she is connected to others. The female detective is shown to be part of a network of people from whom she can gain information, emotional support, and sometimes a hot meal. This network often supplants the detective's family and is intergenerational, multiethnic, and supportive. With this gender shift comes a need to renegotiate power relations. The female detective must contend not only with the bureaucratic (male) world, but also with a society that would relegate her to the roles of victim, girlfriend, or criminal.

Furthermore, the sexual relationship serves a number of functions for the female detective that are both positive and negative. Not only does it demonstrate that the detective is capable of more than work, but it also underscores the important role that her work assumes in her life because she is often forced to choose her work over her relationship. Thus the introduction of women into the genre makes visible areas where women have faced difficulties in their transition to a work environment. This can be seen through the relations that the female detectives have with men in the novels. While some critics argue that a woman in detective fiction needs to have a sexual relationship because it is an indicator of "worldly experience," others suggest that such a relationship keeps her "real" and makes her "human."[6] In rewriting the hard-boiled genre, therefore, women authors have retained the sexual relationship but for different reasons. Rather than representing power over (feminine) disorder, the female detective's sexual relationship, even the "one-novel stand," demonstrates her connectedness, albeit fleeting, with other characters.[7] Nevertheless, this relationship cannot end in marriage, which would jeopardize the woman's ability to do her job, compromising her independence and self-reliance.

Catharine MacKinnon has argued that women acquire their gendered identity through uneven power relations with men since "what women learn in order to 'have sex,' in order to 'become woman'—woman as gender—comes through the experience of, and is a condition for, 'having sex'—woman as sexual object for man, the use of women's sexuality for men."[8] Contemporary Anglo-American women's detective fiction challenges this notion of women as sexual objects for men by offering images of women in sexual control, selecting their own relationships, and trying to reclaim sexual pleasure and sexuality for themselves. (Perhaps the clearest example of this is the creation of the lesbian detective novel, which avoids the problem of male sexual contact entirely.) Thus, the short-term relationships that the female detective has in Anglo-American detective fiction affirms the detective's agency by reinforcing her autonomy and the pleasure she derives from these relationships. In the following pages, I explore how Kirino and Shibata's detectives strive to follow this model but end up subverting it.

Controlling Sex

Kirino Natsuo's *Her Face, Veiled in Rain* tells the story of how Miro became a detective. The daughter of a retired private detective, Miro has been widowed in her early thirties and has quit her marketing job. While mourning her husband's suicide, she learns of the disappearance of her friend Usagawa Yoko, a freelance writer, along with 47 million yen. Miro has two clues to Yoko's whereabouts: research on Berlin that Yoko had been doing when she left is missing, and there is an invitation to an S & M performance, the focus of Yoko's research. As Miro searches for her missing friend, she meets the dashing and dangerous Naruse Tokio, whose combination of raw sexuality and violence sweeps her off her feet. He accompanies her on her search through the S & M bars and seedy bookstores of Tokyo, where she meets a range of people never before encountered in her sheltered life. She also discovers that Naruse has a darker side to his charming personality and finds, as she learns more about him, that he may know more about Yoko's disappearance. Ultimately she discovers that Yoko's disappearance with the money had little to do with her research and everything to do with one man's desperate attempt to survive an economic downturn.

In the sequel, *Tenshi ni misuterareta yoru* (Night abandoned by angels), Miro is a full-time detective, using her father's old contacts and working out of her apartment. She is approached by Watanabe, the editor of a small feminist press, who has seen a pornographic video depicting a young woman being gang-raped by a group of faceless men. The amateurish quality of the video and the emotions shown by the actress, Isshoku Rina, have convinced Watanabe that the rape is real, and she hires Miro to find the actress so that she can convince Rina to press charges. Miro's investigation leads her into the dark realm of the adult video business in Japan, in particular the alleged production of illegal, under-the-table videos featuring "real" gang rapes.[9] Miro soon discovers that Watanabe has been hired by a wealthy socialite to find the actress, and as she is getting closer to uncovering Rina's whereabouts, Watanabe is mysteriously killed. Aided by her father and her gay neighbor, Miro succeeds in solving the case, unearthing secrets that hit far too close to home.

In contrast to Miyabe's psychologically complex but sexually "pure" female heroines in *All She Was Worth*, Kirino's independent and sexually experienced female private detective represents a shift in the portrayal of women both as sexual beings and as professionals. With the exception of Shibata Yoshiki's police officer Murakami Riko, Kirino has created a woman who is closer to the Anglo-American hard-boiled female detectives than any other character examined thus far. Murano Miro is different from the other Japanese female detectives in age, the type of case that she solves, and the fact that she is the first professional private detective. In *Her Face, Veiled in Rain* she has not given any thought to pursuing a career as a detective. Like many fictional amateur private eyes, Miro gets involved by looking for a missing person—in this case, her best friend. Since Miro is widowed and unemployed, she has the time to search for Yoko, and since she is in her early thirties, she does the bulk of the investigative work herself. When *Night Abandoned by Angels* opens, Miro is a struggling professional private investigator who cannot afford to be choosy about the work she accepts.

Murano Miro thus is a woman attempting to establish herself in a new profession that is removed from the comfortable middle-class life that she has enjoyed. The independence of being a private detective allows her to have greater control over the people she meets and the situations in which she finds herself, a control demonstrated in several ways in the novel. First, the point of view lets the protagonist/narrator define what the reader sees, documenting the detective's struggles against objectification. Second, the detective's use of language—in particular her verbal sparring with the men in her life—reveals a level of expressive agency and active engagement with others. Finally, the detective's sexual encounters serve to embody Miro's control over herself and her partners.

Since both novels in the Miro series are narrated in the first person, the reader is privy to Miro's thoughts, feelings, and reasons for making the choices that she does. Unlike police procedurals, which emphasize their protagonists' institutional affiliations, private detective (and in particular, hard-boiled) novels use first-person narration, a practice first standardized by Raymond Chandler and Dashiell Hammett and now almost the norm for writers of women's mysteries.[10] The first-person narration encourages the reader to identify with the narrator/detective, develops the character, and explains her actions and motivations. This "autobiography" of the detective not only instills greater attachment between the reader and the character, but also demonstrates the detective's agency and subjectivity.[11] When women's detective fiction uses the first-person perspective, moreover, the gaze and the voice is female; thus, the woman's body is "not presented as object, as are the dead bodies of many mystery stories, or as the eroticized 'to-be-looked at' body of the *femme fatale*. Instead, the readers are offered through the conventions of the private eye novel a position of subjectivity embodied in the feminine autobiographical voice."[12]

The efforts of women to reclaim this subjectivity in the face of a fictional context of "woman-as-object" highlight how women's detective fiction is not merely an "inversion" of the male genre, with women taking the place of men. Rather, the introduction of women in a previously "masculine" genre serves as a metonymic portrayal of women's position within society at large, bringing the problems of uneven power relations to the fore. The female detective has developed a way to look and talk back in an attempt to right the imbalance. Through first-person narrative, the author is "us[ing] the reflexive possibilities of the 'I' narration either explicitly or implicitly to subject the gaze to investigation and reformulation."[13]

Miro struggles to avoid the stereotypical image of the submissive woman who does not talk back. Lacking the wisecracks characteristic of American hard-boiled writers like Raymond Chandler and Sue Grafton, Kirino has produced this independence of expression by having her detective speak out about what she sees as wrong or unjust. This is made manifest through the dialogue, and in particular the verbal sparring in which Miro engages with the men in her life—a discourse marked by blunt demands and a prose style lacking in poetic niceties. Miro's discussions about her relationships thus lay out the parameters of what she wants to do and have done to her. In the first novel, she argues with her lover Naruse about how the investigation should be conducted and stands up to him even when he hits her in frustration. She also holds her ground against Naruse's shady boss, Uesugi, who admires her spirit even though he threatens her and orders her to be beaten:

> Kimijima opened the envelope. It seemed he couldn't read Kawagoe's terribly broken characters, so he passed it over to a resigned Uesugi. When Uesugi read it, he muttered "Son of a bitch!" Kimijima opened my notebook and started reading it in fits and jerks.
>
> "What, can't read my handwriting?"
>
> When I said that, Kimijima suddenly slapped my face with his open palm. It hurt ten times worse than when Naruse hit my left cheek. I couldn't hear anything in my right ear (185).[14]

Even Naruse, who claims to like strong women, does not like to have them talk back to him; as Miro flatly acknowledges at the end of the novel, however, "We argued all the time" (312). She does little to change her ways, and when she meets Yashiro in the second novel, she challenges him as well—this time over her distaste for his profession and because pornography sickens her with its potential for exploiting women.

The inclusion of and emphasis on Miro's sexual relationships, although these are not graphically described, allow Kirino to demonstrate agency. Kirino has created a female detective who, by virtue of her age and widowhood, escapes the normal pressure on young women to form an attachment that will lead to marriage. Freed from these constraints, Miro is able to have a relationship with anyone that she chooses, and by asserting her choice, she also can control the outcome of her relationships. The likability of the men Miro selects is not at issue here, but rather her decision to enter and end the relationship. This ability is not always welcomed by her partners, and she is criticized by one for "using" him for sex. She makes her choice based on the man's attractiveness and the physical satisfaction he will give her, not on the potential for a long-term relationship. She emphatically does not, however, use her body as a means to get information from suspects—she is too competent at her job to resort to such tactics.

For all her conflict with Naruse and Yashiro, in general Miro is not confrontational with the other people in her life. Her clients, the people she investigates, and her friends and family all receive the proper measure of courtesy, and she uses the appropriate level of politeness. It is only with men with whom she is sexually active that the verbal disagreements begin, when Miro perceives that her mastery of the situation can be wrested away. Miro's attempts to maintain control over her investigation and her body thus result in conflict with the men she thinks can take these away from her. In both novels, Miro has a sexual relationship with men she meets in the course of her investigation. The men share similar characteristics—they are violent and dangerous and possibly suspects in the crimes she is investigating—and her affairs with them are brief and full of passion and rancor. For Miro, mistrust and the threat of violence seem to act as aphrodisiacs, propelling her into the arms of the man who is threatening her, thereby complicating the message of independence.

In *Her Face, Veiled in Rain,* Miro begins a relationship with Naruse Tokio, Yoko's boyfriend, while they are investigating her disappearance. Naruse, who is forty-two, is the owner of Naruse Motors, a foreign car dealership. Agitated by a loss of money, which he borrowed from a shady investment company, Naruse treats Miro roughly at the beginning. As Miro spends more time with him, she recalls Yoko's comments about his violent behavior and his possible ties to gangsters. When she questions him, Naruse tells her that he used to be a student radical while at Tokyo University; arrested and jailed, he lost any chance at a respectable career. While in prison, he met a man who offered to set him up in a car dealership—one of his more legitimate businesses. Naruse's combination of good looks and violence proves to be tantalizing for Miro, and she proves susceptible. Much of the attraction between the two, however, is cloaked in verbal sparring and mutual mistrust. Since Yoko was so close to Miro, Naruse is immediately suspicious of her and spends most of his time with her in case Yoko should try to contact Miro. For her part, although Miro finds Naruse attractive, the more time she spends with him, the more she understands Yoko's growing fear of him.

In a scene that depicts the two characters consummating their attraction for the first and last time, Naruse kisses Miro on the way to her apartment.

She returns the embrace. Since Miro has not had any sexual contact since her husband's suicide, she expects to feel guilty but does not.

> I invited Naruse over to the bed. He sat down and took off my clothes. He carefully undid every button and lowered the zipper. When he pulled the legs of my cotton slacks, Yoko's pendant fell out of the pocket. He suddenly looked at me, but then he began to fondle my body and forgot all about it. . . . I surrendered myself to the pleasure that was coming. Years now separated me from my pain over Hiro, yet I understood that I could not separate myself entirely from him.
>
> "So. . . ."
>
> "Shush, I don't want to talk anymore."
>
> Naruse laughed and grabbed my breasts. I wanted to forget quickly. I wanted him so much it was like I was on fire. I pulled his head close and our lips met. Naruse's fingers softly brushed my cheek and then moved down to my breasts (222).

Here both Miro and her partner want to have sex, and the encounter is neither unpleasant nor exploitative. Miro is in control of the situation and initiates sexual contact by moving Naruse to the bed and kissing him. In contrast to many scenes in Japanese movies and television dramas that portray women fighting against sexual contact, she does not act as if she is being taken against her will. Since they are both involved in the case, Miro is not using sex to glean any information from him, nor is she using their encounter to demonstrate her dominance over him. The language used to describe this scene is descriptive but not graphically so. Miro responds emotionally to Naruse, and her thoughts are on the pleasure they share. The act of penetration remains unstated, occurring somewhere between Kirino's description of the foreplay and the following scene, where Miro and Naruse continue their investigation. After this single encounter, there is never any chance for them to resume their relationship, but Naruse also never again treats Miro with the brusqueness he exhibited at the beginning of the story. In the end, Naruse, who has lost his dealership, decides to emigrate to Canada and invites Miro to come see him off at the airport. Miro, who has continued her search for Yoko's killer, accepts his invitation but uses it as a means to confront him about Yoko's death. The final scene of *Her Face, Veiled in Rain* reproduces the standard image of judgment in the hard-boiled detective novel, in which the justice-seeking detective conquers the criminal in a scene full of righteousness and a shade of regret:

> "Early this morning, Yoko's body was found in a net in Ago Bay. She's coming home after all."
>
> "Yoko?" Naruse asked.

"Yes. Isn't it great that it happened before you left the country?"
Naruse stood up uneasily, as if he was about to bolt.
"All those years in a prison cell—won't it be hard?"
Naruse ran, giving me a menacing look that I'd never seen before.
"Good bye, then," I said (345–346).

In the sequel, *Night Abandoned by Angels,* Miro has an affair that, while similar to the one with Naruse in the first novel, involves the far less pleasant character of Yashiro. While he never physically hurts Miro, he frightens and embarrasses her; nevertheless, she finds herself attracted to him and his "overt sexuality" from the moment they meet (124). When she sees him again several days later and he asks her to sleep with him, she tells him that she cannot trust him. "It wasn't an empty statement," she confesses. "It was a synonym for fear. I am afraid of people that I instinctively can't trust" (190). As they continue talking, she decides that she will sleep with him, but she lays down the ground rules:

"Why won't you sleep with me? You probably don't have a man."
"And you don't have a woman. If I sleep with you, I don't want you to think that we're the same. I have a request. If I sleep with you, don't think that you can control me."
"I don't think that," he said with a serious expression. "I only want to do it. What about you?"
Without waiting for my answer, he kissed me. . . .
"Well?" Yashiro asked, gently.
"OK. . . ."
At this, Yashiro nodded as if he had won. Afraid that I might change my mind, he undid a button on my shirt with a practiced hand.
"I can take my own clothes off. . . ."
After we both had showered, I sat wrapped in one of the sheets, smoking a cigarette. How did this happen? I couldn't believe it (193–194).

This episode is characterized by Miro's ambivalence; each of Yashiro's advances is countered with conditions and the fixing of boundaries. While Yashiro does not make any move without her permission, she still narrates the encounter in terms of winning and losing, as if it were a battle with an outcome that must be determined. After they finish, he departs without saying much, leaving Miro to ponder her actions. Although she continues her investigation, his attraction is too much for her to withstand, and she goes to see him one more time at his apartment. As she interrogates him about the video and denounces rape as reprehensible, Yashiro listens calmly, as if he had heard it many times. In the middle of her tirade, however, he stops her:

Yashiro grabbed my collar with his left hand, and with his free hand pulled down the zipper of my suit pants. When I groaned, "Stop!" he moaned, "You stop it." He released my collar, still pulling us to the sofa. I was certain that I'd be raped.

"I hate rape. If you try, I'll go home!"

Yashiro quickly released me, took my head in both hands, and kissed me roughly. It was enough to stop the talking. Our eyes met.

"I like you," Yashiro whispered, as, then and there, we had sex on the couch.

"I like you too, but I hate your work" (209).

Other than this brief and unsentimental description *(sono mama sofaa de seikō shita)*, little more is said about Miro's sexual encounter with Yashiro. Later they resume their sparring since Miro is convinced that he knows the location of Isshoku Rina. Tired of the verbal battering that he is taking, Yashiro accuses her of using him for sexual release, just as a man would. Indeed, Miro chooses with whom she is going to sleep, and she ensures that her relationships are ones from which she will be able to extract herself without becoming scathed either emotionally or physically. Although she is initially wistful after leaving Naruse at the end of *Her Face, Veiled in Rain,* her sadness solidifies into anger once she realizes that he killed her friend. In turn, Yashiro's marriage and child help to guarantee that their relationship will never develop, and they part in anger when she lies to the police about their encounter, denying him a desperately needed alibi.

Pornography, Violence, and the Limits of Autonomy

While it is possible to understand why Miro is attracted to Naruse, her fascination for the vile Yashiro is puzzling. In particular, this relationship has the potential to sabotage not only her relationship with her father, who is angry at her for lying to the police and contributing to her client's death, but also her entire investigation. Miro is not merely counterposed to Yashiro as a sparring partner; rather, her sexual liaison with him is in tension with her stated abhorrence for sexual violence and her desire not to be controlled in her relationships. This paradoxical relationship, however, begins to make more sense when it is seen in the context of Kirino's treatment of pornography—a treatment that in many ways epitomizes the complicated relationship among sexual expression, subjection, and violence in women's detective fiction.

Pornography, which has been defined as a "coincidence of sexual phantasy, genre and culture in an erotic organization of visibility,"[15] is in fact a discourse, a way of representing sex.[16] As a medium centered on the woman's body, pornography presents a male fantasy of that body and what constitutes pleasure for it. This objectification of the female body typically is accomplished through depictions of the coercion and subjugation of women, although critics in the United States as well as Japan are strongly divided over the degree to which pornography requires or promotes female degradation.[17] While Anglo-American treatments of pornography in women's detective fiction have tended to criticize its exploitative nature, Kirino's use of pornography is less straightforward. Indeed, two opposing views of pornography are at play in *Night Abandoned by Angels.* In one, pornography is seen as exploitative and degrading to women, especially those who work in the profession. It is an object of critical scrutiny, a mode of representation, and a practice that the protagonist actively opposes and criticizes. Miro is troubled by the loss of autonomy and potential violence that pornography represents, and throughout her investigations she struggles with these issues in relation to the woman for whom she is searching. In the other, pornography represents an arena in which women can act out fantasies of sexual autonomy and pleasure. It is a discourse within which Miro is implicated by the author. Miro thus is part of the problem she is trying to solve, her desire for the sexually attractive Yashiro tempered by her fear of losing her autonomy. While Miro remains unconvinced that there is any redeeming value to pornography, her affair with Yashiro suggest that she is susceptible to both the sexual excitement and the exploitative potential that it represents.

In one respect, Kirino's decision to set her novel in the world of pornography actually enhances the heroine's independence and sense of subjectivity. As Priscilla Walton and Manina Jones suggest, "Novels that address prostitution or pornography most obviously develop the capacity of the narrating 'I' to examine and reposition the power dynamics of the gaze, though in a sense this theme is simply an extension of the private eye novel's reflexivity about looking and its implications."[18] Told in the voice of the detective, in other words, the narrative not only offers us a deeper look into Miro's motives, but also bolsters her control of the story since she is allowed to determine both what is told and what is seen. This is crucial, particularly since, while the detective has always been the "eye" in a genre that is about seeing, more often than not that eye has been focused on women.[19]

In *Night Abandoned by Angels,* the gaze of the adult video industry's camera focuses on female victims. These are not only the professional actresses, who receive money for their work, but also the victims of the *urabideo* (videos made under the table), which feature abortions, gang rapes, and suicides. Miro's search for the source of one such video takes her to the headquarters of the Create Company, where Yashiro is president. Upon first meeting Yashiro on the set of one of his films, she is told to stay and watch a woman performing oral sex on a man, who then proceeds to ejaculate on her face. When the action is finished, Yashiro turns to her and tells her that he wants her to star in one of his movies. As she refuses, a man enters and starts trying to rip off her clothes, having confused her with an actress in the film. Yashiro leaves his camera running, doing nothing to help her. Miro, enraged, turns to the camera and shouts, "I am Murano Miro. I am a private detective. I am searching for an actress who starred in Create's film "Ultra Rape." Now I have been tricked by Create's Yashiro Sen and Yamada Kaijin, who are trying to rape me. Although I have taken my clothes off, I did not want to do it. It is disgusting to have to fight, and it is disgusting that men enjoy men who like to rape women. I do not want to be made to enjoy this. Do not laugh at my unhappiness. I am naming names. You, Yashiro—go ahead and film this" (110)! Miro's reaction amuses Yashiro, who for a moment stares at her in her underwear, but he shows her an empty camera, revealing his actions were meant merely to taunt her.

Despite the threat that she faces, Miro thus refuses to allow herself to be a victim. When Yashiro attempts to film her, Miro transforms the camera from an instrument of female objectification that would make her the passive victim of pornography to a witness of her resistance and subjectivity. Yet the following scene encapsulates the contradictions of pornography: despite Miro's anger and resistance to Yashiro's advances, she ends up having sex with him in a fashion that recalls standard pornographic scenarios. The author clearly does not depict her heroine as raped or coerced into having sex, but rather as engaging in sex for her own physical satisfaction. Nevertheless, this scene is unsettling because Miro finds herself strangely attracted by her antagonist's blatant sexuality. This is made clear when he shows up at her home, ostensibly to apologize for his earlier behavior. They talk for a while before he asks her to sleep with him. She wavers until he leans over to kiss her, and reluctantly she decides to have sex because she is attracted to him. "I broke away and said, 'I think you have a hidden camera somewhere. That's totally gross'" (193).

Miro, in other words, is still afraid of being exploited in the same way she was at Yashiro's studio, and she wants to make it clear that she is not going to be treated as if she were an actress in one of his movies. Yet she then goes on to narrate their encounter in a way that makes this very connection explicit: "I pulled back the bedspread and undressed myself. Yashiro watched from the doorway as if he were framing a shot. When I slipped between the cold sheets, Yashiro took off his own clothes. I was startled by the passion that welled up when he pressed his body next to mine" (194). While the act was ultimately her choice, Miro is taken aback by her sexual response to Yashiro and by how he takes charge of the encounter despite her attempts to stay in control. Much of this feeling is caused by his tendency to turn the focus on Miro herself, making her no longer an active investigator but the object of his own (bodily) investigation. Indeed, it is striking that the action and the perspective of the story here follow the plotline of a sexual encounter in a pornographic movie, where the focus is all on female pleasure until the final moment, when the male ejaculates.[20]

This ambivalence about pornography within Kirino's novel is also due, I would suggest, to detective fiction's complicity with pornography at a number of levels. In part because of its relentless realism, as Dennis Porter has noted, detective fiction is the most voyeuristic genre outside of pornography: it allows the reader into the characters' private lives, unearths their secrets, and airs their dirty laundry.[21] Particularly within the *noir* tradition, the scopic pleasure associated with detective fiction is directed at women, especially at the sadistic violence inflicted upon them.[22] In addition, detective fiction shares with pornography what Norma Field has felicitously described as a "lust for knowledge." In both cases, this knowledge is intimately linked to the faculty of vision, either directly or metaphorically. The detective, through the agency of eyewitnesses, as well as his own investigations of the scene of a crime and the evidence left there, attempts to envision what took place, to "see" the crime and its commission. Likewise, as Linda Williams has observed, pornography "obsessively seeks knowledge, through a voyeuristic record of confessional, involuntary paroxysm, of the 'thing' itself."[23] This "thing," or orgasm, which is hidden in women, becomes pornography's object of discovery, and the purpose of pornography is to make visible this hidden pleasure, a feat rendered structurally impossible. Thus, the "truth" of pornography remains forever hidden, a fact that drives the genre into striving endlessly to bring it to light.

Finally, the connection that Kirino makes between the detective's own sexuality and pornography's distortions of women's sexuality reinforces the position of the detective as both social observer and social critic. While problems of sexuality and women's place in society stand at the forefront in Kirino's novels, they have no solution. Rather like Sara Paretsky's V. I. Warshawski series, the novels exhibit what Tzvetan Todorov calls a "double architecture," with endings that partly demand closure and partly depend on its lack.[24] The solution to the plot, in other words, does not require a solution to the problems that inform it.

Detective fiction's relationship to pornography is disturbing, especially since so much of women's detective fiction in Anglo-America as well as Japan is premised on liberal fantasies of women's empowerment. That pornography features similar theoretical underpinnings seems to undermine the positive message of independence that, on first sight, detective fiction seems to provide. One possible rejoinder to this view can be found in the work of

Linda Williams, who argues that due to the increasing number of women viewers, there has been a shift in pornography away from violence to fantasies where women create safe spaces in which they can engage in sex without guilt or fear.[25] Such a shift might explain similar changes in women's detective fiction—that is, the increasing insistence upon depicting sexual relationships in the detective novel represents a desire to render visible a woman's pleasure in the sexual act. Certainly carnal satiation is not the sole reason for a sexual relationship in women's detective fiction. The insistence of female hard-boiled authors on its inclusion, however, could signal a greater interest in transforming the traditional relationship between sex and knowledge in novel ways.

At the same time, despite Williams' positive outlook on women's pornography, the shift from women being seen to women showing their bodies still leaves the female body as an object of the male gaze. The idea that pornography is a portrayal of women's pleasure is both compelling and repulsive, especially in light of its capitalization in the media as a marketing tool or a shorthand for depicting all women. Moreover, Naruse and Yashiro's presence as *hommes fatals* compromises Miro's chances for real sexual freedom. Although occupying the same role that the self-interested and sexually charged *femme fatale* plays in hard–boiled detective fiction, the *homme fatal* demonstrates that a complete inversion of male-female coordinates in detective fiction is not possible. While the traditional *femme fatale* represents an unsettling, disruptive, or threatening irruption of (female) sex-as-unreason into the world of (male) rationality and autonomy, Naruse and Yashiro present a constant threat of violence, sexual and otherwise—violence that makes female sexual independence practically impossible. The fear that at first acted as an aphrodisiac for Miro ultimately overwhelms her pleasure, causing her to abandon the relationship. Additionally, the loss of approval from her father, which occurs after he learns of her relationship, adds to her realization of the dangers that this type of relationship brings. It is this potential for exploitation and violence, in the end, that makes the connection between pornography and detective fiction so fraught and unsettling.

The Lesbian Detective

While Kirino's conflicted heroine decries sexual violence even as she is seduced by its practitioners, Shibata Yoshiki's protagonist, Murakami Riko, presents us with an arguably darker view of (hetero)sex and the violence inherent in it. In *Riko—Forever Venus* the author uses a polyphonic, multi-genre approach not typically found in detective fiction. While the overarching structure is that of a detective novel, Shibata draws heavily from *manga* (comic books) and popular women's fiction to tell her story. The plot is drawn from the standard police procedural scenario, in which a team of detectives is involved in solving a crime. When the author begins to examine the character's nonworking life, however, there is a genre shift—a technique found nowhere else in Shibata's oeuvre. This use of multiple genres both gives the novel its feeling of opaqueness and clarifies certain aspects of the heroine's personal life. At the heart of the baroque plot, in turn, lies a discussion of gender relationships and the byzantine negotiations that make up sexuality.

Riko—Forever Venus is a turbulent novel, and Shibata's portrayal of a policewoman is almost lost amid cartoonlike violence and graphic sex scenes. Often it seems that the emphasis is not upon solving a murder case but upon resolving the heroine's personal life. On the surface, the readers are presented with the story of a woman in a highly masculine environment trying to solve a case. The crime that she is solving, however, and her convoluted personal life intersect in ways that make sexuality a pervasive medium for a variety of social relations and conflicts. Every relationship in the book is mediated in some manner by sexual intercourse, often nonconsensual and violent. From Riko's various heterosexual relationships to the homosexual rapes of the young male victims that she is investigating, Shibata depicts sexual relationships with men as dangerous, destructive, and violent for the people involved. In contrast to the male/male pairings, which are indisputably criminal because they are rapes and which horrify the male characters, the violence inflicted on the female character is accepted by them with near indifference. Unlike Kirino, however, who depicts her heroine using sex as a means to personal pleasure and asserting her independence from her lovers, Shibata counters these violent male liaisons with a sexual alternative—lesbianism.

Riko—Forever Venus, the first Japanese detective novel whose protagonist is involved in a serious lesbian relationship, is significant for its treatment of female homoeroticism, a trait far more common in Anglo-American detective fiction. The growing popularity of the lesbian detective in mainstream Anglo-American detective fiction has led critics to see this phenomenon as more than just an example of growing "inclusiveness" within a formerly white, male genre. As I mentioned above, the addition of women to the hard-boiled novel requires not merely the switching of pronouns, but also a reconfiguration of some of the basic characteristics of the archetypal figure of the detective. The suggestion that the female detective is fundamentally a contradictory figure, seemingly progressive but ultimately conservative, raises the possibility that female detectives, despite their outward independence, are still conceived of in the same bourgeois and paternalistic terms traditionally applied to women. In contrast to this contradictory character, Sally Munt's lesbian detective (a descendant, perhaps, of Walter Benjamin's "heroine of modernism . . . the woman who bespeaks hardness and mannishness") escapes the contradictions inherent in the woman detective.[26] No longer is the detective a woman acting like a man, signaling an incomplete inversion of the genders of the detective; rather, the lesbian is a natural extension of the hard-boiled sleuth, a figure standing on the outskirts of society who does not participate but only observes. Munt thus believes that the figure of the lesbian is analogous to that of the hard-boiled detective, able to observe what she calls "the vagaries of institutional heterosexuality" without being an active participant, and hence well situated to criticize society.[27]

The lesbian detective is also seen as a transgressive figure in Anglo-American detective fiction because the lesbian detective (and more specifically the lesbian police officer) is most disruptive when she enforces the prevailing social codes of behavior and belief yet ultimately challenges those codes by remaining personally agnostic about them. The transgressor is both integrated into the community and separated from it. Thus, as Phyllis M. Betz puts it, the lesbian police officer's "public responsibility demands the maintenance of the dominant community standards, but [her] private life severs all connections with them."[28] Indeed, despite the increasing numbers of Anglo-American lesbian detective novels, the transgressive nature of these novels' protagonists has not diminished.[29]

In contrast to the transgressive nature of lesbianism in the United States, lesbianism in Japan generally has not been seen as "perverted" or "abnormal." In the absence of religious prohibitions of same-sex erotic ties, it has not been an issue in a society where many activities are segregated by sex. As Jennifer Robertson has noted, "provided sexual practices neither interfered with nor challenged the legitimacy of the twinned institutions of marriage and household, nor competed with heterosexist conventions in the public sphere, Japanese society accommodated (and still does) a diversity of sexual behaviors."[30] These practices, however, must be seen as only temporary, so that when a woman marries, her lesbian tendencies are resolved. Moreover, these practices must be kept out of the public eye because of the overwhelming pressures on women to marry and produce children.[31]

In this sense, lesbianism has been understood simply as a phase to be outgrown. It was not until sexually mature women wanted to reveal their relationships publicly, either by living together or by dying together, that lesbianism became socially disruptive. Such public identification as a lesbian, making sexuality a part of the construction of the social self, has not fit with the dominant, traditional notions of femininity.[32] Rather than a way of being, sexuality is seen here as a performance; thus, a person's sexuality does not prevent him or her from performing other roles within the society, allowing a public hetero-normative sexuality to coexist with other, private ones. There is, then, also a pattern or a code to the deployment of different sexualities in different narrative or life circumstances. It is only when a person fails to play the proper role in the proper venue that problems arise since refusal to adhere either to a hetero-normative sexuality or to a sexuality that is appropriate to one's age or gender may hinder the ability to carry out one's other social roles.

As a result, lesbianism serves a different function in Shibata's novels than it does in Anglo-American detective fiction. As long as it does not disrupt social norms, lesbianism poses little threat. Shibata foregrounds the lesbian relationship in the novel as a suggestion of how her heroine might escape the violent heterosexual relationships in which she is engaged. Since there have been no lesbian detectives in Japan, however, Shibata turns to other genres to address female-female relationships in literature, as well as to talk about violence. Thus, while the genre of the detective novel provides a narrative structure for solving the mystery, other genres such as the *shōjo shōsetsu* (girls' stories) and *manga* enrich the portrait that Shibata is painting—influences seen in the language of the novel, the thematic development of its subplots, the level of violence it contains, and its discussion of romantic love.

Shifting Genres and the Language of Sex

Among Murakami Riko's relationships, the most compelling is that with a female member of the patrol division, Tōyama Mari. When the novel opens, Riko is involved in two sexual affairs, one with Mari and the other with a male colleague from the Shinjuku precinct, Ayukawa Shinji. Riko and Ayukawa are working together on a case involving the abduction and videotaped homosexual rapes of young men, and they have drifted into a sexual relationship developed enough that both have keys to the other's apartment. Yet while Mari knows about Riko's relationship with Ayukawa, he is unaware that Riko and Mari are sleeping together. As the novel unfolds, Ayukawa is murdered, and Riko resumes a relationship with Andō, her old supervisor with whom she had an adulterous affair several years before. When Riko discovers that she is pregnant, she is horrified to realize that she does not know the identity of the child's father.

Throughout all this, Riko continues her relationship with Mari. Upon learning that Mari and Mari's male lover were leaders of a crime ring designed to humiliate the police, Riko resigns from the force and decides to commit suicide with Mari at a mountain retreat near Mount Fuji. They make love, and Riko decides that they will climax together and then kill themselves. Mari, however, has other plans. Once Riko has had an orgasm, she is incapacitated by Mari and her male lover, and they attempt to take Riko with them as they flee Japan. Their plans are foiled by Andō, who has been tailing Riko ever since she turned in her resignation, and Andō shoots Mari and her lover. Subsequently, Andō comes to visit Riko at the hospital, bearing details of Mari's death and an offer of marriage.

This novel takes more than the structure of its plot from the genre of the mystery story. Mari-as-*femme fatale* reinforces *Riko—Forever Venus*'s ties to classic hard–boiled detective fiction. As Marty Roth notes, the unsettling and transgressive presence of the *femme fatale* in classic detective fiction reminds the detective of his own criminality and reveals to him that "the extent of her depravity equals his investment in her."[33] This villainous woman is often coded as either a bitch or a lesbian, and it is intriguing to have these characterizations transposed into a novel where the protagonist is also a female. Mari's seduction of Riko in order to get information and her callous murder of Riko's other lover, Ayukawa, reveal the depth of her evil. Like other *femmes fatales*, Mari is the one who initiates sexual contact and controls the ebb and flow of the relationship, using that control to keep Riko in a state of heightened sexual anticipation by sweetly and sadistically touching and stroking her all night so that she is incapable of sleeping. Unlike the archetypal lesbian *femme fatale*, she is not "charged with a repulsive sexuality" in Shibata's depiction;[34] nevertheless, like many other fictional women before her, she must be destroyed in the end since "she is not just a criminal; she poses a larger danger, outside of and threatening to the social order itself. . . . Her desire (usually represented as both sexual and materialistic) is both attractive and threatening, because it exceeds the structures of social control."[35]

In order to narrate this destruction, Shibata turns from detective fiction to another genre—that of the women's novel. Despite its convoluted and lurid plot, *Riko—Forever Venus* is reminiscent of the *shōjo shōsetsu*, an earlier form of popular literature that some scholars have suggested contains lesbian subtexts. *Shōjo shōsetsu* appeared in the women's magazines that flourished in the 1920s and 1930s and dealt primarily with love and romance described from a woman's point of view.[36] Yoshiya Nobuko (1904–1973) popularized the form, and many of her texts, while not explicitly lesbian, contain erotically charged scenes that many times take place in the bathhouse.[37] The language and style of these stories, as well as the general contours of their plots, bear a striking resemblance to those in *Riko—Forever Venus.*

Riko's planned double suicide with Mari, as well as her vague fantasies about living with Mari and raising Riko's soon to be born child, reflect not only stories on this and similar themes by Yoshiya and others, but also the highly publicized lesbian suicide scandals of the 1920s and 1930s. Jealousy and betrayal are key components of the published accounts of lesbian suicides, a phenomenon that reached its peak in the Kansai region during the early Showa era.[38] The Japanese media at the time were fascinated by these events and when there were rumors that one was to take place, the couple was often hounded.[39] The reason given for these suicides was the impossibility of the couple living together openly in society. Notably, such suicides were often characterized by the different gender configurations of the participants, with one of the partners usually adopting the clothing and naming practices of males. This gender switching in practice was reiterated in the texts that accompanied the events. As Jennifer Robertson has noted, "Lesbian suicide as parasuicide letters and accounts collectively constituted another voice, whether explicitly controversial or defensive, or both, in heated public debates about the articulation of sexuality, gender ideology, cultural identity, and (inter)national image."[40] A notable literary reflection of the lesbian love suicide phenomenon is Tanizaki Junichiro's novel *Manji* (Quicksand), which was serialized in *Kaizō* from 1928 to 1930.[41] *Quicksand* describes the love triangle among a housewife, her husband, and a young female artist and the jealousies, rivalries, and suicides that arose from it. Written during the height of media coverage of lesbian suicide, Tanizaki's novel is narrated in a style that echoes the hypersensitive, emotionally charged writing of Yoshiya.

In addition to its employment of plot devices and themes found in the *shōjo shōsetsu* and lesbian suicide texts of an earlier age, Shibata's *Riko—Forever Venus* also features strikingly similar language to that used by Yoshiya and others—breathless, fast-moving sentences; female-centered descriptions; and multiple adjectives—helping to create what might be called a poetics of women's sexuality. References to flowers and their scents, for instance, are a recognized trope in writing about women's sexuality due to their symbolic association with female genitalia and fecundity. Thus, activist and author Miyamoto Yuriko's story "Ippon no hana" (One flower) is replete with images of opening flowers and flowering buds, which, when compared to the closed tree leaves of marriage, signify a flourishing female sexuality.[42] This symbolism is also found in later works by Enchi Fumiko, who in her 1958 novel, *Onnamen* (Masks), uses the image of flowers to represent ideal feminine beauty.[43] In turn, Yoshiya's story "Kiiroi bara" (Yellow roses) not only uses the flowers of the title to denote its young schoolgirl characters, but also includes references to the Greek female poet Sappho, whose name became shorthand for denoting same-sex sexual practice.[44]

The type of language that Shibata employs in *Riko—Forever Venus* changes over the course of the novel, depending on the dramatic and emotional context. In most cases, the criminal investigation is related in a straightforward, even spare fashion, with the bare-bones descriptions and detached tone characteristic of standard detective novels. Shibata's use of third-person narration reinforces this sense of detachment, both from the crime being investigated and from the tangled relationships of the protagonist. It is unusual, however, that the third-person narration is suddenly interrupted by the protagonist's own thoughts, described in the first person. Thus, while the narrator/author consistently refers to her protagonist as "Riko," never using the pronoun *"kanojo"* (she/her), the first-person narration is marked by a shift to the informal pronoun *"atashi"* (I/me).[45] These first–person, almost stream-of-consciousness meanderings serve as a barometer of Riko's emotions, providing the reader with an insight into the turmoil that she is (often silently) suffering—her trauma from a past rape, exacerbated when she has to work with the man responsible; her attraction to Mari; and, when one of her lovers is murdered by an overdose of heroin, her private grief amid accusations by her colleagues that she is unfeeling.[46]

More intriguing (and maddening) are the author's graphic descriptions of Riko's sexual liaisons, the language of which is manipulated to depict sex as either pleasurable or a vehicle for humiliation. In particular, sex with men, whether engaged in by the protagonist or by crime victims, is portrayed in such a way that even when it is consensual, it is not gratifying. Penetration is thus equated with pain and ultimately betrayal, while sex between women is intimate, organic, and pleasurable.[47] This dichotomous construction of sex and sexuality, while owing much to earlier popular writers such as Yoshiya, is equally indebted to *manga*. Many different kinds of *manga* are sold in Japan, highly specialized and targeted to every demographic group. A preponderance of *manga* written for men, however, contain graphic sex and a high degree of violence toward women.[48] As Anne Allison has noted, "Whether pleasure is depicted for her or not, the woman experiences some form, often many, of brutalization and humiliation that is visually or textually inscribed as an important element in the coding of the sex itself."[49] The use of sex to humiliate and the violence (often sexual) directed at women that are characteristic of *manga* can be found as well in *Riko—Forever Venus* in the two cases in which Riko was sexually assaulted (discussed in chapter 3). Riko is not only gang-raped, but is also later attacked by one of the suspected kidnappers for whom she has been searching. No other police officer is harmed in this attack, while Riko's clothes are torn off and she is almost raped again. More humiliating for a police officer, her own gun is used in the attack. However, she is able to escape before being raped and is able to regain control of her gun.

The conventions of *manga,* as well as of the earlier female erotic literature, are likewise used by Shibata to create sex scenes for her characters. At the beginning of the novel, Riko has no illusions about the power of sex. Constantly reminded about her past sexual transgressions, she has developed a studied indifference to social limitations on women's sexuality that reflects both the masculine world of the police department and the work that she does in the sex crimes division. Her attitudes about romantic love have been shattered by earlier events in her life (the affair with Andō and the rape), leading her to adopt what can be seen as stereotypically masculine beliefs about sex. In the first novel, therefore, Riko's attitude toward sexual intercourse with her male partners is that sex is a "stress releaser"; in other words, she has sex with men for the release that orgasm brings but does not consider it to be a sign of love. Her male colleagues accuse her of being "cold" and "incapable of being in love," accusations that give her only brief pause before she ignores them:

> From the time she was a school girl, she never believed that you needed to be in love with the person you were sleeping with. . . . After all, things like purity and chastity did not have any meaning for a vanquished Amazon. Riko did not know to what extent she would deny it, but she was subject to being mentally stoned with the term "shameless hussy." Perhaps it could be said that, in a certain sense, Riko's moral outlook had changed. Riko believed that sex was pleasurable and a stress reliever, and she remembered the pleasure (38).

Yet despite Riko's assertions that sex is a stress reliever and her insistence upon maintaining control of her sex life, every sexual encounter with a man eventually causes Riko to flash back to when she was raped or recall the painful memory of being stabbed by a lover's angry wife. Penetration causes the suppressed memories of her rape to surface, making it hard to understand why Riko continues to be promiscuous:

> Shinji's fingertips blocked Riko's memories.
> Riko stopped thinking about unpleasant things and concentrated on Shinji's caresses. But she couldn't. When Shinji entered her, the memory of Mari's touches was destroyed, and a forgotten, terrible feeling gripped her heart. Riko suddenly tried to persuade her body that it was Shinji inside her, but her body had already stiffened and was refusing him. Riko concentrated with all her might, but her hateful body was forcibly pushing him away, as if the strength was coming from somewhere outside.
> Because of the unbearable memories and because she didn't want to hurt Shinji, Riko used all her concentration to force her body to accept him.
> What a strange rape (72).

Each sexual encounter with Shinji is described in similar terms, and Riko's liaison with Andō Akihiko later in the novel—an affair that she is rekindling after it almost destroyed her career years ago—comes across as far from enjoyable. While the sensory images are more pleasant (e.g., "[his] scent, which she loved so much, lightly enveloped Riko's body" [142]), their sexual contact is abrupt and rough: "Without a word, Akihiko grabbed

Riko's arms and pulled her to him, embracing her while roughly sucking her lips. With his left hand he grabbed her hair so hard it hurt, and without letting her go, his left hand busily moved up and down her back and slid down into her underpants. She stopped him only with difficulty" (137).

With the introduction of Riko's relationship with Mari, however, the language and the tone of the sexual narrative change. Gone are the almost defensive assertions of pleasure and the nightmarish flashbacks to the rape; they are replaced by languorous and almost lyric descriptions of Riko's being touched by Mari. The pacing of the encounters changes as well since the author creates new images of pleasure for her heroine, albeit banal, melodramatic, and generally predictable:

> She thought that [her love for Mari] was a natural thing, like fruit from a mature tree falling to the ground. The first time Mari's slender arms embraced Riko, Riko was surprised, yet she realized that she unconsciously had anticipated it. This heat . . . Riko felt it from deep inside Mari's eyes, a heat that wasn't suffocating like a man's. Moist and sweet, and when it was there, it was pleasurably cool.
>
> Even the touch of Mari's lips on the nape of her neck, modest and delicate, excited her with its pleasurable smoothness. It was like touching an expensive mink coat at a department store's fur salon. Gentle, wherever she touched felt gentle. Riko was never wounded, never hurt, and never broken, a feeling that made her believe she was loved.
>
> Riko was happy.
>
> Sex that would never break you . . . it was the first time Riko had encountered such a thing (39–40).

The metaphorical language used in earlier semi-erotic women's writing, including the inevitable comparisons to fruit and flowers, is found here as well. Shibata's use of nature motifs to describe the relationship between Riko and Mari likewise presents it as "natural," although she does not propose a binary opposition in which heterosexual sex is figured as "unnatural." Furthermore, the "naturalness" of the lesbian relationship, while not wrong per se, is counterposed to Riko's more "legitimate" (but less pleasurable) relationships with men—an interesting take on the nature/culture dichotomy since, unlike in the West, the idea of lesbianism as an unnatural state is never raised.

A similar type of metaphor is that linking a mink coat to a woman's touch. Initially, the natural image of the softness of the mink fur begs the connection between woman and nature; this image, however, contains what George Lakoff and Mark Johnson call a metaphorical "entailment" of the high cost of the mink and the fact that it is located in a department store.[50] A woman's touch, then, is also rare and luxurious, evoking the stereotypical connection between women and shopping, as well as that between women and the consumption of luxury goods. The image of the mink coat thus serves not only to associate a woman's touch with animal sensuality, but also to suggest that the relationship is a "high end" luxury that only a member of an elite class, whether in economic or "lifestyle" terms can afford.

Shibata's purple prose is employed to full effect in two sexually explicit scenes in *Riko—Forever Venus:* the one mentioned above and the final, climactic episode that marks the end of Mari and Riko's relationship. As noted, Riko, who has resigned her position on the police force, has decided to take justice into her own hands by killing Mari and then herself. The scene is set for their demise: "Mari looked at Riko with an expression of surprise. The sun, making its longest sojourn of the year, cast its rays over the lake as if reluctant to set. Framed by the glowing red sky, Mari's beautiful face shone softly, and Riko gazed happily upon it" (336). Later, "The blues of the sky were extinguished, and gold, red, and violet were woven into a rainbow behind the two of them. . . . When they lay down on the dewy grass, they knew that night was creeping across the earth" (337). Placing the women's final encounter against the backdrop of the setting sun and the rapidly approaching night reinforces the earlier connection that the author has made between the women's lesbian relationship and nature. After this introduction, the sex between the two women is described in torrid prose:

> Riko rose under Mari's fingertips, drunk with the sweet taste of despair.
>
> Mari tortured Riko's little bud, and Riko become excited, the sound of her own breathing echoing in her ears. Ecstasy lay within reach—Riko could feel it. . . .
>
> Mari's right hand moved, grabbing the fingers of Riko's left hand, and the caresses stopped.
>
> "Do you want to come?"
>
> When Riko murmured this, Mari smiled. "Of course, I want to come with you. Shut your eyes. I am going to enter you. Can you feel it? Can you feel me" (338)?

While Riko and Mari are making love, however, the narration switches from what Riko is feeling to Riko's own thoughts, told in the first person. No longer are the readers presented with a description of Riko's actions. Instead, her relationship with Mari is framed in terms of the physical differences between homosexual and heterosexual sex, as well as the social problems that arise from those differences. Ultimately, Riko describes their pleasure as fleeting or transitory, lending a vaguely Buddhist air to the affair: "We are not permitted to have the happiness made out of two different pieces, but we can only sigh about this, since we are joined only for a fleeting *[setsuna teki]* moment of happiness" (347). In the end, Riko realizes that a part of Mari's evil has remained within her (literally, *atashi no naka ni iru*), a dark remnant that ultimately works to her advantage. Having a deeply personal knowledge of evil gives the detective a better understanding of the people he or she is trying to catch, so this balance of opposites, like yin and yang, enables Riko to be more sympathetic to the characters that she meets in her later work.

Lesbianism and Its Discontents

Until Riko establishes her relationship with Mari, she steadfastly maintains a laissez-faire attitude toward sex. Her protestations notwithstanding, for all the characters sex is power, although for some more explicitly so than for others. Shibata has created several oppositions in her characters based on sex and gender. One, that between the roughness of the men and the gentleness of the women, the author then subverts with Mari's betrayal of Riko. Women, despite their gentleness, can betray and cause pain, a point Shibata makes through her creation of a series of female criminals. Thus while all three of the Riko novels contain male thugs who brutalize women, the primary criminal in each case is a female who uses either her wiles or cash to get an assistant to help her.

At the beginning of the first novel, Riko has attempted to sever the idea of romantic love from sexual intercourse. Her early affair with Andō, and the public condemnation when it was brought to light, had suggested that romantic love could not solve her problems. Dogged by rumors and working in a male-dominated workplace, Riko thus insulates herself from her abusive past and stressful present by redefining sex as nothing more than a "stress reliever," allowing her to control any sexual encounter by minimizing her psychic investment in it. This detached attitude to sex is attacked by Takasu, who angrily accuses Riko of being incapable of romantic love: "Don't you understand what you say. . . . For you, love only means sleeping together. Don't you know the meaning of love" (57)? Mari levels a similar charge at the end of the novel: "You walk around with your mouth half open and a look of desire on your face. Then when a man comes nosing around, you say, 'It's not my fault,' as you enjoy yourself. For you it's not serious. . . . Don't laugh. You don't know what love is" (339). Yet while Riko is able to ignore Takasu, her response to Mari is tears and reproaches. She asks Mari why she even wants to have anything to do with her, but Mari reassures her that she loves her *because* Riko is the worst kind of person—"*Saitei da kara, daisuki.*" Riko accepts this because she knows that Mari is responsible for Shinji's death, but she also realizes that she loves her nonetheless:

> Mari is a cold criminal. At the same time, she is the woman that Riko loves from the bottom of her heart. I love her. . . .

That's right, I love Mari *[So, atashi wa Mari o aishite iru]*.
Riko thinks that her heart can't lie. She couldn't truly love Shinji, nor
could she accept Akihiko's marriage proposal, one she had wanted so
much—all this because of Mari (343–344).

Ultimately, however, the union of romantic love and sex that Riko finds
with Mari turns out to be unattainable. Andō kills Mari, Riko accepts his
offer of marriage, and in the subsequent novels her sexual energies are sublimated in caring for her child. Shibata's negative resolution of her heroine's
same-sex relationship, and her decision to direct Riko down the more traditional path of marriage and childbearing, I would argue, represent not only
her ambivalent attitude toward lesbianism and homoeroticism as tenable
alternatives to the potential violence of heterosexual life, but also more general misgivings about the possibility for female sexual independence. It is
telling that Shibata refuses to use the word "lesbian" to identify Riko, telling
us only that she is "in love" with Mari. Many times throughout the novel,
Riko muses about her attraction to Mari and wonders if it is *hentai* (perverted), but she dismisses the thought almost as soon as it arises.

The touch of those lips—for Riko it was a pleasurable feeling, one that she
wanted to savor forever.
Is this perverted?
Riko thought about it many times after that evening, but she never found
an answer. Maybe it is not normal, but Riko didn't have any interest in what
is normal in the first place. I feel joy and I don't think that it is strange or
different—it's just one way of doing things.
Mari's hands are warm and her fingers are hot.
Her body is soft, and her voice is sweet (40–41).

Nowhere in the text are the words "lesbian" *(resubian)* or "homosexuality" *(dōseiai)* used, although in the beginning Riko hears gossip that Mari
is bisexual. Riko's relationship is about desire, without any political sense of
identity or interest in being different, and she feels no guilt about it. As a
result, since the author goes to great lengths to insist that her heroine is not
a lesbian, Riko's social identity is clearly marked as intrinsically heterosexual. Yet while Shibata employs lesbian sex not in order to mark identity but
rather as a means of control, such sexual contact must still be ended in order
for the character to be recuperated into the heterosexual economy.

This break, to be sure, is not absolute. Indeed, there are subtle but constant reminders throughout the series of Riko's love for Mari. Once Mari
dies, Riko is not interested in any other women, and when Shibata introduces
another female policewoman, Miyajima Shizuka, in the second novel of the
series, her relationship with Riko is initially antagonistic. Shizuka is clearly

not a lesbian, and her hostility springs from competition with Riko over a man. Shibata calls forth the specter of Riko's past relationships in a scene where Riko is comforting Shizuka and smells her perfume.

> Unconsciously, a scent from the past struck Riko's nostrils. It was the smell of lilies of the valley. Lilies of the valley, muguet.[51] I know that smell well. It was her smell. She always wore it—a sweet, cute, pure smell. It didn't match her makeup, the style of her clothes, her words, or her life. It was the smell of an innocent young girl. . . . But she wasn't an innocent anymore. She was no longer pure. She was a witch.
>
> "Is that Diorissimo?" she asked. . . . "It suits you."[52]

This specter is banished when Riko realizes that Shizuka is an innocent, where Mari was not. From that point onward, Riko and Shizuka develop a professional friendship. Although in the later books Riko has no more affairs with women (or for that matter, men) and devotes herself to her child and her relationship with Andō, there are brief interjections that recall Mari's perfume or how much Riko loved her.

Although much of Anglo-American detective fiction written by women does not involve lesbian ties, the relationships described between women often exceed mere friendship, leaving the heroine to ponder the nature of her sexuality. This situation has prompted Walton and Jones to observe that "[The] investigation of the nature of sexual desire [is] a central component of the narrative" in detective fiction.[53] What this also reveals is the paucity of language available to describe the many gradations of relationships between women in literature. As Luce Irigaray has suggested, "Phallocentrism has eliminated meaningful words for autonomous female sexuality," and detective fiction has long been a particularly phallogocentric genre.[54] To be sure, contemporary women writers have been constantly reworking the language in their books, and the situation of having a previously heterosexual character muse about her own sexuality is not unusual in Anglo-American detective fiction, even when the detective is not identified as a lesbian.

This kind of appeal to the "language of pleasure, or the fact that another woman has literally and figuratively gotten under her skin,"[55] has been far less common among Japanese writers. It is this fact, perhaps, that forces the author to rely on other genres to create a relationship that exceeds the parameters of affairs described in Japanese detective fiction thus far. Such stylistic cross-fertilization, however, also ultimately obfuscates the author's stance on lesbianism, reducing it to merely a titillating storyline. It is as if the author is unsure of who her audience is. This uncertainty extends to the way that the book was critically received. While it won a prize the year it was published, most of the reviews focused on the fact that Riko is "an uninhibited, sexually liberated protagonist."[56] The book's jacket describes it as *"seiai shōsetsu ya ren'ai shōsetsu"* (a story about sex and a story about love) but does not mention what kind of relationships comprise the "sex." The lesbian relationship is addressed in a longer review in *Misuteri besuto 201,* but this brief acknowledgment is accompanied by a discussion of the horrific rapes of the male victims.[57]

This critical avoidance of the novel's lesbian (sub)text was echoed by Shibata herself, who took pains to point out that the second book in the series, *Madonna's Abyss,* featured "a new Riko" who was completely different from the old: "This novel is a sequel to *Riko—Forever Venus.* This, however, is a *new* novel. The protagonist, Murakami Riko, is not the same as she was in the first novel. She's changed. The people and the places around her have changed in the two years that have gone by."[58] Yet while the author claims that the protagonist is different—and it is true that she has changed (she is a mother)—subtle hints in the subsequent novels that Mari is still in Riko's thoughts remind the reader of the events in *Riko—Forever Venus.* Furthermore, Riko's past experience makes her aware of and sympathetic to a variety of marginalized figures, including a transgendered woman and a police detective who quit because of his yakuza boyfriend. It is this trait that makes her more understanding than the other police detectives on the force.

With Mari's death in the end of the first novel, not only is the *femme fatale* destroyed (as she is in all *noir* detective fiction), but this destruction also ensures that the lesbian relationship does not pose a serious challenge to the heterosexual order. In the beginning of the novel, the lesbian relationship was positioned as an alternative to the violence Riko experienced in her relationships with men. Her attempt to maintain herself and her autonomy in the face of attack causes her to cast a cynical eye on the sexual economy. The author proposes an escape through alternative sexualities that allow for a rejection of male dominance. In this construction, sexual intercourse is construed in a simple binary: women are gentle and men are violent. This construction, however, is shown to be inadequate since Shibata cannot commit to lesbianism—in fact, she cannot even use the word in regard to her own character. In the end, Riko is allowed to challenge the order of things only in the arena of the workplace, as her love affair with a woman and her dream of setting up a house together cannot be realized. With her options foreclosed in this way, Riko can be recuperated into the heterosexual world as mother and wife.

In the end, then, heterosexuality appears to be inescapable, and Shibata's novels ultimately validate the status quo. Recuperation is achieved through accepting social norms. On every level, the author demonstrates how patriarchy and heterosexuality structure everyday life and how any disruption of this order, either willing or unwilling, must be punished. While Shibata's series of novels charts Riko's transition from single woman to married mother, it also reflects the changes in her sexual existence. No longer is Riko a sexually active, or even sexual, woman. Once her son is born, her energies shift to balancing child care and work, and even when Andō moves in with her, only once does Shibata mention that they have sex—a button-popping experience, quickly concluded. In the final novel of the series, *Diana's Daydream*, Riko plans to quit in order to devote herself to being a mother and wife, but after she solves a case, she finds she cannot bring herself to abandon the work she loves. (Significantly, as noted, she is severely burned and her jaw is broken while she is capturing the criminal.) Riko's ultimate professional affirmation, therefore, is accompanied by the final stage in a process of desexualization. Her sexual energies first bridled and then sublimated, Riko loses in the end her very existence as both the subject and object of libidinal desire.

Sex, Deviance, and Tolerance

As I have shown, Riko's acceptance of Andō's marriage proposal marks a shift in the series away from her sexual exploits and toward her roles as wife, mother, and worker. This move away from sexuality, however, does not characterize Shibata's novels as a whole. In fact, the pages of the Riko series, as well as the Miro series, are filled with sadomasochists, necrophiliacs, and transgendered characters, as well as more run-of-the-mill gay men and pornographic actors. The presence of such marginal figures in women's detective fiction, in fact, is not a new phenomenon. In Japan, a country where the body, sexuality, and desire have not tended to be common topics of discussion in the mainstream media, other fora exist for the treatment of these issues—most notably the *manga*, which have long been a site for discussing and imaging sexual practices.[59] Detective fiction, as well, has a long tradition of employing images of sexuality and the body as fodder for its plots and settings. In the Taisho period, which witnessed the popularization of detective fiction in Japan, many detective stories either used sexuality and sexual obsession as themes or included descriptions of sexual relations.[60] It was during this time as well that the language of sex and sexuality became standardized and that interest in sex was captured in various forms of popular culture.[61] This fascination is epitomized in the phrase *"ero-guro-nansensu"* (erotic-grotesque-nonsense), which applied to much of the earlier detective fiction as well as more serious fiction.

The *ero-guro-nansensu* aesthetic, which emerged at the same time as new ideas about women's agency and sexuality, was taken up by authors such as Edogawa Rampo.[62] He and a number of his contemporaries extended this grotesque sexual sensibility to the use of "weird" sexualities as a fictive milieu. Rampo's *Kuro Tokage* (Black Lizard) is perhaps the best-known example of this practice, a mystery story populated with characters of differing sexual proclivities and identities.[63] The detective, Akechi, is challenged by a young woman, the Black Lizard, who is able to adopt the persona of any man or woman in order to get what she wants. Like a pair of crafty chess players, Akechi and the Black Lizard plot their moves across Japan until Akechi corners the Black Lizard in her lair, a museum filled not only with beautiful artwork, but also with naked specimens of men and women (collected from all parts of the world), who live in cages or are transformed into living wax statues.

Setting a detective novel within such a milieu does more than simply shock or titillate the audience—it also serves to reinforce the detective's ability to interact with all levels of society and thus becomes a shorthand for the detective's experience in the world. But while the female detective's worldly experience can likewise be discerned from the people that she meets and the places she goes, the inclusion of marginal characters and places in the contemporary detective fiction of Shibata and Kirino goes beyond the Taisho *ero-guro-nansensu* tradition, which was marked by a highly masculine, often voyeuristic treatment of women's bodies and sexualities. Unlike Rampo's atmospheric presentation of a circus of weirdos, both Shibata and Kirino flesh out their minor characters, endowing them with complex motives, carefully exploring their differences, and portraying them neither as freaks nor as aberrations.

More significant, these marginal characters are often kinder, more likable people than the more "normal" individuals who turn out to be the criminals. While one could explain away these characters as devices meant to show that the detective knows and is effective in dealing with a variety of people, both Riko and Miro are more sensitive in those dealings because they too occupy a place at the margins of society, as women doing a man's job. Moreover, the treatment of these marginal characters also serves the didactic purpose of introducing readers to the motivations and the problems that such people face. Thus in Riko's final sex scene with Mari, Riko is led to reflect upon sex with women and the problems particular to a lesbian relationship: "Mari and I, we have bodies that cannot be placed on each other, hearts that cannot enter one another. We are 'the same thing.' We are not permitted to have the happiness made out of two different pieces" (347).

In *Night Abandoned by Angels* Kirino devotes several pages to the life story of Tomo, Miro's next door neighbor, who provides her with the support and nurturing she has been lacking. Attractive and sympathetic, Tomo stands in stark contrast to the heterosexual males in the novel, who are violent, predatory, and deceitful. Miro's relationship with Tomo, however, troubles her since she cannot conceive of him apart from the standard roles of lover or husband. In the beginning of their relationship, she is curious about his homosexuality and wants to know more about how he became who he is. A former salaryman turned bar owner, Tomo is wary about Miro's potential homophobia, only to find that as a child of Shinjuku ni-chome, she is not scared by gay people.[64] Still, his apparent celibacy intrigues her, and as he begins to satisfy more of her emotional needs, she expresses the familiar lament, "Why does Tomo have to be gay?"

Tomo plays a role different from that played by gay men in Anglo-American detective novels written by women; the latter tend either to serve as "sensitive" male foils for the female protagonist or, as Sally Munt has argued, to demonstrate that "homosexuality is the threat that must be expunged by a heterosexual hero."[65] Instead, Kirino uses Tomo to reinforce the idea that heterosexual sex complicates the relationship between men and women, ultimately denying women autonomy and agency in their relationships. Miro's relationship with Tomo thus demonstrates the limitations of heterosexual relationships since he provides the companionship that she cannot get from the men with whom she has a sexual relationship.

It is not merely the gay characters that receive such treatment, however; transgendered individuals make their presence felt as well. Riko is introduced to Isojima Yutaka in *Madonna's Abyss* when (s)he is arrested for attempting to buy drugs. Riko's macho cop partner does not believe Isojima's story and threatens to perform a cavity search to ensure that she does not have any drugs on her. When the woman starts to cry, however, Riko steps in. The story Isojima tells her, while central to the development of the plot, also provides a sympathetic account of the transgendered experience of sex, sexuality, and gender:

> This year I met someone and we began dating. Of course, it's a man. From junior high on, it has almost always been men that I think I like. . . . I haven't been honest because I don't want men to find out that I am not a woman. I'm most afraid of being called a fag. When someone says that, everything goes black. Don't get me wrong; it's not whether or not there's prejudice against gays. I hate the fact that only women with women's bodies are supposed to like men. Please realize that I am a woman; still, when it's taken for granted that it's normal to like men, I just can't support that. But . . . people who seem to be interested in me all change their attitude and think that I'm just a fag.[66]

As she listens to this, Riko tries to make sense of what happens when one's gender and sex do not match up:

> Isojima Yutaka was born with the consciousness that she is a woman. Of course this means that as a heterosexual she is a woman, and as a hetero-

sexual she will be attracted to men. But Yutaka's body has the capabilities of a man. She does have both kinds of body parts, but she is clearly a man. As far as other men are concerned, though, Yutaka is a homosexual. . . . Despite looking like a woman from the outside, fundamentally she cannot perform the same sex acts as a woman. Yutaka and the men who have sex with her have to do it like homosexuals do.[67]

In Japan, where the Takarazuka and the kabuki theater regularly feature performers who have been assigned a gender different from their own, this kind of reflection is not so outlandish. Moreover, these musings are articulated in such a way that the characters are not belittled for their choices or made into objects of ridicule. This is not to say, however, that everyone shares this view. Shiromoto, Riko's partner, is extremely unhappy about having to deal with Yutaka and threatens to crush his testicles. His angry attitude is deflected by Riko's two-page explanation of the difference between transgendered and transsexual persons. The presence of these marginal characters, therefore, does more than simply reveal the effectiveness of the detective. Instead, the discussions of sexuality they provoke serve to enrich and expand the larger debates that the authors have laid out.

Both Kirino and Shibata have used the genre of detective fiction to create compelling yet problematic portrayals of female sex and sexuality in contemporary Japan, manipulating genre conventions in a variety of ways. In particular, both authors play with the erotically charged figure of the *femme fatale,* inverting it (in the form of an *homme fatal*), subverting it (in the form of a sexually liberated protagonist who uses sex to thwart male power), or displacing it (in the guise of Riko's sinister lesbian lover). Each author likewise offers an alternative to heterosexual violence, represented by abusive lovers, sexually predatory colleagues, and the pornography industry—aggressive sexual independence in the case of Miro and a homosexual liaison in the case of Riko. In a place like Japan, where the pervasive image of women and sexuality is exploitative and violent, the fact that Kirino and Shibata attempt to propose such alternative visions is significant, particularly in light of the fact that it was not until the mid-1980s that Japanese women began to speak out in an organized way about pornography and its link to sexual violence. Both authors cast a critical eye upon sexual exploitation, and both attempt to openly and positively address female sexual desires and the problems women face in their sexual relationships.

In the end, however, both Shibata and Kirino suggest that such alternatives are untenable or deceptive and that outside of the traditional institutions of marriage and motherhood, sex and danger will remain unavoidably linked—a conclusion bolstered by their portrayal of violence and particularly sexual violence toward women. As Sue Grafton has noted, "Detective fiction is the stuff of violence, so you'll always be dealing with some form of it."[68] In these novels, however, the threat of violence against women is omnipresent. Miro is roughed up by gangsters in the first novel and later faces threats and random violence. Riko is attacked while hunting a subway pervert, abducted, has a finger broken by a yakuza, and is beaten and left in a burning building. Both Miro and Riko deal with this nonsexual violence in a professional manner, and it does not deter them from completing their tasks. While the level of violence inflicted upon Miro is minor in comparison to the beatings that Riko endures over the course of her three novels, Miro is still a more physical creature than the other female detectives in Japanese detective fiction. In *Her Face, Veiled in Rain* Miro takes a beating at the hands of thugs with a combination of insouciance and stoicism, while the intimidation in *Night Abandoned by Angels* proves unsettling but not incapacitating. Both detectives handle the violence as something that comes with the job.

Still, as David Glover points out, "The all pervasive presence of male violence acts as a brake upon the narrative, a limit upon movement and access, threatening to hold the investigation back by transforming the heroine into a victim, interrogating the meaning of suspense in the process."[69] This is particularly true in the case of sexual violence. While violence in tandem with sex is standard fare for hard-boiled detective fiction, in the context of women's detective fiction both take on different meanings. The intertwining of sexuality and violence in these novels shows that while women might be the instigators of sexual contact, they remain the targets of physical domination and, in the case of pornography, of a mode of representation that "mak[es] it appear that violence is intrinsically erotic, rather than something that is eroticized."[70] Kirino strives to avoid this problem by creating a heroine firmly in control of her body and her sexuality. Nevertheless, the fear that Miro feels during her involvement with Naruse and Yashiro is not a fear of violence itself but of the loss of self and of symbolic domination. Riko is raped, an ordeal that turns the detective from an active agent into a victim and that is used by the author as a graphic reminder of the differences between sex with men and sex with women.

CHAPTER 5

Sexing the City

Bodies and Space
in the Work of Matsuo Yumi

Here was a town of pregnant women. Women who had another life inside them could leave their homes and their jobs for a while, congregate here and live peacefully. It was a perfect environment, safe and secure. . . . Some called it a "people ranch," and certain men called Balloon Town a form of sex discrimination. Such an advantageous living situation certainly had its charms, but there wasn't a huge rush of people who wanted to live here.

—Matsuo Yumi, *Murder in Balloon Town*

Matsuo Yumi's 1994 collection of short stories, *Baruun Taun no satsujin* (Murder in Balloon Town, 1994), is set in a Tokyo of the near future divided into special wards, each dedicated to a specific function such as industrial production or commercial activities. One of these is the Special Seventh Ward, nicknamed "Balloon Town"—a place designated for pregnant women who leave their homes and families to live in this ward before they give birth. The stories in *Murder in Balloon Town* focus upon the resolution of a crime through the discovery of one key clue, a discovery that requires the skills of a knowledgeable "insider." In the first story, the eponymous "Murder in Balloon Town," a man is stabbed to death in front of Balloon Town's main gate, and Detective Eda Marina of the Tokyo Metropolitan Police is sent undercover to find the murderer. Assisted by her old college friend Kurebayashi Mio, a Balloon Town resident, Marina solves the crime by means of an unusual clue—the shape of a pregnant woman's stomach. Each of the other stories in the collection follows a similar pattern, as Mio's personal experience of pregnancy provides the key to a series of vexing mysteries until at last she gives birth to a little boy.[1]

Matsuo Yumi was known primarily as a science fiction writer until the publication of *Murder in Balloon Town,* which was billed as a "science fiction mystery." Despite its futuristic setting, however, this collection of stories is firmly grounded in the traditions of detective fiction. In particular, Matsuo's work emphasizes one of the defining aspects of that genre: its focus upon lived space—and more specifically upon the urban environment—not only as "context," but also as a crucial aspect of the story itself. Indeed, the subject of Matsuo's stories often seems to be a place—Balloon Town—rather than people and the mysteries surrounding them. This highly developed sense of space and attention to its many nuances and details serve in turn as the points of departure for a parodic critique of gender relations and politics in contemporary Japan. In this chapter, I will focus upon Matsuo's detective fiction and its treatment of the central issues of "space," the body, and the intersection of the two.

Detective Fiction and City Spaces

Detective fiction is concerned with the solution of a crime, the discovery and unmasking of the criminal, and the restoration of matters to the status quo. It is a genre that relies upon digging into the past, uncovering what had been concealed, and reconstructing what was lost from sight in order to reveal the truth "in light of reason" and to "inculcate a sense of order."[2] In particular, appearing as it did at the same time that Europe's major cities were expanding, detective fiction has always been intimately linked to the urban environment.[3] Rapid urbanization bred chaos and crime, making it a place unknowable and disordered—a place that required logic to restore order and detailed observation to gain useful knowledge about its hidden nooks and crannies.

In the West, the detective story first appeared in the early 1840s, with a trio of short stories by Edgar Allen Poe. Set in Paris, Poe's stories used the city streets to show the dangers of urban life. In particular, "The Mystery of Marie Roget" (1842–1843), which was based on the real life murder of Mary Rogers, a New York shop clerk, articulated the dangers that city streets posed to women and to public safety in general. In the stories of Arthur Conan Doyle, the dark, foggy streets of London, lit by street lamps, became indelibly associated with detective fiction. In Japan also, writers such as Edogawa Rampo took advantage of the urban setting of prewar and postwar Tokyo. Rampo's stories described the rapidly changing metropolis, documenting the ruins of Edo architecture and the new buildings of the modern era.[4] Each of these authors demonstrates how important space is for describing the mood of the city and, in certain cases, providing impetus for the narrative itself.

One aspect of detective fiction that reveals its uniquely "modern" nature, therefore, is the role of city space. In addition to detective fiction's historical and conceptual ties to the city, physical space is privileged within the genre because of detective fiction's emphasis on "realistic" emplotment and description. The texts must continually refer to actual places, people, and organizations in order to reinforce the genre's mimetic qualities. In turn, this sense of authenticity and feeling of participation are large parts of the pleasure of reading.[5] As the pages of a detective novel describe the streets and buildings of different parts of a city, the city thus becomes central, serving both as a narrative setting and as subject matter.[6] Yet the spaces that detective fiction delineates are not just the physical topographies of the city, but also the social as well as bodily spaces of the characters themselves. The social spaces are the homes and offices where the characters live and work and where their interactions produce the clues and the information that help the detective solve the crime. It is in these spaces that the mundane details of lived experience are transformed into answers to the detective's questions. The bodily spaces of the characters are also important to the functioning of detective fiction. The appearance of a body, either living or dead, marks the beginning of the detective story. Furthermore, it is the traces of the body—the fingerprints, the bloodstains, and (more recently) the DNA samples—that furnish the detective with clues to solve the mystery.

These disparate elements are united by the figure of the detective, who has knowledge of the city and the ability to read its spaces, enabling him to discover what is hidden beneath the surface. The detective's desire to unearth what was concealed and to gather the pieces of evidence together to assemble a whole is dependent on his knowledge of where to look—knowledge that must be wide and is necessarily uneven since the detective must know others better than they know him. This knowledge, furthermore, is of people as "individuals—that is, in their rich circumstantiality and idiosyncrasy—and as members of particular groups or occupants of particular social roles, who thereby possess the special knowledge associated with the group or role—especially the knowledge of the cultural rules that structure and inform role-specific behavior."[7] Therefore, it is both the detective's distance from the people that he is studying and his closeness to the crime that he is investigating that allow him to piece the clues together and solve the crime.

Parodying Space

Matsuo's fictional Balloon Town, and the ways in which it is depicted clearly are related to the broader spatial strategies and concerns of detective fiction. These stories, however, are interesting not because they are concerned with space, but because of the unique way that conceptions of space are defined, discussed, and manipulated. In particular, Matsuo uses the detective form in order to parody the themes, descriptive conventions, and narrative devices of detective fiction itself.

Parody as a literary strategy incorporates the target genre's own materials and structure in order to make its point. In particular, familiar structures of the genre may be deliberately brought to the foreground by being made more obvious, more complex, or more confusing.[8] This foregrounding highlights how these structures are augmented, condensed, or juxtaposed in order to give the genre a more complex or perhaps ambivalent focus.[9] This strategy gives parody the ability to recreate and imitate certain norms (both generic and social) in order to attack or defend them. As Judith Butler puts it, "To enter into parody is to enter into a relationship of both desire and ambivalence. . . . Parody requires a certain ability to identify, approximate, and draw near; it engages an intimacy with the position it appropriates that troubles the voice, the bearing, the performativity of the subject such that the audience or the reader does not quite know where it is you stand, whether you have gone over to the other side, whether you remain on your side, whether you can rehearse that other position without falling prey to it in the midst of the performance."[10]

Notably, Matsuo does not directly challenge the conventions of detective fiction and the way that space is represented; rather, she takes the traditions of detective fiction and displaces them. In other words, Matsuo constructs her stories using the conventions of detective fiction, but by exaggerating or displacing these features, she makes explicit detective fiction's use of space as a setting and as a plot device. The familiar world of the detective, for instance, is intensely masculine—a place where loners go head to head with criminals in a dark, urban landscape. In Matsuo's stories, however, the central figure of the detective is realigned and recast within an explicitly, even absurdly, "feminine" space. Matsuo's Detective Eda is a woman in a woman's world, rather than a man in a man's world. In turn, by creating a place for women only, in which a uniquely feminine process, reproduction, is the primary activity, Matsuo accomplishes another displacement that parodies urban spatial practices. Through this kind of play with the gender conventions of detective fiction, therefore, the author creates an imaginary space in which the situation of women, their bodies, and their reproductive functions becomes dramatically clear.

The division of Tokyo by function is one example of how Matsuo's displacement of the "normal" processes of the city serves as a critique of urban space. As Elizabeth Grosz points out, the city has always been a place that "orients and organizes family, sexual, and social relations, insofar as the city divides cultural life into public and private domains, geographically dividing and defining the particular social positions and locations occupied by individuals and groups."[11] One of the central divisions in urban space takes place along gender lines, as particular spaces or categories of space are associated with the gender of those who occupy them or are delineated as being proper to one gender or another. Yet while the gendering of space is not a new phenomenon, Matsuo explores it in new and different ways. Her explicitly feminine space, Balloon Town, is not assimilated to the "private" or "domestic" arena; instead it is a public place that is wholly under the aegis of the government of Tokyo. Yet this "public" place, because of its function, is gendered female and is used for a "private," "bodily" function.

This distinction indicates the connection that long has existed between public and private functions and the gender of the people associated with them. Traditionally, in both Japan and the West, this link has been firm. With the development of the modern industrial city, the existing demarcation of spaces for men and women was solidified. The home became the site for women's work as new technologies and regimes of production took men away from the hearth and sent them to the factories and offices. The division between the interior, private space of the home and the public space of the city had further consequences. In contrast to the domestic arena, the public arena became defined as the sphere of reason and universal freedom, of autonomy and creativity, and of education and rational debate.[12] The public arena also was a place for the production and exchange of goods and money.[13]

Conversely, the "domestic" sphere of activities was linked to the space of the home with "femaleness," defined by reproduction and motherhood, emotional relations, domestic labor, and illness. This was thus the sphere of the body and bodily relations that prevented women from participating in the public arena.[14] As Elizabeth Grosz has noted, "Men produce a universe built on the erasures of the bodies and contributions of women/mothers and the refusal to acknowledge the debt that they owe to the maternal body. They hollow out their own interiors and project them outward, and require women as supports for this hollowed space. Women become the guardians of the private, the interpersonal, while men built conceptual and material worlds."[15] The domestic sphere, supported and run by women, also was a haven for men; women, however, were deterred from venturing out into the world of the public. The home was the location for women, both metaphorically and physically. Of course, women were not confined at all times to their homes; however, even places outside the home where women frequently went, such as department stores and restaurants, were distinctively marked by this association with women and could thus be classified as "women's spaces."[16]

The division of space in Japan has been equally gendered, although at certain times women have had more access to the public arena. During the

Tokugawa period (1603–1868), the woman, at least in samurai households, was bound within a Neo-Confucian hierarchy that often made her position little more than that of a servant.[17] Early in the Meiji period, some attempts were made to educate women, and there was a movement for women's suffrage, but toward the end of the nineteenth century, the Japanese government added Article 5 to the Meiji Civil Code, which prevented women from having the right to vote, joining political associations, or even attending a political meeting.[18] Furthermore, the Meiji Civil Code solidified the position of the patriarchal head of household, who "controlled the family assets, managed his wife's property, and approved marriages of women under twenty-five (and men under thirty) years of age."[19] The articulation of the concept *"ryōsai kenbo"* (good wife, wise mother) around 1899 made the "domestic destiny" of women an element of state ideology discouraging women from public life until after World War I.[20] Virtues such as submissiveness, modesty, and chastity were stressed, and in lieu of academic training young women were prepared "to contribute to society and the state through household management and child rearing rather than political, artistic or economic activity in the public world."[21] While *ryōsai kenbo* remained a potent force in the socialization of women, it was not monolithic, and after World War II it gradually fell out of favor. Nevertheless, while society has changed over the years in Japan and despite the many strides that women have made, the division of the spaces that men and women inhabit has been slower to disappear. The home and family still are seen as the woman's domain, and despite the 1985 Equal Employment Law, many women are still expected to quit their jobs in order to raise their families.

Within this context, the parodic quality of Matsuo's "female space" becomes more apparent. The Special Seventh Ward, which is Balloon Town's proper name, was created by the metropolitan government in response to women's demands to be able to control their bodies. In the latter part of the twentieth century, natural childbirth has disappeared in favor of a system in which a baby is gestated in a controlled environment outside of the mother (known as AU, or artificial uterus).[22] This system quickly spread and became institutionalized, but some women were dissatisfied and campaigned to return to the old ways of natural childbirth. Once they did, the Tokyo metropolitan government made a commitment to them and decided to reorganize the city. The city center was emptied while various governmental and commercial activities were regrouped and reassigned to different parts of the metropolis, leaving Tokyo for a time in a state of chaos. Yet while this reassignment caused outrage among the citizens, ultimately the government won out with its argument that Tokyo should "aim at being people friendly" (14), and the construction progressed.[23]

Balloon Town is open to all women from their fifth month of pregnancy until they give birth. Since it is run by the metropolitan government, women are able to use their national health insurance to pay for most of the fees, making it accessible to any woman who, in the protagonist's jaundiced view, "want[s] to put up with the months of doubt and endure a deformed body and the painful experience of childbirth" (15). The residents of Balloon Town include wealthy women and full-time housewives, as well as career women. Everything is designed to ensure that there is strict equality among them. There are no wide economic discrepancies since the same services are available for each woman at the same price.

Despite its status as one of Tokyo's wards, Balloon Town limits the number and kind of people who can enter. There are two entrances to the ward: a special gate requiring an ID card that only the pregnant women carry and a regular security gate for employees and visitors. This system ensures that the women are safe without the added distraction of police or other surveillance within the ward itself. Aside from family members and friends, there are few visitors to Balloon Town. The creators of Balloon Town, in other words, have envisioned a place that would be secure and free from all harm.

Upon entering Balloon Town, a visitor is in a thickly wooded park. In the center of the park, there is a large pond dominated by a six-meter-high stone statue. Called the "Good Vessel," it depicts a very pregnant woman "carved in deep relief . . . [with] flowing hair and a body shaped like a pear. Clad in light clothes, she was posed with her hips slightly swiveled" (19). The residents are housed in cookie-cutter apartments, each of them light and airy, with cheerful flowered curtains and blond wood furniture. If a woman is not satisfied with her apartment, we are told, she easily can move to another one with a better view.

The creation of Balloon Town serves, in effect, to render what we consider a "private" function associated with the domestic sphere—reproduction—into a public one. Yet, despite the fact that the Seventh Ward is one of the main wards of Tokyo and under government administration, access is deliberately controlled, making it in fact semiprivate. With the whole city organized by function, these new spaces become easier to control because it is easier to discern who belongs and who does not. To this end, it is clear how thoroughly the designers have engineered a place for a particular function in order to ensure that every need is met.

Everything in Balloon Town has been constructed for the comfort and convenience of pregnant women. Although Matsuo's Tokyo is several years in the future, her detailed description of Balloon Town makes it clear that it occupies the area of present-day Aoyama.[24] Building on the existing hills and using the walls of the old city, the government authorities have constructed a new town. The green spaces in the area (perhaps including Meiji jingu, the shrine dedicated to the spirit of the Meiji emperor) have been turned into parks, the area has been closed off to through traffic to reduce carbon monoxide (which could damage the fetuses), and buses have been replaced by trolleys. The subway lines that had provided access to the area have been closed down, not only so that the women would be shielded from their electromagnetic rays, but also so that they would feel safe and secure. The Seventh Ward is located conveniently next to the business ward, so that husbands can visit easily, while Suitengu Shrine, long a destination for expectant mothers seeking divine protection during pregnancy and childbirth, has been relocated to provide direct access for Balloon Town's residents.[25]

Not only has the ward been redesigned to protect the pregnant women from harmful substances, but it also provides them with a variety of activities, all geared to producing a better child. The motto of Balloon Town is "Be a Good Vessel," suggesting that these women should conceive of their surroundings as a way to enrich themselves for their children. Thus there are theaters and eateries that cater to the needs of pregnant women. The cafés serve caffeine-free herbal teas and *konbu cha*, a fermented tea purported to have medicinal properties, as well as snacks to sate hunger pangs. Moreover, it is impossible to buy an alcoholic beverage in Balloon Town, as Detective Eda finds to her chagrin. Because of pregnant women's frequent need for restrooms, these are provided on every corner. Furthermore, there are activities and sports meant to educate the mother and nurture the baby once it is born. These include knitting, yoga, and watercolor painting, as well as classes geared toward bodily care, such as breathing and breast massage (50).

To further ensure that there will be no need to leave Balloon Town, the stores and boutiques have been transformed into emporia catering to the needs of pregnant women—maternity formal wear, maternity lingerie, shoes with special buckles designed to expand with the foot—while supermarkets have been provided for the women to do all of their shopping. There is a ready supply of leisure activities, such as concerts, theater, and (as we have seen) shopping, and everything is set up so that women do not need to change their habits in their new neighborhood. The decor of all the apartments and buildings is dominated by pastels, flowers, and soft designs. As Matsuo writes, "Flowers grew on every street corner, and the buildings looked as if they belonged in a fairy tale *[meruhenchikku]*. . . . The supermarket's bird-shaped weather vane annoyed Marina" (29). The gendered quality of the space extends to the clothing that each woman wears. Even with the general lack of variation in maternity wear generally, Balloon Town is marked by a style of clothing that amounts to a uniform: a jumper skirt and a blouse for cooler months and the jumper by itself (worn as a sundress)

Suitengu Shrine, Tokyo. Here women come to buy amulets and pray for safe pregnancies and births, especially on each month's "Day of the Dog."

for hotter weather. These outfits come in a range of colors (most are pastels with floral patterns) and can be purchased in Balloon Town's stores, the most famous of which is Coquille d'Oeuf (The Eggshell).[26]

Bodies and Space

As we have seen, the gendered space in which these stories are situated is intimately linked to the physical dimensions and requirements of the female body, and especially the pregnant body. This relationship, however, is not confined to Matsuo's fictional universe. Rather, as scholars increasingly have argued, cities comprise spatial regimes for the bodies of their inhabitants: they order and organize the unrelated bodies of different classes of people, and the city becomes the context and frame for the body, a place where the body is socially, sexually, and discursively produced.[27] In general, the development of city space has largely been for the benefit of the people participating in commerce and production; a look at recent developments in any modern urban center reveals the trend toward privileging the spaces of business and commerce.[28]

Matsuo's organization of the future Tokyo, however, and her situation of Balloon Town within it can be seen as both an inversion and a reinforcement of this conception of the city. Her new corner of Tokyo resonates with the functioning of the pregnant human body and privileges childbearing over business or trade. At the same time, the structure of the city as a whole makes it clear that forms and modes of "production" ultimately comprise its organizing principle. Within this context, childbearing itself *is* production, not simply in a bodily but also in a political and economic sense. In short, Balloon Town is "[the] reflection, projection or product of [the] bodies" that reside within its borders.[29]

The corporeal aspect of the residents, then, defines what might be called the "bodily space" of Matsuo's stories. As noted above, all detective fiction is, to some extent, about the body—from the motivating presence of a dead body to the physical identification of the murderer. Whether fingerprints or furtive glances, bloodstains or whispered secrets, each clue to the mystery can be traced back to the body directly or indirectly. In Matsuo's series of stories, too, it is the knowledge of the body that provides the key to the mystery in each case. Yet this emphasis on knowledge of the body is another element of Matsuo's parodic strategy since she makes the connection much more visible by introducing a world that is *centered* on the body. The whole landscape of Balloon Town is dominated by the stone statue of "the Good Vessel." Indeed, the entire town focuses on women's bodies, in particular their bulbous stomachs. Not only is the environment influenced by the body, but also the body itself, and in particular the pregnant body, figures in all aspects of the detection and crime solving carried out by the protagonists in each story.

Within this gendered space, moreover, all conversations and activities are centered around being pregnant. One of the first conversations that Marina overhears is a discussion of how to put on a *hara obi,* or "belly band," a strip of unbleached cotton material that is wrapped around the stomach to protect the belly and to ease the burden of the growing baby. There follow discussions of what other women's stomachs look like and how advanced one's pregnancy is. Conversations about the changes in a woman's body during pregnancy involve not only the residents of Balloon Town, but also the staff members and shopkeepers in the stores that line the streets. When Marina attempts to buy a bra in her own, unpregnant size, the clerk reminds her sternly that she must take account of the fact that her bra size will increase during pregnancy and afterward. At the next shop, the shoe salesman points out the benefits of shoes that can expand to accommodate the swelling foot. As Marina pointedly concludes, "In this town, it was generally assumed by everyone that various parts of a woman's body would gradually be swelling" (44).

This emphasis on the ungainliness of the pregnant body forces us to confront the corporeality, or the physicality, of pregnancy in a way seldom portrayed in literature. In contemporary magazines or other popular cultural representations, pregnancy is glossed over in a diaphanous or dreamlike way that does not make readers aware of its more earthy aspects.[30] Here, the author confronts the readers with the visible otherness of pregnant women, as in her description of Balloon Town's health club: "Tropical plants were placed around the sides of the pool, giving it the appearance of a watermelon patch. Women lay around on deck chairs, nearly all of them wearing brightly colored or flowered bikinis. Their stomachs were exposed to the sun, as if it had some special kind of significance. With their sunglasses on, you couldn't tell whether or not they were sleeping, save for their protruding belly buttons, which moved up and down" (52).

This connection between "natural" surroundings and pregnancy is reinforced throughout the text, where pregnant women are compared to such things as watermelons, pears, and animals. Matsuo thus joins her gendered treatment of space to a consensus on the "naturalness" of women's pregnancy and childbirth. Detective Eda repeatedly comments about how the pregnant women look like sheltered animals in an exotic park or how they resemble a carton of eggs when they are sitting on the trolley. These wry observations about the women's appearance, however, are accompanied by obvious fear and discomfort about "natural" pregnancy. By presenting a character with such mixed feelings, Matsuo reveals to readers how quickly attitudes toward pregnancy and birth change. By emphasizing the naturalness of pregnancy, she points out how the elaborately constructed surroundings are nothing more than that, since in the past pregnancy and childbirth have not inhibited women. Moreover, the insistence on having a natural pregnancy becomes a way to control women in Balloon Town since any "unnatural" activity would be noted and talked about and the woman harassed.

Matsuo, in other words, uses the character of Detective Eda Marina to demonstrate to the readers the strangeness of pregnancy. Since pregnancy in the novel is not a choice made by many Japanese women and was unheard of in the previous generation, it is profoundly foreign to a young, unmarried professional woman like Marina. The option of becoming pregnant is not one that many women take; thus, when Marina arrives, she is overwhelmed by the fact that pregnancy is almost the only topic of conversation. From the moment she learns that she is to be sent to Balloon Town, Marina is horrified. On her first trip to Balloon Town to meet with the head of security, Ms. Takayama, she walks through a park where many pregnant women are strolling along the wooded paths. Gazing at their "protruding bellies" and "massive proportions," she is struck by their "clumsy appearance" and by the "terrible, uniformly contented expression" on their faces, and she feels like she is in a nightmare (20).

The more she learns about the customs of Balloon Town, such as turning one's head away when someone sneezes in order to give her some privacy to check her sphincter control, Marina's revulsion grows. This feeling reaches its peak when, on the first night of her undercover work, she reads through the two books that every woman who comes to Balloon Town receives as a gift from the ward. She ignores the first *(A Good Vessel)* and begins to browse through the other, *The Pregnancy and Birth Handbook:* "Without thinking, she returned to the beginning and began reading again. Covering her mouth with her hand, she was unable to tear her eyes away. When she came to the pages filled with pictures and graphs about birth, Marina's body became rigid. Vaginal deliveries. Cesarean sections. They were equally barbaric" (45).

Once she meets her old college friend, Kurebayashi Mio, who is living in Balloon Town, this revulsion is tempered by a sense of irony. By the end of the first story, Marina realizes that for the residents of Balloon Town, being pregnant is a part of their identity, and the minute differences in the shape of a woman's body become markers of individuality. This point becomes clearer when she starts to interview witnesses to the murder. She is frustrated when the women are unable to provide a detailed description of the suspect and can focus only on the shape of the woman's stomach, leaving her with a profile of a "female, pregnant, approximately 28 to 30 weeks, with a *togari* [pointed] stomach, medium build, medium height, wearing a salmon pink sun dress" (33). In Balloon Town, as it turns out, women have eschewed the modern convenience of learning the sex of one's baby before it is born, preferring to rely on the traditional method of determining it by the shape of the woman's stomach. A *kamebara*, or turtle-shaped belly, means that the child will be a girl, while a *togaribara*, a pointed or beak-shaped belly, means that the child will be a boy. This detail is more than simply diagnostic, however; women themselves are categorized by the shape of their stomachs.

This focus on the body and its functions, moreover, defines the crimes that are committed in the novel and the clues that are needed to solve them. All of the crimes in Matsuo's series center around pregnancy and secrets involving pregnancy. The first is a murder to protect a secret, the second an assault to advance a career, and the third and fourth are industrial and political intrigues. Knowledge of pregnancy, which is unavailable to outsiders, become the key to solving these crimes. Despite being a capable detective, Marina is befuddled and cannot comprehend the meaning behind what the women are saying. Ultimately she cannot crack the case without the privileged information provided by her pregnant friend Mio. While Marina and the other members of the Metropolitan Police Force are frustrated by unending references to how large women's pregnant stomachs are, Mio is able to recognize that this is the clue to the entire mystery. Traditional knowledge and superstitions about pregnancy also play a role in the story. For instance, Mio solves another case because only she realizes that powdered coral, when consumed by a pregnant woman, is reputed to guarantee the birth of a son.

The inability of the detective to solve the crimes by "reading" the physical and social environments is another one of Matsuo's inversions of genre conventions. The detective, an observer and interpreter of the city, normally is easily able to move about the urban landscape and among its denizens, thus linking the disparate parts of the city into a whole. Through his contact with the streets and their people, the detective accumulates a wealth of knowledge about the city and the connections that form it. Thus, the detective's "power [is] based solely in knowledge, founded in observation and description rather than lived experience."[31] Here in Balloon Town, Matsuo's detective, Eda Marina, is incapable of solving three out of the four crimes because she lacks this fundamental characteristic of the detective. Despite Marina's determination to solve the crimes—even to the point of living in Balloon Town—she is unable to bridge the gap between herself and the pregnant body. Therefore, knowledge of the city streets here does not translate into the lived bodily knowledge that is crucial to solving these crimes, and Marina, a young woman with no understanding of the pregnant body, cannot begin to read the situation in Balloon Town. It takes Kurebayashi Mio to discern the indications of wrongdoing. In each case, it is the awareness of small things—for example, the shape of a pregnant woman's stomach or the traditional folk practice of determining the child's sex—that solves the case.

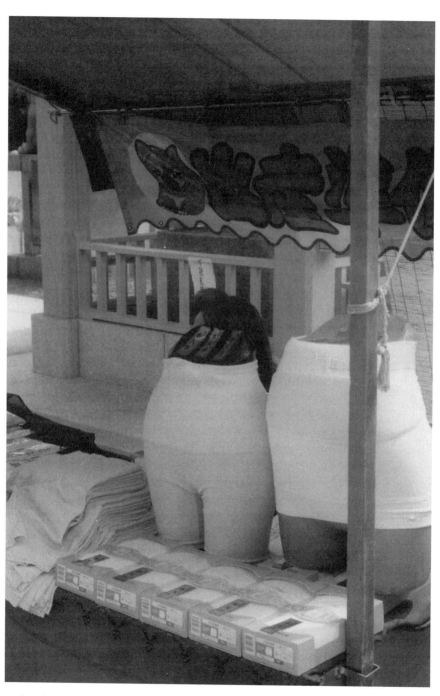

Modern *hara obi*, or "belly bands." These, as well as traditional *hara obi*, are sold at Suitengu Shrine on the Day of the Dog.

Bodies, Production, and the Past

As we have seen, the Special Seventh Ward was created explicitly to serve the needs of a specific population—women who have chosen to carry a child in their wombs. The spaces of the city have been reconfigured in order to respond to the needs of its citizens, concentrating resources for each different type of production in a single locale and thus making the use of space more efficient. To this end, Balloon Town has been laid out in such a way as to provide every comfort to the women, creating a physical environment that caters to their bodily needs. The women, in turn, use this new space in the city to produce better babies. The idea of linking the spaces of the city to the spaces of the body is not new. The new spaces in Balloon Town are a manifestation of this relationship, which is best described by Elizabeth Grosz in her seminal essay, "Bodies/Cities": "The city is made and made over into the simulacrum of the body, and the body in its turn is transformed, citified, urbanized as a distinctly metropolitan body."[32] Thus in Balloon Town, the pregnant woman is like the space that she inhabits since both function to improve the people they harbor. The city has been crafted into a space that fosters the fosterers, guaranteeing them security and comfort, just as the mothers do for the lives they contain.

The relationship of the body and the city operates on a larger scale as well since the city's structure and its layout also have an effect on the material production carried out by its inhabitants. The merger of town functions with women's reproductive functions can be seen as taking public spaces (where production and commerce take place) and private spaces (the domain for women and reproduction) and combining them. The realignment of Tokyo, which has set aside places for production as well as reproduction, serves to make Balloon Town a place of production, featuring women as the ultimate form of the productive body. The modern city has always been productive (it produces material goods from factories that are staffed by its people), but in this version of production the city produces producers: like a Russian Matrushka doll as imagined by Escher, the city is a series of spaces nesting one inside the other, until the final space is opened to reveal a child, generating further spaces in turn. Unlike the transformative production characteristic of human handiwork (using labor to turn things into other things), this generative production is literally and figuratively internalized. Thus, in Matsuo's *Murder in Balloon Town,* we are presented with a city that is truly crafted in the image of the body.

In their introduction to *The Sex of Architecture,* Diana Agrest, Patricia Conway, and Leslie Kanes Weisman note that in Western architecture, the inscription of the sexualized body is a recurring theme, a "reification of the male longing to appropriate an exclusive female privilege: maternity."[33] An analysis of gender in architecture, they argue, reveals a social system that functions to exclude or control women, giving rise to the equation male: outside::woman:inside. The metaphorical link between contained space and the womb has interested many writers on women and the city. As Christine Boyer notes, "There is . . . a long history to this sexualization of space, conceptualized by and through the body of a woman, and it stretches back at least to the time of Plato, when the metaphoric transference of feminine attributes to spatial concepts appears to have been clearly established."[34] Other urban geographers, such as Edward Soja in his *Postmodern Cities,* have dealt with space as an inert or passive presence or concept, an approach that only recently has undergone critical scrutiny in the work of Christine Boyer and Rosalyn Deutsche.[35]

Given this critical and metaphorical linkage between space and women, both destined to be conquered and filled, Balloon Town can be seen as a hyperversion of this notion—a space filled with the filled. What, then, is Matsuo parodying, and what is the point of her parody? I believe that her purpose is not to envision new options for women but to discuss how space is constructed and allotted in Japan today, making concrete what she believes is the ideological place of women in Japanese society through her depiction of this fictional space. From her parody, one can see that in the popular imagination, women belong in the private spaces of the domestic rather than the public spaces of economics and government and that a woman's function is to be a mother. In *Balloon Town,* women are segregated from the wider realm of politics and government by that very government. Of course, there is a place for women within the boundaries of Tokyo, but it is set apart physically from the rest of the city. Matsuo's book thus raises a number of pressing questions that arise from the political consequences and contexts of the future she envisions and the present in the book has been written and is read. At first glance, *Murder in Balloon Town* seems, in some ways, a utopian vision. The community in which the stories take place is a special place for pregnancy and is affordable for every woman. Constructed as an antidote to the mechanization of birth, it is almost an entirely single-sex environment that effectively is self-administering. For its inhabitants, Balloon Town represents a women-centered answer to the takeover of gestation and pregnancy by the mechanical process of the artificial uterus. Matsuo has, then, created a new world that provides "a viable space and time for women to inhabit as women," one that would neither restrain women nor obliterate them.[36] Balloon Town, to be sure, only serves women for the short time that they are pregnant. Nevertheless, this space becomes an area where women's actions are validated and they are pampered while they are pregnant—something that does not happen in everyday society. Indeed, the pregnant woman's bulging belly becomes an object of overweening care and attention.

In turn, Balloon Town's natural, women-centered overcoming of the mechanization of childbirth reflects themes found in other modern (post-1868) Japanese literature, in particular the contested place of technology in the creation of a better world. Japan's political and economic aspirations to create a better society through modernization and technological development in the years before World War II were echoed to a degree by Japanese writers. As the dark side of technology became more apparent, however, utopian literature began to take on a more pastoral and less futuristic tone. Balloon Town seems to rest squarely in the latter tradition.

Upon closer examination, however, Matsuo's Balloon Town presents us with a more complicated and *dystopian* face. Although women have gained a place of freedom while they gestate, they still are in the grips of a capitalist patriarchal society. Matsuo's stories, that is, show what might occur when women are marked as "bodily" producers. To be sure, Matsuo's stories are far less ominous than Margaret Atwood's classic dystopia about the state's attempts to regulate sexuality and fertility, *The Handmaid's Tale*.[37] The women in Balloon Town strictly watch each other, and anyone who does not conform to the unwritten rules is talked about and criticized, but there is no other punishment. The pregnant heroine, nevertheless, is constantly scolded for her smoking (although the cigarettes do not have any nicotine or carbon monoxide) and for her unmarried status (she is the only single mother), both by her peers and by the unmarried, nonpregnant detective. Regimented through uniform and by activity, the denizens of Balloon Town have little opportunity for personal freedom.

At first glance, *Murder in Balloon Town*'s dystopian quality might seem to be a direct product of the author's choice of the genre, detective fiction, which contradicts the goals of utopian literature—not least because of its unrelenting realism and its focus on the darker elements of human nature. Yet detective fiction by itself is not anti-utopian; indeed, much of what makes the genre work is quite compatible with utopian fiction and its conventions. As a conservative genre oriented toward the resolution of trouble and the restoration of the status quo, detective fiction might provide an ideal forum in which the accomplishments of a utopian society are preserved and defended. In turn, the figure of the detective, the outsider who questions and observes, is analogous to the figure of the "interested outsider" journeying to a different world, a common trope in utopian and dystopian literature. The problem, then, is not detective fiction per se, but rather the way in which Matsuo situates her utopian society vis-à-vis both its own society and its own history. For one thing, Balloon Town is not in fact a new order but a sequestered space within a preexisting order. In fact, despite the Tokyo metropolitan government's support for Balloon Town, the society in which Balloon Town is embedded is opposed in a number of respects to its goals and ideology. As a result, the resolution demanded by the narrative is intrinsically opposed to the utopian character of its setting because the detective's status quo is predicated on a system of values extrinsic to the site of her investigations.

Moreover, Matsuo inverts the temporal-ethical matrix of utopian fiction in a crucial way. In most utopian literature, social change is organized along the temporal axis—in other words, the movement from crisis or problem to solution (utopia) is coterminous with a movement from present to future. In Matsuo's literary world, however, the opposite is true: the imputedly problematic social practice (that is, the mechanization of childbearing) is situated in the future, while the solution to that problem is found in the narrative past. This inversion is not, by itself, a violation of the utopian narrative; the "good old days" have a long history of being the source of solutions to modern woes. What is decisive is the fact that the narrative past here is equivalent to the reader's present—the ideal solution for the residents of Balloon Town, in other words, is a hyperbolic version of things as they are for contemporary Japanese readers.

This inversion thus turns utopian fantasy on its head: rather than solving today's problems with tomorrow's solutions, the women of Balloon Town hope to solve tomorrow's problems with today's status quo. This technique, however, does more than simply provoke an ironic chuckle. Rather, it allows the reader—even forces her—to consider the ways in which the "brave new world" of Balloon Town is in fact a pastiche of practices, beliefs, and programs from Japan's own past, remnants and recasts of earlier models of control, segregation, and oversight.

A closer look at the structures and assumptions that have guided the construction of the fictional Balloon Town, furthermore, reveals the extent to which this future world recycles elements of Japan's own history and traditions. It is precisely the existence of these structures that makes Matsuo's parody so sharp since it is within these structures that the utopian/dystopian critique lies. By explicating the social and historical antecedents to Balloon Town, we can see more clearly how *Balloon Town* serves as a critique of Japanese society—a feature Matsuo's book shares with recent feminist detective novels in England and the United States.

Physically reconfiguring the urban environment to match a change in the social structure, for instance, recalls the spatial practices of Edo-era castle towns, in which one's physical proximity to the castle reinforced one's position in the Neo-Confucian hierarchy. This stratified, four-tiered class structure divided up cities in Japan. The first class, the samurai, occupied the inner ring around the lord's castle, while craftspeople and merchants lived in concentric circles radiating from the castle. Edo's natural topography enhanced this division; the warrior class inhabited the hills around the castle, while the farmers, artisans, and merchants lived along the river plains below.[38] Additionally, the Tokugawa-era divisions also paralleled the development of Balloon Town with the Yoshiwara, or pleasure quarters, that were placed outside of the city precincts. The Yoshiwara, where the courtesans held sway, was an area where private acts and bodily functions became public. Rather than a site for reproduction, however, the Yoshiwara was a place where pregnancy was feared and often meant the end of a woman's life. This class-based social geography endured well into the nineteenth century, and traces of it still remain in present-day Tokyo. Notably, despite the almost wholesale devastation of the city caused by the Great Kanto Earthquake in 1923 and the bombing campaigns of World War II, the scale of the Tokugawa-era reorganization of Edo has never been matched.

Likewise, the governmental involvement in female sexuality and fertility found in Balloon Town reflects a tradition of state supervision dating back to the Meiji period. As Sheldon Garon has pointed out, it is difficult to discuss the history of Japanese women without reference to the state.[39] Legally, politically, and socially, the Japanese government has long intervened in women's lives, with a special focus on the regulation of women's fertility. The production and nurturing of children was seen as the woman's primary function, and a woman's role as mother assumed a mythic aura that persists to this day.[40] During times of political and economic instability, the slogan *"ryōsai kenbo"* was employed to exhort women to bear more children, part of an explicit political appropriation. Perhaps the most extreme example of this occurred during the fifteen-year span of Japan's Pacific War, when the government adopted policies that promoted motherhood in order to increase its demands for manpower.[41] Coupled with a suppression of the birth control movement and the continuing illegality of abortion, there were few options for women but to bear children.[42] Furthermore, despite the social and political changes that followed the war, *"ryōsai kenbo"* remained an influential concept until the late 1980s.[43] As Kathleen Uno has shown, motherhood rather than wifehood became the dominant image for Japanese women since the development of the Japanese nuclear family, which took the husband away from the family, and the popularization of time-saving consumer goods made a woman's primary concern the welfare of her children.

Bodies, Production, and the State

In the end, Matsuo does not tell us whether her Tokyo of the near future is a utopia or a dystopia. The reason, I would suggest, is that Matsuo takes elements of both in order to pursue her real goal: a critique of the ways in which women today are conceived of and function within Japanese society. Balloon Town is predicated on an old yet urgent question: to what lengths would the government go to convince women to bear children in an era where the Japanese birthrate has fallen to the lowest level of most industrial nations?

Written in 1994, when the Japanese government was trying to boost the sagging birthrate (which at that point had fallen to 1.53 children per couple), *Murder in Balloon Town* parodies the lengths to which the government would go to ensure that women would have children. Realizing the failure of social pressure, government officials resorted to direct exhortations to women. On 2 March 1990 Prime Minister Kaifu Toshiki told the Diet that "we must strive to increase the desire of our young to have children."[44] A few months later, Minster of Finance Ryutaro Hashimoto placed the blame for the plunging birthrate on too many women pursuing postsecondary education, and even suggested that the government should take strong measures to discourage women from continuing to pursue college and specialty school degrees.[45] Although Hashimoto's comments were mocked both at home and abroad, causing him to amend his original message a number of times, they provided clear evidence of the instrumental attitude toward women that many Japanese leaders continued to foster. While "good wife, wise mother" had become an anachronism for many young women, it lived on as part of state ideology, underpinning the perception of women as producers of children rather than parts of the workforce.

It is notable that natural childbirth in Matsuo's Tokyo receives eager support from the metropolitan government. In the first kind of birth technology that had been implemented women were unencumbered by gestating a child, so they could continue with their careers. With natural childbirth, however, women had to leave their jobs and spend time at home. Yet the government in this book is happy to accommodate these requirements, perhaps suggesting that if society wants women to "produce," then all it has to do is provide them with the resources to do so properly. Since the Japanese economy was in a downturn in the early 1990s, having women leave the workplace to bear and raise children takes on clear political and economic overtones.

With Japan's rapid postwar economic growth and the increasing educational and professional opportunities for women, Japan's birthrate has continued to decrease, taking with it the efficacy of governmental suasion efforts. Despite public speeches by politicians who are trying to exhort women to leave the workplace and have more children and despite the marriage of the Harvard-educated, career-oriented Owada Masako to the Crown Prince, women have not been leaving the workplace to start families in droves.[46] Certainly one reason that women have been having fewer children is the increased educational and work opportunities they now enjoy. While traditional avenues for careers in the big Japanese companies have been drying up due to the worsening economic situation, there are still opportunities for women in smaller companies, foreign companies, and the burgeoning freelance translation and interpretation fields.[47] Another reason is that after the burst of the bubble economy, lifetime male employment can no longer be taken for granted, making the two-income family more common than ever before.

In her book *Japan: The Childless Society,* sociologist Muriel Jolivet discusses some of the factors that contribute to Japan's plummeting birthrate. Her work, based on interviews with young women in Tokyo and its environs, examines the expectations and conditions of Japan's young mothers and the problems women have in coping with them. In a society where husbands are still kept away from the families both by culture and by the demands of the workplace, women bear the brunt of raising children, which consists of getting children into school, college, and a career, as well as raising them to be well balanced and happy.[48] According to Jolivet, women who have jobs they enjoy often do not want to leave them for the relative isolation of raising a child. Often the long hours of child care, uninterrupted by adult companionship and support, can become quite alienating.[49]

Far more interesting in relation to Matsuo's novel is Jolivet's analysis of the literature on childbirth and child raising that is available to Japanese women. In her chapter on advice by leading pediatricians, Jolivet notes that "the various theories fostered by pediatricians are presented in the form of [an] oppressive Decalogue," with a view to illustrating more effectively their part in the Japanese reluctance to have children.[50] Some of the "Ten Commandments" to Japanese women preparing to give birth elucidate the system of beliefs underlying the practices of Balloon Town. The first is "Thou shalt bond with thy fetus *[taikyo].*" The pregnant woman is enjoined by her doctor to lead a stress-free life, eat well, and develop a good rapport with the fetus. The second is "Thou shalt lovingly develop thy fetus' IQ." Thus, from conception, the mother is responsible for educating her child, and to this end, there are books and CDs recommended for the fetus.[51] The third is "Thou shalt give birth in pain." As Jolivet explains, "In Japan, the most difficult path is always the most favorable and labor is no exception to this rule. Mothers are therefore not spared from being told of all risks that they would be exposing their unborn child to if they requested an epidural (which very few hospitals in fact administer), it being understood that pain had a value per se, inasmuch as it is supposed to create the bonding between mother and child."[52]

The fourth commandment is "Thou shalt breast-feed thy child day and night for a whole year." While Japanese women used to breast-feed as a matter of course, in the 1960s this ceased to be the case; indeed, when Empress

Michiko decided to do so for her son, it was considered outlandish. Now breast feeding is on the rise again, and there are schools that teach women how to breast-feed and perform weekly breast massages.[53] The remaining commandments, such as the insistence on using only cloth diapers, result in more work for the mother, and all are aimed at creating a bond of maternal devotion to the child and fostering selflessness.

This overbearing process, designed to link mothers and children, is borne out in both social and economic policy. The Japanese system of childbirth and child care is premised on the assumption that the mother is the wife of a white-collar employee and devotes her time to raising her children. Employees receive household allowances as part of their monthly wages, and all other support is funneled through the head of the family.[54] In addition, the government makes the mother-child tie stronger through the *boshi techō* (mother-child handbook) issued to each expectant mother.[55] The linguistic pairing of mother and child extends beyond the mother-child handbook since the term *"bosei kango"* (maternity nursing) is used by the medical establishment to refer to the entire childbearing and child-rearing process.[56]

The time-consuming dictates of Japanese motherhood, as well as their socioeconomic underpinnings, are recast and replayed in Balloon Town. The devotion to the development of one's child even while in utero, the careful maintenance of one's surroundings, and the detailed attention to the techniques and materials of pregnancy have turned gestating a child in Balloon Town into an artistic enterprise. This image of craftsmanship is not new; as Kawamura Kunimitsu has observed, pregnancy and giving birth were treated as artisanal activities in the mid-eighteenth century, while the image of the "good vessel" was current in Tokugawa discourse.[57] Faced with the possible extinction of the handmade articles of everyday life in the 1920s, Yanagi Sōetsu, the founder of the *mingei* movement, transformed them from utilitarian objects to art. Likewise, the creation of Balloon Town is justified in large part as the recuperation of practices identified as "traditional" (and hence threatened by the tides of technology and modernization), a recuperation that depends upon depicting those practices as valuable elements of the national culture.

The nativist and naturalizing tendencies of Yanagi's *mingei* movement, as Julie Christ has suggested, were intimately linked to the wider discourse of prewar Japanese imperialism—an ideological context that resonates strongly in Matsuo's novel as well.[58] Indeed, recrafting the notion that pregnancy and childbirth must be nurtured and developed like an *objet d'art* is accompanied by an attempt to naturalize the return to gestation within the body and away from artificial gestation. "'I want to raise my child in my womb,' these women said. There was no particular logical reason for this. Still, 'of course' women wanted it this way" (4). Thus, traces of the history of the movement and dissent against it were repressed from public view, and the creation of Balloon Town was presented to women as satisfying what they had always wanted.[59] The Tokyo government's fictional facilitation of the return to the time-consuming methods of gestation and childbirth, therefore, becomes symptomatic of the real-life movements and exhortations to regulate women's fertility for the benefit of the state, but these efforts are placed within a more sinister tradition of ideological manipulation and control.

The divisions in Balloon Town only serve to reinforce this message, representing as they do an exaggerated and explicitly spatial version of the historical segregation of women and children in Japanese society. Indeed, Balloon Town can be seen as an updated version of an ancient Japanese practice, the social separation of pregnant women in *ubuya*, or parturition huts.[60] A woman retreated to the *ubuya* during the impure time of menstruation or childbirth, in order that she not defile the rest of society.[61] Not only was the pregnant woman required to live separately from the main dwelling, but she was also required to eat food prepared separately.[62] Thus, women were literally cast out of society, cordoned off, and sealed in a place of pollution and danger.[63] Notably, parturition huts endured into the modern period, persisting until the latter half of the twentieth century in rural areas like the Tsugaru Peninsula in northern Aomori Prefecture.[64] Matsuo's fantastic urban space, therefore, is at the same time a recycled and expanded version of an ancient, yet not so distant, Japanese tradition that adds overtones of ritual purity (and danger) to the complex ideology underlying Balloon Town.

The ideological matrix is shaped, finally, by another important social phenomenon: consumerism. As a result of the heavy expenses involved in bearing, raising, and educating a child, children in contemporary Japan become a consumption choice. In this light, it is telling that Balloon Town, the center of reproduction, is located in Aoyama, the contemporary center of luxury consumer culture. With its boutiques and cafés, Aoyama today is a place for elegant, high-class consumption, in contrast to the trendy centers of youth culture nearby, such as Shibuya and Harajuku. By transforming this mecca of conspicuous consumption into a community devoted exclusively to childbearing, Matsuo ironically shows us how bearing a child might be seen as a form of "conspicuous reproduction." Within the functional arrangement of this fictional future Tokyo, the production of children has become analogous to the contemporary demand for expensive consumer goods. Being pregnant, a visible activity, is a way to demonstrate one's commitment to natural pregnancy and to be marked as an artisan, a producer of Japan's new generation.

Matsuo's parody of the genre reinforces the efficacy of detective fiction as a form of cultural critique; she highlights the various metaphysical underpinnings of the genre in order to show how they are implicated in maintaining the status quo. *Murder in Balloon Town* as detective fiction also demonstrates how Japanese culture—or culture in general—informs the underlying system of knowledge that the detective must have to solve the mystery. In this case, Marina's lack of specific cultural knowledge, resulting in her inability to know Balloon Town, demonstrates how particular knowledge is necessary. Matsuo's parody, moreover, is ironic in two senses. First, it is not the detective who possesses the knowledge that leads to the unraveling of the mystery but the sidekick. Second, the solution of the biggest secret of Balloon Town, the sex of Mio's baby, is at the mercy of wholly natural forces since it can only be found at the end of the pregnancy. In fact, Matsuo shows that popular wisdom ultimately cannot be trusted as the *kamebara* Mio gives birth to a son. That Mio, the pregnant Watson character, is the only person capable of logically solving the problem is also ironic since women are rarely associated with logical thinking (and pregnant women even less so).

The force of the parody shifts the reader's attention away from the traditional violations found in detective fiction (murder, maiming, and blackmail) to the violence of a natural act that humanity takes for granted. Within Matsuo's fictional setting, the obvious irony of a bearer of new life taking the life of another is overlaid with the detective's even greater astonishment (and repulsion) at the very fact of a pregnant woman. From the chain-smoking Mio to the graphic descriptions of bodily functions, the living human body thus becomes figured as more horrifying than murder itself. Ultimately, Marina is able to adapt to the challenges of Balloon Town through her relationship with Mio, only to discover that the heroine she so admired has feet of clay since the child Mio was carrying was not conceived as a political statement but because of a birth control failure. Inertia and fear brought Mio to Balloon Town, and Marina, who has not entirely become accustomed to the strangeness of pregnancy and perhaps is looking for some kind of resistance to (or at least ironic distance from) the perky oppressiveness of Balloon Town, is disappointed. Marina's discontent, prompted by what she feels is Mio's complicity with the tenets of Balloon Town, thus calls into question an underlying truth of detective fiction: the detective ultimately supports the status quo.[65]

Within this context, the boundaries of Matsuo's parody become clearer. Here, the force of her parody lies not in the inversion of any of the rituals and information surrounding the traditions and practices of pregnancy in Japan but in emphasizing these practices and beliefs and presenting the reactions of an explicitly nonpregnant woman in order to produce parodic effect.[66] By creating a space where the only topic of conversation is aspects of pregnancy, Matsuo cleverly exploits the socio-critical potential not only of detective fiction, but of science fiction as well. In particular, her novel draws upon historical and current realities to create an extreme yet believable vision of the lengths the government will go in order to maintain a satisfactory material and sexual economy. Despite the fact that the new technologies of birth ensure that the birthrate would remain stable, the government's involvement in the return to the old ways indicates a desire for women to be predominantly (re)productive members of society.

At the same time, Matsuo's parody of detective fiction points out the genre's flaws, in particular the problems of women's precarious situation within the city discussed by so many Western critics. While Crawford has argued that women's detective fiction allows any woman a vantage point to analyze and interpret the city, Kathleen Gregory Klein concludes that all detective fiction featuring women detectives amounts to parody since it is an adoption of the genre that changes only one element. In Klein's view, this parodic situation can be remedied only by adding more realism to the genre.[67] Yet Sally Munt, in her reexamination of women's detective fiction, argues that detective fiction *as a genre* is by nature satirical, "evoking the Medusan laugh of feminism, which exposes through ridicule. The defining act of the detective is to reveal the real and sordid nature of the world, but this is achieved obliquely, through the sideways glance of satire."[68] In this sense, Matsuo's *Murder in Balloon Town* might in the end be seen as a double parody—a parody of a form that is, by definition, a parody.

Afterword

Bobbie Ann Mason has suggested that detective fiction is like a sonnet, "endless variations on an inflexible form."[1] We have traced these variations in the work of Miyabe Miyuki, Nonami Asa, Shibata Yoshiki, Kirino Natsuo, and Matsuo Yumi. While these writers have in some ways critiqued the structures and assumptions of women's detective fiction, they also have exploited its resources to discuss issues important to them. In particular, these authors are aware of the socio-critical potential inherent in the genre, an aspect that is not lost on literary critics, who have created the new rubric, *shinhonkaku-ha,* to describe the combination of social criticism and more traditional puzzle mystery that characterizes this new brand of detective fiction. Despite the fact that certain Anglo-American critics believe that women's detective fiction is doomed to be a parody, I would argue, therefore, that such an approach fails to consider what women's detective fiction *can* do. Each of the authors studied here has addressed issues of particular concern to contemporary Japanese women: consumerism and the crisis of identity, discrimination and workplace harassment, sexual harassment and sexual violence, and the role of motherhood and childbearing. Their stories, by drawing upon the genre's unique combination of realism, historical specificity, social commentary, compelling characterizations, and stylistic flexibility, provide insights into these problems that journalistic reporting or sociological research cannot.

These authors share with their Anglo-American counterparts the creation of flawed but persevering female characters, women looking for answers and struggling, often with little assistance, to make their way in a hostile environment. Each of the five present us with women who work in nontraditional jobs, are competent at what they do, and support themselves. Even in her conservative depiction of society, Miyabe Miyuki, although she does not feature a female detective, does not limit her other female characters; rather, she is critical of a society that tends to treat women and the jobs that they do as fungible. Indeed, within *Kasha* there are a number of strong professional women whom the main character, Honma, professes to admire: his doctor, his best friend's wife, and a businesswoman.

These five authors differ from their Western counterparts, however, in their treatment of women's private lives. Their emphasis upon women's economic vulnerability, the threat of male violence, and isolation contrasts with the network of interpersonal relations that characterizes Anglo-American women's detective fiction. To this prevailing sense of loneliness, moreover, is added the difficulty in establishing female sexual freedom in a society that still views women as either sexual objects or mothers. Thus, while Kirino and Shibata initially seem to revel in developing sexually autonomous protagonists, it soon becomes clear that such an endeavor is fraught with difficulty.

The difficulty can be seen most clearly in Kirino's recent work, *Rōzu gaaden* (Rose garden), a collection of short stories meant to fill in the gaps in Miro's life story, and her novel *Out,* the story of four women who work the night shift in an *obento* (lunch box) factory. In *Rose Garden*'s title story, Kirino portrays Miro as a victim of molestation by her stepfather in order to explain why she later becomes attracted to dangerous and potentially violent men.[2] By locating the roots of sexual independence in childhood sexual exploitation, Kirino suggests that Miro's behavior toward men results from her being damaged, rather than from a principled desire to seek sexual autonomy and equality in her relationships with men. Instead, childhood trauma leads to risky attachments that can never achieve real intimacy or satisfaction. The story further emphasizes the notion that heterosexual relations are antagonistic, by making Miro's relationship with her gay neighbor the only one not fraught with tension and violence. Kirino's conflicted perspective on gender, sexuality, and violence is made even more explicit in *Out,* with its gritty yet surreal portrayal of factory women whose side business involves dismembering and disposing of corpses. Here, the stereotypically male realm of violent crime is made into a site for women's solidarity and resistance, a transformation rendered problematic by the novel's graphic finale, in which one protagonist affirms her violent rape as a sexually liberating moment. (Notably, the film version of Kirino's novel, released in Japan in October 2002, was made more palatable to a mainstream audience by replacing the violent sexual episode with an ending in which the four friends simply flee to Hokkaido to watch the aurora borealis.)[3]

In contrast to Kirino's continued attention to women and sexuality in her work, Shibata Yoshiki has not revisited her police detective, Riko, since the final volume of the series, *Diana's Daydream.* Leaving Riko married but continuing with her career, the author seems to say that marriage is a safe haven from sexual violence for women. Yet Shibata destabilizes this message by raising doubts that Riko's new husband will remain faithful. In the last section of the final book, Riko sees him in a cab with another woman, but the episode is never addressed, leaving both Riko and the reader in doubt over his intentions. In the end, then, we are left with the impression that it is only work and career that can compensate the female police detective (and, by extension, the single working woman) for her lack of a private life, a point made forcefully as well in the works of Nonami Asa.

One feature that joins all of the authors in this study is the social and political overtones of their work, albeit expressed in sometimes radically different ways. Thus, while both Miyabe and Matsuo use detective fiction's critical potential to talk about Japan's return to its "traditional" past, Matsuo takes a much more critical view of the use of "tradition" as a means to control women and fertility. Although *Baruun Taun no tejinashi* (The sorcerer of Balloon Town) and *Baruun Taun no temari uta* (Handball songs of Balloon Town), the sequels to *Murder in Balloon Town*, lack the dystopic and heavily parodic quality of her debut work, Matsuo continues to focus less upon mystery per se and more upon the real-life problems faced by her characters. *The Sorcerer of Balloon Town*, for instance, focuses upon Eda Marina's friend Mio and the challenge she faces trying to balance work, family, and her ongoing relationship with her child's father. Matsuo thus continues to exploit the social and political potential of detective fiction in order to address the questions and concerns of women in Japan today. Notably, Matsuo's blend of politics and clever storytelling has caught the eye of Western literary critics, and her appearance in a special issue of the *Review of Contemporary Fiction* on new Japanese writing (alongside more renowned writers like Murakami Haruki, Shimada Masahiko, and Kasai Kiyoshi), including a full-length interview, has made her work more accessible to an English-language audience.[4]

In turn, Miyabe Miyuki has continued to blend social commentary and popular fiction in an immensely successful fashion. Following the publication of *The Reason* in 1997 and its subsequent Naoki Prize, Miyabe went on to release a stream of best-selling novels, helping her to establish a veritable publishing juggernaut (including an artistic and business partnership with two other authors, the so-called "Osawa Office") and allowing her to branch out into other media, including the creation of a storyline for the Play Station 2 video game "ICO." In 2001, Miyabe's sprawling two-volume detective novel *Mohohan* (The copycat) was released and went on to sell over 1.2 million copies in hardcover.[5] Unlike her earlier works, *The Copycat* features the most nuanced female character that Miyabe has ever created, journalist Maebatake Shigeko. Like *All She Was Worth* and *The Reason*, however, *The Copycat* focuses squarely upon the problems besetting contemporary society, this time taking aim at the destructive effects of the media and media feeding frenzies upon crime victims in particular and the Japanese people more generally. The novel's popularity was boosted even further by the release in June 2002 of a cinematic adaptation, a box office success (albeit critical flop) featuring high-profile stars like Yamazaki Goro (featured frequently in the films of Itami Juzo) and Nakai Masahiro (perhaps best known as a founding member of the performing group SMAP).

Despite the strengths and potential of women's detective fiction and the recent success of its practitioners, there have been some signs that its place within the Japanese literary world is contested. This was demonstrated most dramatically in 1997, when Takamura Kaoru announced that her latest novel, *Reidi jokaa* (Lady joker), would be her last work of detective fiction. Despite the success she had achieved, she did not feel, as Matsumoto Seichō had, that she could reconcile her politically motivated commentary with her detective fiction. More pointedly, she explained that detective fiction did not allow her the scope to explore the deep problems of guilt and punishment that now interested her; instead, she announced that she would focus her energies on a study of the origins of guilt as reflected in the works of Dostoyevsky. Thus, rather than gaining insights from her own writing career and the real world, she needed to turn back to what she felt was a purer, more literary source of authority, reinforcing the standard critical conviction that detective fiction, as *taishūbungaku*, is not able to describe social problems or realities in a suitably serious or meaningful way.

Detective fiction's "popular" status also has posed another set of challenges, stemming from the emphatically market-driven nature of mainstream publishing in Japan (a situation, it should be noted, that has come to the fore in Europe and the United States as well). As with other areas of the recessionary Japanese economy, the book trade has become increasingly sensitive to small changes in consumer tastes and interests, leading marketing departments to push authors toward new genres and themes.[6] The most notable example of this shift has been the attempt to maintain and expand readership by merging detective fiction with another popular genre, the historical novel *(jidai shōsetsu)*. This new category of so-called "folklore literature," in which a plot, either romantic or mysterious, is set in earlier Japanese history (usually in the Meiji or Taisho periods), has enjoyed tremendous success, indicated not only by the large sales of novels by writers like Ono Fuyumi and Nashiki Kaho, but also by the recent awarding of the Naoki Prize to works in this vein by Yamamoto Fumio and Yuikawa Kei.

The popularity of this new folklore subgenre in a time of unrelenting economic distress is as significant as the popularity of women's detective fiction in the beginning of the previous decade. Rather than critiquing society as it is, these new novels implicitly contrast the problems and traumas of contemporary existence with a world in which life was "simpler," using historical time to provide the reader with a kind of comfort zone. This reflects larger cultural movements in Japan, most notably the rise of a "nostalgia industry," which, unlike earlier efforts to reclaim old Japan through trips to the countryside or historic sites, provides easy access to the past in the form of consumer items and even consumer sites, like a shopping mall in Daiba, Tokyo, that doubles as a historical theme park.[7]

Yet while the authors studied here have not been immune to the appeal of new genres or to the market shifts that support them—Miyabe with her "magical history tour of Japan," *The Heisei Traveler's Diary*; Kirino with 2001's *Gyokuran* (Orchid), a historical time traveling romance set in prewar Japan and today; Shibata with her recent entry into the world of psycho-horror fiction; or Matsuo with her continuing efforts to straddle the line between mystery writing and science fiction—it also seems clear that detective fiction, and in particular women's detective fiction, will continue to be a creative and attractive literary force for years to come. Although Takamura found mystery writing an insufficient vehicle for her intellectual aspirations, many other authors have continued to find ways to expand the genre, use it in new and compelling ways, and appeal to a broad audience. Nonami Asa has spent the time since her success with *Frozen Fangs* working exclusively on mysteries, many of them paperbacks featuring female protagonists in which family problems, rather than the mysteries per se, take center stage, and her motorcycle-riding detective, Otomichi Takako, has continued to capture the imagination of the reading public, not only in a collection of short stories and two full-length novels, but also in a number of made-for-television movies as well. Likewise, Miyabe has remained committed to detective fiction (a com-mitment rewarded by *The Copycat*'s enormous sales), while Kirino's recent publication of a third Miro novel, 2003's *Dark*, makes it clear that she has not forgotten what made her a best-selling writer in the first place. All in all, then, these women's use of detective fiction's critical potential, their willing-ness to adapt the genre to new voices and new approaches, and the example that they provide for future generations of writers suggest that Takamura's misgivings are not only premature, but ultimately unfounded.

Notes

Chapter 1: Introduction

1. Sakata Makoto, *Sengo o yomu: Gojussatsu no fikushon* (Reading the postwar: Fifty works of fiction) (Tokyo: Iwanami shisho, 1995), 174–177.

2. Yamamae Yuzuru, *Aka no misuterii: Josei misuterii sakka kessaku* (Red mystery: A collection of women's mysteries), and *Shiro no misuterii: Josei misuterii sakka kessaku* (White mystery: A collection of women's mysteries) (Tokyo: Eibunsha, 1997).

3. See, for example, Tom Gunning, "Tracing the Individual Body: Photography, Detectives and Early Cinema," in *Cinema and the Invention of Modern Life*, ed. Leo Charney and Vanessa L. Schwartz (Berkeley: University of California Press, 1995), 20, and more generally Ernst Mandel, *Delightful Murder: A Social History of the Crime Story* (Minneapolis: University of Minnesota Press, 1984).

4. On this phenomenon, see Mark Silver, "Purloined Letters: Cultural Borrowing and Japanese Crime Literature," Ph.D. dissertation, Yale University, 1999.

5. Itō Hideo, *Taisho no tantei shōsetsu* (Taisho-era detective fiction) (Tokyo: San'ichi shobo, 1991), 12, mentions Ruikō. Shinpo Hirohisa, however, suggests that Okamoto Kidō's (1872–1939) *torimonochō* (case book or police blotter) stories, featuring an Edo-era policeman *(meawashi)*, were the first real detective stories, although they have been categorized as historical novels *(jidaishōsetsu)* on account of their sentimental themes. Shinpo Hirohisa, "Parallel Lives of Japan's Master Detectives," *Japan Quarterly* 47, no. 4 (October–December 2000): 52–53.

6. Kazuo Yoshida, "Japanese Mystery Literature," in Powers and Kato, eds., *Handbook of Japanese Popular Culture*, 277.

7. Mark Silver, "Crime and Mystery Writing in Japan," in *The Oxford Companion to Crime and Mystery Writing*, ed. Rosemary Herbert (Oxford: Oxford University Press, 1999), 242.

8. For more on Anna Katharine Green's career and oeuvre, see Catherine Ross Nickerson, *The Web of Iniquity: Early Detective Fiction by American Women* (Durham, N.C.: Duke University Press, 1998), 60–116.

9. Hirabayashi Hatsunosuke, "Nihon no kindaiteki tantei shōsetsu—toku ni Edogawa Ranpo ni oite" (Japan's modern detective fiction—in particular, Edogawa Rampo), *Bungei hiron zenshū*, 3: 221 (Tokyo: Bunseido shoten, 1976). Unless otherwise noted, all translations are mine.

10. Karatani Kōjin, *Origins of Modern Japanese Literature*, trans. Brett de Bary, et al. (Durham, N.C.: Duke University Press, 1993), esp. chs. 1–3.

11. Yoshida, "Japanese Mystery Literature," 276.

12. *Ugetsu monogatari* was translated into English by Kenji Hamada as *Tales of Moonlight and Rain* (New York: Columbia University Press, 1972).

13. Tanizaki Junichiro, "The Secret," translated by Anthony Hood Chambers in *New Leaves: Studies and Translations of Japanese Literature in Honor of Edward Seidensticker,* ed. Aileen Gatten and Anthony Hood Chambers (Ann Arbor: University of Michigan Center for Japanese Studies, 1993), 157–173, and "The Incident at the Willow Bath House," translated by Phyllis I. Lyons in *Studies in Modern Japanese Literature: Essays and Translation in Honor of Edwin McClellan,* ed. Dennis Washburn and Alan Tansman (Ann Arbor: University of Michigan Center for Japanese Studies, 1997), 321–339. Itō gives a complete list of the twenty stories by Tanizaki that may be considered his detective oeuvre; most of these were published in leading newspapers and magazines of the time. Itō, *Taisho no tantei shōsetsu,* 192–193.

14. "Edogawa Ranpo" is a transliteration of Edgar Allan Poe, Hirai's main artistic inspiration. I have chosen to use the form "Rampo" rather than the normal romanization "Ranpo" since the former is the English spelling used by both Frederick Dannay (a.k.a. Ellery Queen, in the special issue of *Ellery Queen's Mystery Magazine* devoted to Rampo) and Rampo's English translator, James B. Harris.

15. Silver, "Crime and Mystery Writing in Japan," 242.

16. Matsuyama Iwao, *Ranpo to Tokyo: Toshi no kao* (Rampo and Tokyo: The face of the city) (Tokyo: Chikuma Gakugei Bunko, 1994), 15.

17. Yoshida, "Japanese Mystery Literature," 278.

18. For more about *Shinseinen's* impact on the study of modern Tokyo, see Shinseinen kenkyukai, *Shinseinen yomihon* (A *Shinseinen* reader) (Tokyo: Sakuhinsha, 1988).

19. For an analysis of Raichō's translation, see Inoue Ken, "Honyaku sareta gunshū: 'Gunshū no hito' no keifu to kindai nihon" (Translated crowd: The geneology of "The Man in the Crowd" and modern Japan), *Hiten bungaku kenkyū* 69 (December 1996): 37–66.

20. Hirabayashi Taiko, "Supai jiken" (The spy incident) and "Irezumi jiken no shinsō" (The truth about the tattoo affair), in *Hirabayashi Taiko zenshū,* 1: 14–19 and 32–39 (Tokyo: Asahi shuppansha, 1979).

21. Yukiko Tanaka, "Hirabayashi Taiko," in *To Live and Write: Selections by Japanese Women Writers, 1913–1938,* ed. Yukiko Tanaka (Seattle: Seal Press, 1987), 65–73.

22. See Yamashita Takeshi, "Joryū tantei sakka daiichigo: Ogura Teruko" (The first woman mystery writer: Ogura Teruko), in *"Shinseinen" o meguru sakkatachi* (Authors of *Shinseinen*) (Tokyo: Chikuma shobo, 1996), 153–196.

23. See, for example, Okamoto Kidō, "Umoregi"(Buried tree), *Shufu no tomo* (August 1924): 5.

24. See Hayashi Eriko, *Onna tantei monogatari: Serisawa Masako no jikenbo* (A tale of a woman detective: The record of Serisawa Masako) (Tokyo: Rokufun shuppan, 1990).

25. Sugiyama Tamae, "Aru katei ni okotta futatsu no tantei hiwa" (Two secret investigations in a certain household), *Shufu no tomo* (April 1924): 236–242. My thanks to Sarah Frederick for this reference.

26. Itō Hideo, *Showa no tantei shōsetsu* (Showa-era detective fiction) (Tokyo: Sanichi shobo, 1993), 325.

27. On the circumstances of the translation, see James B. Harris' preface to Edogawa Ranpo, *Edogawa Rampo: Tales of Mystery and Imagination*, trans. James B. Harris (Rutland, Vt.: Charles E. Tuttle, 1956).

28. Mamie Kamada, "The Awkward Writer: Opinions about and Influence of Matsumoto Seichō," *Japan Interpreter* 8, no. 2 (spring 1978): 149.

29. Matsumoto Seichō, "The Face" (Kao), in *The Voice and Other Stories*, trans. Adam Kabat (New York: Kodansha, 1989), 27–62.

30. Kamada, "The Awkward Writer," 152.

31. Mark Schreiber, *Shocking Crimes of Postwar Japan* (Tokyo: Yenbooks, 1996), 78, 92–99; Kamada, "The Awkward Writer," 161.

32. John G. Cawelti, *Adventure, Mystery, and Romance: Formula Stories as Art and Popular Culture* (Chicago: University of Chicago Press, 1976), 34–35.

33. Priscilla L. Walton, "Identity Politics: April Smith's *North of Montana* and Rochelle Majer Krich's *Angel of Death*," in *Detective Fiction and Diversity*, ed. Kathleen Gregory Klein (Bowling Green, Ohio: Bowling Green State University Popular Press, 1999), 130.

34. Cawelti, *Adventure, Mystery, and Romance*, 35.

35. Margaret Crawford, "Investigating the City—Detective Fiction as Urban Interpretation: A Reply to M. Christine Boyer," in Algrest et al., eds., *The Sex of Architecture*, 119.

36. Edogawa Rampo, "Yaneura no sanpōsha," in *Edogawa Ranpo meisakushū* (Best-known works of Edogawa Rampo), 3: 143–185 (Tokyo: Shunyōdo, 1959).

37. Matsuyama has convincingly argued that "Imomushi" is a sympathetic portrait of the plight of workers in the 1920s, as well as a critique of the government's failure to provide adequate unemployment or health services for them. Matsuyama, *Ranpo to Tokyo*, 223–224.

38. According to critic Kasai Kiyoshi, there have been three distinct periods of *honkaku-ha* writing. The first begins with Edogawa Rampo and is more aptly referred to by the rubric *"henkaku"* (transformation) owing to its combination of fantasy and suspense. The literature of this period is deeply influenced by Poe and other Anglo-American writers. The second period begins with the end of the Pacific War and represents a reaction to prewar Anglo-American detective fiction; the third comprises the literature of the 1970s and later. Kasai Kiyoshi, "Tantei shōsetsu no chisōgaku" (Excavating mysteries), in Kasai Kiyoshi, ed., *Honkaku misuteri no genzai*, 13–14.

39. Edogawa Rampo, *Tantei shōsetsu yonjūnen* (Forty years of detective fiction) (Tokyo: Chūsekisha, 1989), 140.

40. A point made most forcefully by Matsumoto Kenichi, "Modanisumu kara fuashizumu e: *Shinseinen* to Ranpo/Kyūsaku" (From modernism to fascism: *Shinseinen* and Rampo/Kyūsaku), *Kokubungaku* 36, no. 3 (March 1991): 24; see also Yoshikuni Igarashi, "Edogawa Rampo and the Excess of Vision," paper presented at the annual meeting of the Organization for Asian Research, Chicago, 29 March 2001.

41. Deductive detective fiction, which features an all-knowing detective, was made famous by Arthur Conan Doyle and reached its height in the interwar years. In contrast,

inductive-style detective fiction, where the detective has access to the same information as the reader, was popularized by the writers of the hard-boiled tradition. Inductive detective fiction is most common in contemporary Japan and Anglo-America.

42. Franco Moretti, "Clues," in *Signs Taken for Wonders: Essays in the Sociology of Literary Forms*, trans. Susan Fischer, David Foryacs, and David Miller (London: Verso, 1988), 137.

43. One exception to this rule is Dashiell Hammett's *Red Harvest* (1929), in which the detective, the "Continental Op," becomes embroiled in the internecine struggles of a corrupt town. This exception proves the rule since the Op's close involvement results in the utter devastation of the town and its inhabitants.

44. Sally R. Munt, *Murder by the Book? Feminism and the Crime Novel* (New York: Routledge, 1994), 124.

45. Matsumoto Seichō, *Points and Lines (Ten to sen)*, translated by Makiko Yamamoto and Paul C. Blum (Tokyo: Kodansha, 1986).

46. Kasai, "Tantei shōsetsu no chisōgaku," 14. On the costs of Japanese economic growth, see Koji Taira, "The Dialectics of Economic Growth, National Power and Distributive Struggles," in Gordon, ed., *Postwar Japan as History*, 167–189, as well as Gavan McCormack's examination of Japan's current economic dilemmas and their historical antecedents in *The Emptiness of Japanese Affluence* (Armonk, N.Y.: M. E. Sharpe, 1996).

47. For what follows, see Kamada, "The Awkward Writer," 150–152.

48. Kato Hidetoshi, one of the editors of *Handbook of Japanese Popular Culture*, opposes the use of "popular" as a translation of the term *"taishū"* since "popular" in English has the connotation of "nonserious." Instead, he points to the Buddhist, egalitarian inflection of the term, according to which "there is no distinction between 'elite' and 'mass,' 'literate' and 'non-literate' and so on." See "Some Thoughts on Japanese Popular Culture," in Powers and Kato, eds., *Handbook of Japanese Popular Culture*, xviii. On the other hand, Marilyn Ivy translates *"taishū"* as "mass" in order to highlight its identification with that which is "administered, commodified . . . pretargeted and produced for large numbers of consumers." "Formations of Mass Culture," in Gordon, ed., *Postwar Japan as History*, 240.

49. The exemplary form of *junbungaku* is commonly identified by Japanese literati as the *watakushi shōsetsu*, or "I" novel. For an excellent treatment of this distinction and its history, see Matthew Strecher, "Purely Mass or Massively Pure?" *Monumentica Nipponica* 51, no. 3 (autumn 1996): 357–374. Moreover, *junbungaku's* elitism stands in contrast to the more egalitarian aspects of *taishūbungaku*.

50. Hirano Ken, Itō Sei, and Yamamoto Kenkichi, "Junbungaku to taishūbungaku" (Pure and popular literature), *Gunzo*, October 1961, 157.

51. Ibid., 169.

52. Itō Sei, "'Jun' bungaku wa sonzai shiuru ka?" (Does "pure" literature exist?) *Gunzo*, November 1961, 180.

53. This is Edward Seidensticker's translation of *"chūsetsu bungaku."* Not surprisingly, Seidensticker, a translator of many of the classics of the Japanese literary canon, including *The Tale of Genji*, took a dim view of Matsumoto, whom he

describes as a "tireless raker into the fetid mud of the American occupation." Edward Seidensticker, "The 'Pure' and the 'In-Between' in Modern Japanese Theories of the Novel," *Harvard Journal of Asian Studies* 16 (1966): 183.

54. Itō, "'Jun' bungaku," 184.

55. Ibid., 187.

56. The *bundan* (literally, literary guild) refers to a small but influential group of authors and critics that has played a crucial role in determining the course (and definition) of literature in Japan up to the present. The *bundan* was responsible for the success and growth of the "I" novel, which was held to epitomize "pure" literature since it was written for a small, select, and refined audience instead of a mass readership.

57. Strecher, "Purely Mass or Massively Pure?" 363.

58. Ibid.

59. Ibid. Another instance of this phenomenon was the education minister's warning in June 2002 that too many foreign words were entering the Japanese language, threatening to "tarnish" the beauty of "traditional Japanese." See "Experts Sought to Halt Loan Words," *Japan Times Online,* 26 June 2002 (http://www.japantimes.com), and Howard French, "To Grandparents, English Word Trend Isn't 'Naisu,'" *New York Times* (online edition), 23 October 2002.

60. Oe Kenzaburo, "Japan's Dual Identity: A Writer's Dilemma," in Miyoshi and Harootunian, eds., *Postmodernism and Japan,* 190.

61. Hayami Yukiko, "Akutagawa-sho wa tsumaranai" (The Akutagawa Prize is boring), *Aera,* 1 January 1996, 46–52. I would suggest that the controversy surrounding Yu Miri, the 1997 winner of the Akutagawa Prize who faced death threats from right-wing political groups, is an ironic indicator of the vital role of political and social change within literature and literary culture. Yu, a Zainichi Korean, drew the ire of the right wing not only because of her Korean ethnicity, but also her visible success.

62. Interview with Sato Shinichiro, December 1996.

63. While they are not the focus of this book, it should be noted that male writers of detective fiction, including Shimada Sōji, Akagawa Jirō, and Suzuki Koji, continue to produce many books and enjoy considerable commercial success; in particular, Koji's series of horror mysteries—*Ringu* (Ring, 1991), *Rasen* (Spiral, 1995), and *Ruupu* (Loop, 2000)—were best-sellers, with a cinematic English-language version of *Ring* recently appearing in the United States. Nevertheless, these authors have been overshadowed among critics and the press by the recent wave of their female counterparts. Likewise, while female detectives are not the sole province of women writers—Kitamura Kaoru, for example, has made a name for himself with mysteries featuring young female heroines and is often paired in speaking engagements with Miyabe Miyuki, whose fictional detectives (as we will see) are all men—Kitamura's and others' female protagonists tend to fall firmly within the "cozy" tradition of the intelligent but demure amateur, in contrast to the more assertive and hard-boiled women characters of the authors examined here.

64. Kasai Kiyoshi, "Tantei shōsetsu to keishiki" (Detective fiction and its form) in *Nyū weibu misuteri dokuhon* (Reading new wave mysteries), ed. Yamaguchi Masaya (Tokyo: Hara shobo, 1997), 227.

65. Yamamae Yuzuru, "Nihon no josei suiri sakka—taitōki kara seijukuki e" (Japanese women mystery writers—from prominence to maturity), in Yamamae, ed., *Aka no misuterii*, 456.

66. Social criticism was not confined to Niki's works, of course; later in her life, Hirabayashi Taiko wrote an essay criticizing the current state of Japanese detective fiction, noting that it was too plot-oriented and did not pay any attention to social or historical problems. Hirabayashi Taiko, "Tantei shōsetsu mandan" (A chat about detective fiction), in *Hirabayashi Taiko zenshū*, 10: 308–310 (Tokyo: Asahi shuppansha, 1979).

67. Yamamae, "Nihon no josei . . . taitoki," 457.

68. Yamamae suggests that the first of this new wave of women writers was Koike Mariko, whose suspense novel *Tsuma no onna tomodachi* (The wife's female friend) won the Japan Mystery Writer's Association Prize in 1989. I prefer to begin with Miyabe, however, since her works clearly qualify as detective fiction. Yamamae Yuzuru, "Nihon no josei suiri sakka: Zensei jidai no tōrai" (Japanese women mystery writers: The arrival of the golden age), in Yamamae, ed., *Shiro no misuterii*, 491.

69. For an analysis of the prize system and its relationship to the romance novel industry, see Chieko Irie Mulhern, "Japanese Harlequin Romances as Transcultural Woman's Fiction," *Journal of Japanese Studies* 48, no. 1 (February 1989): 50–70.

70. Omori Nozomi, "Miyabe Miyuki," *Marco Polo* 3, no. 8 (August 1993): 22.

71. Yamamae, "Nihon no josei . . . zensei," 494.

72. Sengai Akiyuki, "Kaisetsu" (Analysis), in Shibata Yoshiki, *Riko—Viinasu no eien*, 392.

73. This can be seen from the fact that the media labeled their work as *"joryū"* (women's) mysteries—an intriguing term since neither Takamura nor Miyabe focuses particularly on female characters or women's concerns.

74. Bessatsu Takarajima Henshubuhen, ed., *Kono misuterii ga sugoi! Kessakusen* (This mystery is great! A selection of masterpieces) (Tokyo: Takarajimasha, 1997), 98.

75. "Naoki-sho jushō wa watashi no jinsei no misuterii" (The Naoki Prize is my life's mystery), *Gendai*, September 1993, 105.

76. Quoted in Nonoyama Yoshitaka, "Sakka no 'gimu' wa shōsetsu o koete" (An author's "duty" goes beyond the novel), *Gendai*, December 1995, 68.

77. A notable instance was Takamura's public commentary about the horrific 1997 murder of a ten-year-old mentally retarded child by a fourteen-year-old classmate, who sent the police a series of "clue-filled" letters before he was apprehended. Takamura conducted extensive interviews with noted psychologist Noda Masaaki about the case, arguing that "the boundary between criminals and law-abiding people is becoming blurred" due in part to the effect that sex and violence in literature and the popular media have on individual behavior and perceptions. Takamura Kaoru, "Sakakibara seito wa jidai no ko ka ijōsha ka," *Bungei shunjū* (August 1997): 150–158. Translated into English as "Japanese Society and the Psychopath," *Japan Echo* (online edition), 24, no. 4 (October 1999).

78. Bessatsu Takarajima Henshubuhen, ed., *Kono misuterii ga sugoi!*, 150.

79. See below. Notably, this declaration seems to have done little to alter Takamura's reputation among the reading public (and the literary industry) as a mystery writer—a fact indicated by the prominent placement of her 2002 novel, *Haruko jōka* (Our sweet Haruko), in the mystery section of most of the large bookstores in Tokyo.

80. Omori Nozomi, "Miyabe Miyuki," 26.

81. Miyabe Miyuki, "Mienakute kowai totsukuni" (An unseen foreign land), *Asahi shinbun*, 27 June 1994, 25.

82. Aoki Chie, "Kogoeru kiba," in Ikegami Fuyuki, ed., *Misuteri besuto 201 Nihonban*, 216.

83. Arai Noriko, "Nonami Asa: Kono hito no ikikata ga suteki 42" (Nonami Asa: Great lives, no. 42), *Oggi (Japan)*, March 1997, 158.

84. There are two other novels in the Riko series, *Seibo no fukaki fuchi* (Madonna's abyss) (Tokyo: Kadokawa shoten, 1996), and *Daiana no asaki yume* (Diana's daydream) (Tokyo: Kadokawa shoten, 1998). A movie version of *Riko—Viinasu no eien* was released in Japan in 2000.

85. Yamamae Yuzuru, "Shibata Yoshiki," in Yamamae, ed., *Shiro no misuterii*, 439.

86. *"Kao ni furikakaru ame*, Kirino Natsuo," *Hōseki*, December 1993, 295.

87. Ibid.

88. Yamamae Yuzuru, "Kirino Natsuo," in Yamamae, ed., *Shiro no misuterii*, 367.

89. *"Kao ni furikakaru ame*," 295.

90. Kirino Natsuo, *Fuaiabooru burusu* (Fireball blues) (Tokyo: Bunshun bunko, 1998). The Japanese women's professional wrestling organization offered disgraced skater Tonya Harding a million dollars to wrestle in Japan. Harding turned down the money, but the organization continued to grow.

91. Kirino Natsuo, *Out* (Tokyo: Kodansha, 1997).

92. Ikeshita Ikuko and Kirino Natsuo, "Yonjūdai wa onna no yūjō no migakidoki" (The forties are a time for polishing women's friendships), *Fujin kōron*, March 1996, 117–122.

93. This category was created by publishers as a subgenre of mystery fiction that incorporates supernatural or fantasy elements into its plots; in Japan, it provides a way to classify books that have the structure of a mystery but treat themes in a way different from that of orthodox detective fiction. One of Tokyo's largest bookstores, Yaesu Book Center, has a section of science fiction mystery for books like Matsuo's, as well as other detective stories that have less realistic settings or plot devices.

94. An early, and still valuable, treatment of these issues is Kathleen Gregory Klein, *The Woman Detective: Gender and Genre* (Urbana: University of Illinois Press, 1988).

95. Rosalind Coward and Linda Semple, "Tracking Down the Past: Women and Detective Fiction," in *Genre and Women's Fiction in the Postmodern World*, ed. Helen Carr (London: Pandora, 1989), 46.

96. Munt, *Murder by the Book?*

97. Maureen Reddy, *Sisters in Crime: Feminism and the Crime Novel* (New York: Continuum, 1988).

98. Priscilla Walton and Manina Jones, *Detective Agency: Women Rewriting the Hard-Boiled Tradition* (Berkeley: University of California Press, 1999), 4.

99. Klein, *The Woman Detective*, 18.

100. On the problems posed by the unaccompanied or independent woman in nineteenth-century London, see Judith Walkowitz, *City of Dreadful Delight: Narratives of Sexual Danger in Late-Victorian London* (Chicago: University of Chicago Press, 1992), 45–52.

101. Rosalyn Deutsche, "*Chinatown,* Part IV? What Jake Forgets about Downtown," in Deutsche, *Evictions,* 97.

102. Liahna Babener, "Uncloseting Ideology in the Novels of Barbara Wilson," in Klein, ed., *Women Times Three,* 144.

103. Deutsche, "*Chinatown,* Part IV?" 99.

104. Walton and Jones, *Detective Agency,* 93.

105. Quoted in ibid.

106. Quoted in Ann Wilson, "The Female Dick and the Crisis of Homosexuality," in Irons, ed., *Feminism in Women's Detective Fiction,* 149.

107. Crawford, "Investigating the City," 125.

108. Sabine Vanacker, "V. I. Warshawski, Kinsey Millhone, and Kay Scarpetta: Creating a Feminist Detective Hero," in *Criminal Proceedings: The American Crime Novel,* ed. Peter Messent (London: Pluto Press, 1997), 73.

109. Walton and Jones, *Detective Agency,* 154.

110. Vanacker, "V. I. Warshawski," 79.

Chapter 2: A Home of One's Own

1. "Misuterii no haba hirogaru." Interview with Miyabe Miyuki. *Yomiuri shinbun,* 12 October 1994, 8.

2. *Hōseki* 20, no. 10 (October 1992): 304–305; "Misuterii no haba hirogaru," 8.

3. Miyabe Miyuki, interview by author, Tokyo, 7 February 1997.

4. Ibid.

5. Kasai Kiyoshi, "Tantei shōsetsu no chisōgaku," 12–14.

6. The novel's original title, *Kasha* (Cart of fire), is taken from a medieval Japanese poem. Although "*kasha*" (commonly read as *hi no kuruma*) is a Buddhist term for the vehicle that conveys sinners to hell, here it describes someone in financial straits. The title used here, *All She Was Worth,* is from the translation by Alfred Birnbaum. Birnbaum (or his editor) omitted much of Miyabe's lengthy discussion of personal finance in the original; in addition, he inexplicably changed the names of some of the minor characters, although these names have clear symbolic importance for the author. Therefore, while I have used Birnbaum's translations, I have chosen to revert to the names in the Japanese original.

7. Sakata, *Sengo o yomu,* 174–177. Another of Miyabe's novels, *Sabishi karyūdo* (The lonely hunter) (Tokyo: Shinchosa, 1993), also has been translated into French as *La Librarie Tanabe,* trans. Annick Laurent (Paris: Editions Philippe Picquier, 1995).

8. Namioka Hisako, "Katari to tomoshibi" (Tales and lanterns), in Kasai Kiyoshi, ed., *Honkaku misuteri no genzai,* 255–279.

9. R. Gordon Kelly, *Mystery Fiction and Modern Life* (Jackson, Miss.: University of Mississippi Press, 1998), 26.

10. See the reviews of *Kasha* in *Hōseki*, 20, no. 10, (October 1992): 304–305, and *Chūō kōron* 108, no. 3 (February 1993): 158–159, as well as the more in-depth treatment of Miyabe's works by Namioka, "Katari to tomoshibi."

11. Gillian Rose, "Place and Identity: A Sense of Place," in *A Place in the World?* ed. Doreen Massey and Pat Jess (London: Open University Press, 1995), 88.

12. Ibid.

13. Jonathan Rutherford, "A Place Called Home: Identity and the Cultural Politics of Difference," in *Identity: Community, Culture, Difference,* ed. Jonathan Rutherford (London: Lawrence and Wishart, 1990), 19.

14. "Takamura Kaoru to Miyabe Miyuki supeshiaru taidan" (A conversation between Takamura Kaoru and Miyabe Miyuki), *Shūkan Asahi*, 30 July 1993, 131. In contrast, other authors are deliberately vague about historical and spatial references in order to attempt to achieve a sense of timelessness. An example of this is the Nancy Drew mysteries in the United States or those of Yamamura Misa in Japan. The fact that the period of a detective novel still can be determined despite the author's attempt at creating a timeless setting is an example of detective fiction's ultimate dependence upon historical and social particularities. For more on Nancy Drew, see Bobby Ann Mason, "Nancy Drew: The Once and Future Prom Queen," in Irons, ed., *Feminism in Women's Detective Fiction*, 73–93.

15. Page citations refer to Birnbaum's translation of *All She Was Worth*.

16. David Harvey, *Justice, Nature, and the Geography of Difference* (Cambridge, Mass.: Blackwell, 1996), 100.

17. Igarashi Akio, "'Inhabitant' or 'Resident': Japan's Metropolises at a Crossroads," paper presented at "The Fora on Cities," Seoul, Korea, 10–13 December 1996. The terms "High City" and "Low City" as designations for the Yamanote and the *shitamachi* are used by Edward Seidensticker in his history of Tokyo in the post-Meiji era, *Low City, High City: Tokyo from Edo to the Earthquake* (Tokyo: Knopf, 1983).

18. Quoted in Maeda Ai, "Yamanote no oku" (In the recesses of the high city), in *Toshi kukan no naka no bungaku* (Literature in the context of the city) (Tokyo: Chikuma Shobo, 1989); (unpublished) translation by William F. Sibley, p. 1.

19. There are several guides to the *shitamachi* in Japanese that divide up the area and introduce the reader to the various "traditional" foods and crafts. This is a new development since in the prewar era, the Asakusa area was the center for modern entertainments such as movies and revues. It was only after the war and the devastation that it wrought that Asakusa and the *shitamachi* revived with the rejuvenation of the traditional appellation. This development has gone even further in 2002 with the rebuilding of the area around Sensoji in the brick architecture of the prewar.

20. Susan Stewart, *On Longing: Narratives of the Miniature, the Gigantic, the Souvenir, the Collection* (Durham, N.C.: Duke University Press, 1993), 23. On this issue, compare Kathleen Stewart, "Nostalgia, A Polemic," *Cultural Anthropology* 3, no. 3 (1988): 227–241.

21. Miyabe Miyuki, "Mienakute kowai totsukuni," 25.

22. Doreen Massey, *Space, Place, and Gender* (Minneapolis: University of Minnesota Press, 1994), 121.

23. Literally translated as "old village," *"furusato"* has come to mean a person's place of origin, usually in the countryside, where one has family roots. For a discussion of *"furusato"* and its political uses, see Jennifer Robertson, *Native and Newcomer: Making and Remaking a Japanese City* (Berkeley: University of California Press, 1991), ch. 1.

24. John Clammer, *Contemporary Urban Japan: A Sociology of Consumption* (Oxford: Blackwell, 1997); Theodore C. Bestor, *Neighborhood Tokyo* (Stanford, Calif.: Stanford University Press, 1989); and Robertson, *Native and Newcomer.*

25. It should be noted that such a nurturing community, in which "family" is not coterminous with a nuclear kinship unit, is not unusual among American working-class families. In *The Time Bind*, a study of families and work in a Fortune 500 manufacturing company, sociologist Arlie Russell Hochschild discovers that family and friends among blue-collar workers form an informal domestic "welfare system" to take care of family needs. She finds that this system does not extend to the white-collar workers in the same company, partly because many of them were not locals (as is the case for the blue-collar workers), and partly because their "family needs" are exclusively taken care of by paid services or housewives. The financial situation of the white-collar class erases the need to maintain the extended "family." Arlie Russell Hochschild, *The Time Bind: When Work Becomes Home and Home Becomes Work* (New York: Metropolitan Books, 1997), 168.

26. For this standard definition, see, for example, Bunkyō-ku Kuyakusho, *Bunkyō-ku e yōkoso* (Welcome to Bunkyo Ward), December 1995, 26.

27. Clammer, *Contemporary Urban Japan,* 61.

28. Utsunomiya, in Tochigi Prefecture, has little of the glamor and excitement of Tokyo. The *shinkansen* train does stop there, but it was the housing crunch of the 1990s that placed Utsunomiya within commuting distance to Tokyo. This has made it less of a backwater than Miyabe describes.

29. "Water trade," or *mizu shobai,* is a Japanese term denoting any kind of work in bars and other "entertainment" enterprises.

30. Clammer, *Contemporary Urban Japan,* 131.

31. Clammer points out that in Japan, since class differences manifest themselves differently, one cannot simply apply Pierre Bourdieu's research findings on class and taste in *Distinction: A Social Critique of the Judgement of Taste,* trans. Richard Nice (Cambridge, Mass.: Harvard University Press, 1984), where Bourdieu finds that the possession of cultural capital, or cultural knowledge, permits distinctions between people of similar economic classes. Rather, Clammer suggests that patterns of social classification exist both between classes and within social groups in the same economic position. "The possession of cultural capital—cultural knowledge and competence—allows differentiations to appear among people of the same economic class position." Clammer, *Contemporary Urban Japan,* 103.

32. See Edward Fowler's *San'ya Blues: Laboring Life in Contemporary Tokyo* (Ithaca, N.Y.: Cornell University Press, 1996), a nonfictional treatment of a group of

men who, due to economic circumstance, have created a community of their own. The neighborhood of San'ya is where the day laborers live, and several cheap hotels and boarding houses are located there to serve their needs. Miyabe's portrait of a homosocial community is not unique; what distinguishes it from others is that it is not a formal organization such as a monastery or a jail, although it maintains the same distinct family-like connections.

33. Miyabe Miyuki, *Tokyo shitamachi satsujin bōshōku* (Murders in downtown Tokyo) (Tokyo: Kobunsha bunko, 1994).

34. Jennifer Robertson, *Takarazuka: Sexual Politics and Popular Culture in Modern Japan* (Berkeley: University of California Press, 1998), 86.

35. There are many examples of this archetype of Japanese womanhood. For a send-up of the concept, see Ohba Minako, "The Smile of the Mountain Witch" (Yamauba no bisho), in *Japanese Women Writers,* ed. Noriko Mizuta Lippit and Kyoko Iriye Selden (Armonk, N.Y.: M. E. Sharpe, 1991), 194–206.

36. The "three C's" were modeled on the three treasures of the imperial regalia and denoted three valuable things that consumers prized in the late 1960s. In the 1950s and early 1960s there were the "three S's": *senpūki, sentakki,* and *suihanki* (electric fan, washing machine, and electric rice cooker). In the early 1970s the "three J's" were *jueru, jetto,* and *jūtaku* (jewels, overseas vacations, and a house). For more on this, see William Kelly, "Finding a Place in Metropolitan Japan: Ideologies, Institutions, and Daily Life," in Gordon, ed., *Postwar Japan as History,* 195.

37. Clammer, *Contemporary Urban Japan,* 1.

38. For the rise of this consumer mentality among the postwar *sarariiman* (white-collar worker) class, see Ezra F. Vogel's classic *Japan's New Middle Class,* 2d ed. (Berkeley: University of California Press, 1971), 71–85.

39. Ivy, "Formations of Mass Culture," 253.

40. Clammer, *Contemporary Urban Japan,* 9.

41. Ivy, "Formations of Mass Culture," 254.

42. Lise Skov, "Fashion Trends, Japonisme and Postmodernism," in Treat, ed., *Contemporary Japan and Popular Culture,* 137–168.

43. The magazine *Mono* (Things), for instance, is a seasonal buying guide for trendy items. There also are magazines dedicated to all the product lines released by Hermès (a French accessory company).

44. *"Enjo kōsai"* has been rendered into English by the news media as "assisted dating." A more subtle reading of this phrase might be "beneficial interpersonal relations," which adds to the vaguely social science air of the term. Neither rendition, however, gets at the fact that the phenomenon is undeniably prostitution. I would like to thank William Sibley for his nuanced interpretation of the term. In order to acquire the luxury goods that were currently in vogue, such as the Prada handbag, teenage girls, some as young as thirteen, were prostituting themselves to businessmen. This phenomenon was not widespread, and only an estimated 8 percent of Tokyo's school-girls were thought to have participated. It did, however, capture the Japanese popular imagination and was a theme in many dramas and detective programs. For more, see Valerie Reitman, "Japan's New Growth Industry: Schoolgirl Prostitution," *Wall Street Journal,* 2 October 1996, A8.

45. Despite her protests to the contrary, Miyabe herself is conversant with the world of luxury goods. In an interview with Miyabe and Takamura Kaoru, the term "open heart" (a particular design of necklace by Tiffany that for a time was *de rigeur* for well-dressed young women) came up. Takamura disavowed any knowledge of the term, while Miyabe was able to explain to her what it was. "It is an incredibly popular item. What I thought was scary was that there was an ad saying that men should give these necklaces to women. None of my friends had one, though." She goes on to discuss the gap between information and reality: "I think that only the pure of heart do not succumb to this kind of message." "Takamura Kaoru to Miyabe Miyuki supeshiaru taidan," 131.

46. During the Tokugawa period (1603–1868) and even later, Japanese families sold their daughters into indentured labor. Moreover, the modern Japanese economy was built through the labor of young rural women in the cotton spinning mills. See E. Patricia Tsurumi, *Factory Girls: Women in the Thread Mills of Meiji Japan* (Princeton, N.J.: Princeton University Press, 1990). This rural-to-urban migration of women has not been entirely exploitative in the twentieth century, however; many of Japan's women writers and thinkers, such as Hayashi Fumiko and Itō Noe, came to Tokyo in search of an artistic and intellectual freedom that they were unable to find in the countryside. See Sharon Sievers, *Flowers in Salt: The Beginnings of Feminist Consciousness in Modern Japan* (Stanford, Calif.: Stanford University Press, 1983).

47. Interview with Miyabe Miyuki, Tokyo, 7 February 1997.

48. Clammer, *Contemporary Urban Japan*, 13.

49. Kristin Ross, *Fast Cars, Clean Bodies* (Cambridge, Mass.: MIT Press, 1995), 107.

50. Ibid., 107–108.

51. It is interesting in this context to point out some contemporary figures on home ownership in France, Japan, and the United States. Despite the French penchant for home ownership, more Japanese own their own homes (slightly over 60 percent), making Japan fifth in the world (and just behind the United States' 66 percent; Israel is number one). Jessica Steinberg, "The Homeowner's Land," *New York Times*, 5 August 1998, C1.

52. Gaston Bachelard, *The Poetics of Space*, trans. Maria Jolas (Boston: Beacon Press, 1969), 4–7.

53. Massey, *Space, Place, and Gender*, 5.

54. Klein, *The Woman Detective*, 96–98.

55. Clammer, *Contemporary Urban Japan*, 4.

56. Marilyn Ivy, *Discourses of the Vanishing: Modernity, Phantasm, Japan* (Chicago: University of Chicago Press, 1995), 104.

57. Norma Field, "Somehow: The Postmodern as Atmosphere," in Miyoshi and Harootunian, eds., *Postmodernism and Japan*, 171.

58. Tanaka Yasuo, *Nantonaku, kurisutaru* (Somehow, crystal) (Tokyo: Shinchosha, 1980), 55; quoted in Field, "Somehow," 175.

59. Masao Miyoshi, *Offcenter: Power and Culture Relations between Japan and the United States* (Cambridge, Mass.: Harvard University Press, 1991), 236–237.

60. Certainly Miyoshi is not alone in his disgust. Critical reaction in the United States to Brett Easton Ellis' 1991 *American Psycho,* a novel about a young Yuppie serial killer and the brand-name goods he consumed, was just as violent. Notably, the 2000 film adaptation of Ellis' novel was received far more favorably.

61. Yoshimoto Banana, *Kichin* (Tokyo: Fukutake shoten, 1991); translated by Megan Backus as *Kitchen* (New York: Washington Square Press, 1993), 27.

62. John Whittier Treat, "Yoshimoto Banana Writes Home: The *Shōjo* in Japanese Popular Culture," in Treat, ed, *Contemporary Japan and Popular Culture,* 284.

63. Yoshimoto Banana, *Kitchen,* 4.

64. Treat, "Yoshimoto Banana Writes Home," 296. This lack likewise distinguishes Yoshimoto's object-centered nostalgia from Susan Stewart's account of the use of souvenirs to "evoke a voluntary memory of childhood . . . a childhood manufactured from its material survivals," since the latter process depends for its efficacy upon an act of memory. See Stewart, *On Longing,* 145.

65. Treat, "Yoshimoto Banana Writes Home," 303.

66. See Oe Kenzaburo, "Japan's Dual Identity," 196–197.

67. Moretti, "Clues," 135.

68. See Sievers, *Flowers in Salt,* 116n. As Sumiko Iwao points out, however, the social stigma associated with divorce has largely disappeared in the last few decades; see *The Japanese Woman: Traditional Image and Changing Reality* (Cambridge, Mass.: Harvard University Press, 1993), 119. There also has been an ongoing legal struggle in Japan for women to use their maiden names while they are married, thus undercutting the essentially patrilineal construct of the *ie,* or "household" which the *koseki* is meant to document. Called *fufu bessei,* this movement has met with opposition not only from right-wing groups, but also from the Japanese government. Kyoko Itoh, "Women Ask, 'What's in a Name?' " *Japan Times,* 6 March 1997, 14.

69. Clammer, *Contemporary Urban Japan,* 139.

70. Fowler, *San'ya Blues,* 229.

71. Ienaga Saburo, *The Pacific War, 1931–1945,* trans. Frank Baldwin (New York: Pantheon Books, 1978), 112 and 272 n. 38. The degree to which a person's actions come under observation is a key issue in another detective story, Matsuo Yumi's *Murder in Balloon Town,* which I address in chapter 5.

72. Massey, *Space, Place, and Gender,* 122; compare Harvey, *Justice, Nature, and the Geography of Difference,* 246.

73. Miyabe Miyuki, *Riyū* (The reason) (Tokyo: Asahi Shinbun shuppansha, 1998). This theme is addressed more fully in my forthcoming article, "There Goes the Neighborhood: Community and Family in Miyabe Miyuki's *Riyū.*"

74. Another sign of the *shitamachi*'s increasing integration with the rest of Tokyo is the planned extension of the Hanzomon subway line, which runs through the trendy regions of Shibuya and Aoyama into the neighborhoods of Sumida and Arakawa—a particularly significant development given that these areas are not currently served by the city subway lines.

75. Miyabe Miyuki, *Heisei okachi nikki* (The Heisei traveler's diary) (Tokyo: Shinchosha, 1998).

76. *Chushingura* is perhaps the best-known historical epic in Japan, celebrating the actions of forty-seven *rōnin* (or masterless samurai) who defied their superiors in order to avenge the murder of their lord and were later rewarded for their loyalty by being allowed to commit seppuku on their master's grave.

Chapter 3: Office(r) Ladies

1. Tamae K. Prindle, trans. and ed., *Made in Japan and Other Japanese "Business Novels"* (Armonk, N.Y.: M. E. Sharpe, 1989).

2. Klein, *The Woman Detective*, 6.

3. Robert P. Winston and Nancy C. Mellerski, *The Public Eye: Ideology and the Police Procedural* (New York: St. Martin's Press, 1992), 103.

4. Ibid., 6.

5. Klein, *The Woman Detective*, 24 and 30n. Klein notes that these women predate the existence of real British policewomen, and she suggests that since at this time many police detectives were hired to work privately, such women should be classified as private detectives.

6. Munt, *Murder By the Book?* 6.

7. Janis Appier, *Policing Women: The Sexual Politics of Law Enforcement and the LAPD* (Philadelphia: Temple University Press, 1998), 149.

8. M. H. Abrams, *A Glossary of Literary Terms* (New York: Harcourt, Brace, and Jovanovich, 1993), 174. For more on the use of realism in detective fiction, see Jon Thompson, *Fiction, Crime, and Empire: Clues to Modernity and Postmodernity* (Urbana: University of Illinois Press, 1993), particularly 35–39.

9. Quoted in Dennis Walder, ed., *The Realist Novel* (London: Routledge, 1995), 6.

10. Sandra Tomc, "Questing Women: The Feminist Mystery after Feminism," in Irons, ed., *Feminism in Women's Detective Fiction*, 58.

11. Walton and Jones, *Detective Agency*, 14.

12. Ibid.

13. *Mysteries by Mail* catalog, October 1999.

14. The rebel cop in "Hamidasu deka" is a man who refuses to "play by the rules" and often lets his passions run away with him. While the head of his section is a woman and there is a young woman police detective who often investigates crimes with him, they play supporting roles at best.

15. Interview with Miyabe Miyuki, 7 February 1997.

16. For more on women in the Self-Defense Forces, see "Onna to Jieitai" (Women in the Self-Defense Forces), *Uno!* February 1997, 164–165.

17. In Ikegami Fuyuki, ed., *Misuteri besuto 201 Nihonban* (Tokyo: Shinshokan, 1997), an analysis of the most popular and critically acclaimed mysteries in Japanese reveals that of the entire genre, only 15 percent are termed police procedurals. The police may make a brief presence in other subgenres, such as horror, but are not the focus of the action.

18. The use of a foreign phrase instead of a Japanese word to represent sexual harassment may indicate that the Japanese have refused to naturalize this type of behavior with a Japanese expression. Other types of discrimination have not received this kind of distancing, such as *"jinshu sabetsu"* (racial discrimination).

19. Notably, revisions of the Equal Opportunity Law on 1 April 1999 included provisions for sexual harassment. Additionally, the outcomes of several landmark sexual harassment cases have helped to strengthen laws relating to it.

20. Keiko Karube, "Sexual Harassment at Japanese Colleges and Universities: Causes, Patterns and Some Countermeasures," paper presented at the annual meeting of the Association for Asian Studies, Boston, 13 March 1999.

21. Ibid., 3.

22. Nicole Gaouette, "Japan Abuzz over Sexual Harassment," *Christian Science Monitor* (online edition), 14 April 1998.

23. Tsunoda Yukiko, "Sexual Harassment in Japan: Recent Legal Decisions," trans. Yokokawa Muro Mariko; *U.S.-Japan Women's Journal*, English Supplement, no. 5 (1993): 64.

24. Nonami Asa: *Hana chiru goro no satsujin* (Murder when the petals scatter) (Tokyo: Shincho bunko, 1999); *Kusari* (Chains) (Tokyo: Shinchosha, 2000); *Miren* (Attachment) (Tokyo: Shinchosha, 2001).

25. Nonami Asa, *Kogoeru kiba*. Translations are mine, and all references are given parenthetically in the text.

26. *Terekura* is a form of prostitution in which a man makes contact over the phone (usually a cell phone) with a young woman and, if he finds her appealing, arranges for a rendezvous. Since there is no third party involved, the transaction avoids legal sanction in Tokyo and other localities. The *terekura* (along with *enjo kōsai*) captured media imagination and was featured in several television dramas in the 1990s. For more on *terekura*, see Miyadai Shinji, "'Terekura' no minzokushi" (The folklore of *terekura*), in Ueno Chizuko, ed., *Iro to yoku*, 123–166.

27. Klein, *The Woman Detective*, 162.

28. On the role of interrogation and its central place within the self-image of the Japanese detective, see Setsuo Miyazawa, *Policing in Japan: A Study on Making Crime*, trans. Frank G. Bennett Jr. and John O. Haley (Albany: State University of New York Press, 1992), 159–165, 179.

29. This technique is not limited to law enforcement; rather, it exists in any male-dominated field where women make inroads. The military also has had its share of harassment cases, both publicized and fictionalized. For one woman's story of her own rough initiation into the police force, see Gina Gallo, *Armed and Dangerous: Memoirs of a Chicago Policewoman* (New York: Forge, 2001).

30. As of 1 April 1999, according to a spokeperson for the National Police Agency, there were 8,300 police women and 12,400 women on the general staff in Japan. This is in contrast to 226,400 policemen and 29,351 male police staff.

31. This situation, as sociologist Yuko Ogasawara has shown, is in fact systemic within the Japanese workplace, where differences in age and education levels have long been used to prevent women from organizing to improve their lot, leading most women to seek solitary solutions to their problems rather than attempting to mobilize the public arena to seek redress. Yuko Ogasawara, *Office Ladies and Salaried Men: Power, Gender, and Work in Japanese Companies* (Berkeley: University of California Press, 1998), 47.

32. Hochschild, *The Time Bind*, 35–52.

33. For a treatment of this topic in detective fiction, see Tomc, "Questing Women."

34. See Anne Allison, *Nightwork: Sexuality, Pleasure, and Corporate Masculinity in a Tokyo Hostess Club* (Chicago: University of Chicago Press, 1994), especially 124–141.

35. Appier, *Policing Women,* 156.

36. Sherry Ortner, "Is Female to Male as Nature Is to Culture?," in *Making Gender: The Politics and Erotics of Culture* (Boston: Beacon Press, 1996), 25.

37. Ibid., 30.

38. Nonami Asa, *Hanachiru goro no satsujin,* 309.

39. Ibid., 310.

40. Ibid., 313.

41. Shibata Yoshiki, *Riko—Viinasu no eien* (Riko—Forever Venus) (Tokyo: Kadokawa bunko, 1995), 28–29. Translations are mine, and all references are given parenthetically in the text.

42. Klein, *The Woman Detective,* 169.

43. Competition, both between sections of the police force and among detectives, is endemic in Japan; see Miyazawa, *Policing in Japan,* 176–177.

44. For more on the symbolism of, and women's discontent with, the task of tea pouring, see Ogasawara, *Office Ladies and Salaried Men,* 40–43.

45. On the use of this strategy in the workplace more generally, see ibid., 48.

46. Shibata Yoshiki, *Daiana no asaki yume,* 395.

47. Walton and Jones, *Detective Agency,* 16.

48. These advertisements appeared in May 1997, part of a series that featured well-known people talking about motorcycle riding. Nonami Asa was the only woman who appeared and if not the only author, certainly the only one who writes detective fiction.

49. Klein, *The Woman Detective,* 168.

50. Interview with Narita Akemi, translator of detective fiction, Tokyo, 28 January 1998.

51. A recent ruling shows just how egregious such an act needs to be before it is ruled sexual harassment. In 1999, the governor of Osaka, Japan's second largest city, was forced to resign and pay reparations to a young woman only when it was shown that he had accosted her, thrown a blanket over her, and groped her. Howard W. French, "A Resignation Is Cheered by Feminists around Japan," *New York Times,* 22 December 1999, A6.

52. Paula L. Woods, *Inner City Blues* (New York: Ballantine, 1999), 16–17.

53. Tsunoda, "Sexual Harassment in Japan."

54. Arai, "Nonami Asa," 158.

55. Tomc, "Questing Women," 58.

Chapter 4: Sex and Violence

1. Murano is in fact named after Milo Milodragovich, James Crumley's rough-talking, hard-boiled detective.

2. The notion of single women's sexuality as something over which women exert control or from which women derive pleasure is either glossed over or absent in much

of contemporary Japanese popular culture. It is striking that the majority of so-called *"torendi dorama"* (trendy television dramas) rarely feature any physical intimacy beyond chaste kisses, while comic books, or *manga,* often feature plots revolving around sex. In 2003, due to the popularity of the American cable series "Sex and the City," Japanese television programmers created a new show in which the protagonist is a divorced freelance writer who has affairs with many men. Unlike its American counterpart, however, with its frank and funny discussion of women's sexual and personal lives, "Koi wa tatakai" (Love is a battlefield) seems more interested in revealing (and ridiculing) men's more bizarre desires. (In the first episode the heroine ends up in a hotel room with a lover who wants her to whip him.)

3. Munt, *Murder by the Book?* 31.

4. It is important to note at the outset that while "sex" and "sexuality" are closely related terms, they are not the same thing. Sexuality may overlap with sex, but it is implicated with desire and erotic pleasure in a more complex manner than the merely reproductive. In Rosalind Coward's concise definition, "sex" or "sexual activities" describe the enactment of a person's sensual aims and gratifications; "sexuality" refers to the representation of activities surrounding these aims and gratifications; and "sexual identity" is the public representation of these aims and objectives as they are integrated into the personality. Rosalind Coward, *Patriarchal Precedents: Sexuality and Social Relations* (London: Routledge, 1983), 279. The precise content of these terms, however, is not static, since what is defined as "sexual" and "erotic" varies culturally and historically. Therefore, as Gregory Pflugfelder has noted, it is necessary to acknowledge that "'sexuality' and 'eroticism' are relatively porous signifiers, designating a shifting set of practices and desires without a constant or easily identifiable center." Gregory M. Pflugfelder, *Cartographies of Desire: Male-Male Sexuality in Japanese Discourse 1600–1950* (Berkeley: University of California Press, 1999), 6. See also Robertson, *Takarazuka,* 17.

5. Klein, *The Woman Detective,* 131.

6. Kimberly J. Dilley, *Busybodies, Meddlers, and Snoops: The Female Hero in Contemporary Women's Mysteries* (Westport, Conn.: Greenwood Press, 1998), 109.

7. Ibid.

8. Catharine MacKinnon, "Feminism, Marxism, and Method of the State: An Agenda for Theory," *Signs* 7, no. 3 (spring 1982): 531.

9. The term *"urabideo"* refers to illegally made amateur or underground videos. In this novel, Kirino makes reference to a whole subgenre that features abortions, suicides, and gang rapes, but she fictionalizes the content. In 1992, the AV Human Rights Network was founded after revelations that one video had used actual rape scenes. The network offers assistance to women who have been victims of "involuntary" performances and breach of contract disputes. Tomoko Yunomae, "Commodified Sex (Sexism): Japan's Pornographic Culture," in *AMPO-Japan Asia Quarterly Review,* ed., *Voices of the Japanese Women's Movement,* 108. For more on the history of AV in Japan, see Akagawa Manabu, "AV no shakai shi," (The social history of AV), in Ueno Chizuko, ed., *Iro to yoku,* especially 179–186.

10. A cursory survey of a selection of American women's mysteries reveals that almost 90 percent are narrated in the first person. These include novels by Sara

Paretsky, Sue Grafton, Janet Evanovich, and Patricia Cornwell, as well as by lesser known authors like Linda Barnes, Diane Mott Davidson, and Karen Kijiewski.

11. Walton and Jones, *Detective Agency,* 151.

12. Ibid., 152.

13. Ibid., 159.

14. Kirino Natsuo, *Kao ni furikakeru ame* (Her face, veiled in rain) (Tokyo: Kodansha, 1993). Translations are mine, and all references are given parenthetically in the text.

15. Linda Williams, *Hard Core: Power, Pleasure and the "Frenzy of the Visible"* (Berkeley: University of California Press, 1999), 269.

16. When I refer to pornography in this chapter, I mean hard-core pornography that does not include sadomasochistic elements. Hard-core, which is distinguished from soft-core by the inclusion of close-up scenes of penetration, also includes the "money shot" (a representation of a male ejaculating).

17. For classic statements of this position, see Catharine A. MacKinnon, "Only Words," in Gould, ed., *Gender,* 440-441, and Andrea Dworkin, *Pornography: Men Possessing Women* (New York: Perigee Books, 1979). Two notable challenges to this view are Linda Williams' *Hard Core* and Laura Kipnis' "(Male) Desire and (Female) Disgust: Reading *Hustler,*" in *Cultural Studies,* ed. Lawrence Grossberg, Cary Nelson, and Paula Treichler (New York: Routledge, 1992), 373–404. Similar debates have taken place in Japan, with particular attention by feminists to the imbrication of sex and violence. See Shirafuji Kayako, ed., *Porunogurafuii: Yureru shisen no seijigaku* (Pornography: The blurred line of political science) (Tokyo: Gakuyo shobo, 1992). Particularly helpful are two roundtable conversations in this volume contrasting male and female attitudes on the subject: Shirafuji Kayako and Yamaguchi Bunken, "Ren'ai to poruno no aida fukai dobu" (The chasm separating love and porn), 6–21, and Shirafuji Kayako and Saito Ayako, "*Osama no monogatari* o dō yomu ka" (How to read *The Story of O*), 22–34. On Japan's much stricter censorship of pornographic images and the recent loosening of these restrictions, see Anne Allison, *Permitted and Prohibited Desires: Mothers, Comics and Censorship in Japan* (Boulder, Colo.: Westview Press, 1996), especially 147–175.

18. Walton and Jones, *Detective Agency,* 164–165.

19. Maggie Humm, "Legal Aliens: Feminist Detective Fiction," in *Border Traffic: Strategies of Contemporary Women Writers* (Manchester: Manchester University Press, 1991), 203.

20. Williams, *Hard Core,* 102.

21. Dennis Porter, *The Pursuit of Crime: Art and Ideology in Detective Fiction* (New Haven, Conn.: Yale University Press, 1981), 241; compare Geraldine Pederson-Krag, "Detective Stories and the Primal Scene," in *Poetics of Murder: Detective Fiction and Literary Theory,* ed. Glenn W. Most and William W. Stowe (New York: Harcourt, Brace, and Jovanovich, 1983), 13–20.

22. Walton and Jones, *Detective Agency,* 164.

23. Williams, *Hard Core,* 49.

24. Tzvetan Todorov, *Poetics of Prose,* trans. Richard Howard (Ithaca, N.Y.: Cornell University Press, 1977), 44.

25. Williams, *Hard Core*, 246–264.

26. Walter Benjamin, *Charles Baudelaire: A Lyric Poet in the Era of High Capitalism*, trans. Harry Zohn (London: Verso, 1973), 90.

27. Munt, *Murder by the Book?* 120.

28. Phyllis M. Betz, "Playing the Boys' Game," in Gosselin, ed., *Multicultural Detective Fiction*, 86.

29. The majority of detective novels featuring lesbian detectives are published in the United States by small, feminist presses. Within the past five years, however, a growing number of these novels have appeared from mainstream presses. In general, see Munt, *Murder By the Book?* and Betz, "Playing the Boys' Game."

30. Jennifer Robertson, "Dying to Tell: Sexuality and Suicide in Imperial Japan," *Signs* 25, no. 1 (autumn 1999): 21.

31. Minako Hara, "Lesbians and Sexual Self-Determination," in *AMPO-Japan Asia Quartely Review*, ed., *Voices from the Japanese Women's Movement*, 130.

32. This distinction has not been limited to lesbianism, but applies to homosexuality as well. For more on changing Japanese attitudes toward male-male sexuality, see Pflugfelder, *Cartographies of Desire*.

33. Marty Roth, *Fair and Foul Play: Reading Genre in Classic Detective Fiction* (Athens, Ga.: University of Georgia Press, 1995), 121.

34. Ibid., 123.

35. Walton and Jones, *Detective Agency*, 193.

36. *"Shōjo shōsetsu"* in this prewar context has a meaning different from that given to the term by John Whittier Treat in his study of Yoshimoto Banana. While both refer to literature written for young, unmarried women, Treat's *"shōjo"* (girls) do not produce anything and are nothing but consumers. Furthermore, these contemporary young women are infantilized (by choice) to the point where they are unable to participate in the sexual economy. For more, see John Whittier Treat: "Yoshimoto Banana Writes Home," and "Yoshimoto Banana's *Kitchen*, or the Cultural Logic of Japanese Consumerism," in *Women, Media, and Consumption in Japan*, ed. Lise Skov and Brian Moeran (Honolulu: University of Hawai'i Press, 1996), 274–298.

37. For more on Yoshiya's life and lesbianism, see Jennifer Robertson, "Yoshiya Nobuko: Out and Outspoken in Practice and Prose," in *The Human Tradition in Modern Japan,* ed. Anne Walthall (Wilmington, Del.: SR Books, 2002), 155–174.

38. One explanation for the prominence of the Kansai as a place for lesbian double suicides is the popularity there of the Takarazuka, the all-woman revue that served as a focal point for the nascent lesbian subculture in the region, as well as a stimulus for many of the more notorious suicides and parasuicides. See Robertson, "Dying to Tell." Another theory concerns the prevalence of traveling female salespersons in the Kansai area whose housecalls were said to promote a new kind of female relationship. On this, see Kataoka Teppei, "Josei fuan to dōseiai" (Women's discontent and homosexuality), *Kaizō*, March 1934, 78–84.

39. Robertson, "Dying to Tell," 28.

40. Ibid., 30.

41. Tanizaki Junichiro, *Quicksand (Manji)*, trans. Howard Hibbett (New York: Alfred A, Knopf, 1994).

42. Iwabuchi Hiroko, "Rezubianizumu no yuragi Miyamoto Yuriko 'Ippon no hana'" (The tremor of lesbianism in Miyamoto Yuriko's "One Flower"), in Iwabuchi Hiroko, et al., eds., *Hueminizumu hihyō e no shōtai,* 149–174.

43. See Enchi Fumiko, *Onnamen* (Masks), trans. Juliet Winters Carpenter (New York: Vintage, 1983): "To be supremely beautiful . . . a woman's skin had to glow with the internal life-force of spring's earliest buds unfolding naturally in the sun. But city women, too clever with makeup, lost that perishable, flowerlike beauty at a surprisingly early age. . . . So musing, Mikame gazed fixedly at Yasuko, her face clear and moist as just-opened petals" (15). Compare Enchi's description of the beautiful but simpleminded Harume, "like a large white flower bathed in light, magnificent in her isolation" (39).

44. See Robertson, "Dying to Tell," 9.

45. While the pronoun *"kanojo"* does not appear as frequently in Japanese as does its English equivalent, it is used in similar situations. Although the author does not use *"kanojo,"* she does employ its male analog. This usage changes, however, in the subsequent novels.

46. It should be noted that this violation of Henry James' dictum that point of view is the "fourth unity of fiction" has a precedent in Japanese *junbungaku*—for example, Shiga Naoya's *Anya kōro* (A dark night's passage).

47. Compare here Andrea Dworkin's insistence that penile penetration is "by definition violent," in *Intercourse* (New York: Free Press, 1987), 63.

48. Even within the category of "ladies' comics," a genre designed for women, many styles of sexual intercourse are portrayed. Not all *manga* feature the exploitative male domination of women. For more on the types of "ladies' comics," see Fujimoto Yukari, "Onna no yokubo no katachi: Redeisu komikkusu ni miru onna no sei gensho" (The structure of women's desire: The sexual phenomenon as seen in ladies' comics), in Shirafuji Kayako, ed., *Porunogurafuii,* 70–90.

49. Allison, *Permitted and Prohibited Desires,* 62.

50. George Lakoff and Mark Johnson, *Metaphors We Live By* (Chicago: University of Chicago Press, 1980), 9.

51. Interestingly, lilies of the valley, which denote beauty and gaiety in the West, seem to have a symbolic connection to schoolgirl crushes in Japan, particularly in the works of Yoshiya.

52. Shibata Yoshiki, *Seibo no fukaki fuchi,* 103.

53. Walton and Jones, *Detective Agency,* 104.

54. Luce Irigaray, *This Sex Which Is Not One,* trans. Catherine Porter and Carolyn Burke (Ithaca, N.Y.: Cornell University Press, 1985), 160–161.

55. Walton and Jones, *Detective Agency,* 105.

56. Bessatsu Takarajima Henshubuhen, ed., *Kono misuterii ga sugoi!* 201.

57. Ikegami Fuyuki, ed., *Misuteri besuto 201 Nihonban,* 214. I would suggest that the critical focus upon the novel's male rape scenes, rather than its lesbian plotline, is due to Shibata's use of the language of *manga* for many of her sexual descriptions, thus offering the male reader a voyeuristic glimpse into Riko's sex life. Sex between women is a common trope in pornography and is considered a precursor to a woman being penetrated by a man. The opposite, however, does not hold true. Men

are penetrated by other men only in gay pornography, a type of pornography that does not share the same crossover appeal. Thus, the male rapes strike male critics as unfamiliar, startling, and hence memorable, despite the fact that they are a minor part of the novel. Riko's recuperation back into the patriarchal world by her acceptance of Andō's marriage proposal could be read in this context as the end of the novel's lesbian "foreplay."

58. See Shibata's afterword to *Seibo no fukaki fuchi*, 326.

59. Sandra Buckley, "The Foreign Devil Returns: Packaging Sexual Practice and Risk in Contemporary Japan," in *Sites of Desire, Economies of Pleasure: Sexualities in Asia and the Pacific*, ed. Lenore Manderson and Margaret Jolly (Chicago: University of Chicago Press, 1997), 274.

60. Narita Ryuichi, "The Overflourishing of Sexuality in 1920s Japan," trans. Sarah Teasley, in *Gender and Japanese History*, vol. 1, ed. Wakita Haruko, Anne Bouchy, and Ueno Chizuko (Osaka: Osaka University Press, 1999), 347.

61. Sabine Frühstück, "Managing the Truth of Sex in Imperial Japan," *Journal of Asian Studies* 59, no. 2 (May 2000): 332–358.

62. For more on this topic, see Donald Roden, "Taisho Culture and the Problem of Gender Ambivalence," in *Culture and Identity: Japanese Intellectuals during the Interwar Years*, ed. J. Thomas Rimer (Princeton, N.J.: Princeton University Press, 1990), 37–55.

63. Edogawa Rampo, *Kuro Tokage* (Black Lizard), in *Edogawa Ranpo chōhen zenshū* (Collected works of Edogawa Rampo), vol. 10 (Tokyo: Shunyōdo, 1972), 2–142.

64. Shinjuku ni-chome is a section of the entertainment area of Shinjuku, whose bars and clubs form the epicenter of gay nightlife in Tokyo (if not all of Japan). For a firsthand account of Shinjuku ni-chome and its culture, see John Whittier Treat, *Great Mirrors Shattered: Homosexuality, Orientalism, and Japan* (New York: Oxford University Press, 1999).

65. Munt, *Murder By the Book?* 57.

66. Shibata, *Seibo no fukaki fuchi*, 23–24.

67. Ibid., 24.

68. Sue Grafton and Bruce Taylor, "G Is for (Sue) Grafton: An Interview with the Creator of the Kinsey Millhone Private Eye Series," *Armchair Detective* 22, no. 1 (1989): 12.

69. David Glover, "The Stuff That Dreams Are Made of: Masculinity, Femininity and the Thriller," in *Gender, Genre, and Narrative Pleasure*, ed. Derek Longhurst (London: Unwin Hyman, 1989), 80.

70. Eva Feder Kittay, "Pornography and the Erotics of Domination," in Gould, ed., *Gender*, 431.

Chapter 5: Sexing the City

1. In addition to the four stories published in 1994, Matsuo published one more installment three years later: "Baruun Taun no ura mado" (Balloon Town's rear window), *Shōsetsu tripper*, winter 1997, 66–80. In this story, the characters of Mio and Marina have become legendary, and the puzzle is solved by Mio's apprentice Natsuo,

who is just beginning to test her powers of detection. In 2000, Matsuo published a sequel called *Baruun Taun no tejinashi* (The sorcerer of Balloon Town) (Tokyo: Bungei shunjū, 2000), and in 2002 she published another collection of stories based on the Balloon Town characters called *Baruun Taun no temari uta* (Handball songs of Balloon Town) (Tokyo: Bungei shunjū, 2002).

2. Deutsche, *"Chinatown,* Part IV?" 189.

3. Gunning, "Tracing the Individual Body," 20.

4. See Tomita Hitoshi, *Ranpo Tokyo chizu* (The Rampo Tokyo criminology map) (Tokyo: Sakuhinsha, 1997), which is full of pictures and hand-drawn maps giving specific locations for the stories' settings. For Rampo's relationship to the world of prewar Tokyo, see Matsuyama's *Ranpo to Tokyo.*

5. Munt, *Murder By the Book?* 140.

6. Rosalyn Deutsche, *"Chinatown,* Part IV?" 245.

7. R. G. Kelly, *Mystery Fiction and Modern Life,* 29.

8. Margaret A. Rose, *Parody: Ancient, Modern and Postmodern* (Cambridge: Cambridge University Press, 1993), 52.

9. Ibid., 83.

10. Judith Butler, "Merely Cultural," *Social Text 52/53* (fall/winter 1997): 266.

11. Elizabeth Grosz, "Bodies/Cities," in Colomina, ed., *Sexuality and Space,* 250.

12. Nancy Fraser points out that the phrase "public sphere," when used by contemporary feminists to refer to everything that is outside the domestic or familial sphere, tends to conflate "at least three analytically distinct things: the state, the official-economy of paid employment, and arenas of public discourse." The term that I am using, "public arena," is meant to foreground the physical and imaginary *site* for social, political, and economic activities and discourse. See Nancy Fraser, "Rethinking the Public Sphere: A Contribution to the Critique of Actually Existing Democracy," in *Postmodernism and the Re-reading of Modernity,* ed. Francis Barker, Peter Hulme, and Margaret Iverson (Manchester: Manchester University Press, 1992), 198.

13. Carole Pateman, "Feminist Critiques of the Public/Private Dichotomy," in *The Disorder of Women: Democracy, Feminism, and Political Theory* (Stanford, Calif.: Stanford University Press, 1989), 121–123.

14. Ibid., 125.

15. Elizabeth Grosz, "Women, Chora, Dwelling," in *Postmodern Cities and Spaces,* ed. Sophie Watson and Katherine Gibson (Oxford: Blackwell, 1995), 55.

16. Recent research has challenged this notion. Mark Wigley ("Untitled: The Housing of Gender," in Colomina, ed., *Sexuality and Space,* 327–389) points out that although the home was a place for women, they were not in charge of the house either financially or spatially. Whereas the husband had access to the entire house, there often were rooms (e.g., the study) to which women were denied access. In such male spaces the financial records were often kept. Moreover, department stores were not universally the province of women, as Gail Reekie and Noriko Aso have indicated in the cases of Australia and Japan respectively. Of course, within the department store there are distinctly gendered areas for both men and women. See Gail Reekie, "Changes in the Adamless Eden: The Spatial and Sexual Transformation of a Brisbane Department Store, 1930–1990," in *Lifestyle Shopping: The Subject of Consumption,* ed. Rob

Shields (London: Routledge, 1992), 170–194, and Noriko Aso, "Tradition and Modernity in Pre-War Japanese Department Stores," paper presented at the annual meeting of the Association for Asian Studies, Washington D.C., 26–28, March 1998.

17. Kathleen S. Uno, "Women and Changes in the Household Division of Labor," in Bernstein, ed., *Recreating Japanese Women*, 17–41.

18. Sievers, *Flowers in Salt*, 52.

19. Kathleen S. Uno, "Death of 'Good Wife, Wise Mother,'" in Gordon, ed., *Postwar Japan as History*, 299.

20. Sharon Nolte and Sally Ann Hastings point out that at first this ideology pertained to women in the new middle class since it was not economically feasible for women of lower classes not to work outside the home. After 1900 it was added to the curriculum of elementary schools, thus reaching larger numbers of children. Sharon Nolte and Sally Ann Hastings, "The Meiji State's Policy toward Women," in Bernstein, ed., *Recreating Japanese Women*, 151–174.

21. Uno, "Death of 'Good Wife, Wise Mother,'" 299.

22. Matsuo clearly is influenced here by the writings of Shulamith Firestone, who argues bluntly that pregnancy is barbaric and that childbirth is an unnecessary source of pain for women. Her solution is "cybernation," or an artificial means of gestation that would not only free women from painful childbirth but also provide an alternative to the oppressions of the biological family and allow for a total redefinition of the economy. Shulamith Firestone, *The Dialectic of Sex: The Case for Feminist Revolution* (New York: William Morrow, 1970), 226–230.

23. Matsuo Yumi, *Baruun Taun no satsujin* (Murder in Balloon Town) (Tokyo: Hayakawa, 1994). Translations are mine, and all references are given parenthetically in the text. An abbreviated version of my translation of "Baruun Taun no satsujin" can be found in Larry McCaffrey, Tatsumi Takayuki, and Sinda Gordon, eds., *New Japanese Fiction, Review of Contemporary Fiction* 22, no. 2 (2002): 91–110.

24. In an interview with Matsuo, it was suggested that Balloon Town was based on present-day Aoyama. Akagi Kanko, "Atto Iwaseru Matsuo Yumi no monogatari settei" (Of course! Matsuo Yumi's story settings), *Hayakawa Mystery Magazine* 489 (December 1996): 226. In a subsequent conversation, Matsuo told me that she originally had been inspired by Nerima, near Hikarigaoa Park, but that the description in her novel turned out to be closer to Aoyama than she had realized.

25. Suitengu Shrine, located in Ningyo-cho, Tokyo, is visited by women in their fifth month of pregnancy; in addition to praying, they also purchase *hara obi* (belly bands—see below), *omamori* (amulets) for a safe birth, and maternity clothes and toys. Dogs, due to their purported ability to give birth painlessly, have become symbols of the shrine, and each "day of the dog" on the zodiacal calendar brings especially large crowds. See Hamano Takuya, *Tokyo Suitengu monogatari* (The story of Tokyo's Suitengu Shrine) (Tokyo: Kodansha, 1985).

26. As Matsuo has explained, "I mentioned in the text the maternity dress boutique 'Coquille d'Oeuf' (eggshell) more than once. It was because I was shocked by the name of an existing (or existed, when I myself was pregnant) maternity dress brand 'Blanc d'Oeuf' (white of the egg). Isn't it weird? I liked (or hated) it so much, I parodied it and used it in the book. The real brand 'Blanc d'Oeuf' is a subbrand of

a big fashion brand, 'Comme Ça de Mode,' whose headquarters is, I believe, in Aoyama." Personal communication (in English) from the author, 6 November 1997.

27. Grosz, "Bodies/Cities," 243.

28. Harvey, *Justice, Nature, and the Geography of Difference*, especially 295–299.

29. Ibid., 245.

30. Poet Itō Hiromi's book *Ii oppai, warui oppai* (Good breasts, bad breasts) (Tokyo: Shueisha bunko, 1992) on her own pregnancy is a refreshing change. Dealing with the earthier aspects of pregnancy, birth, and baby care, Ito's book proved popular with readers and was turned into a movie.

31. Crawford, "Investigating the City," 121.

32. Grosz, "Bodies/Cities," 242.

33. Diana Algrest, Patricia Conway, and Leslie Kanes Weisman, "Introduction," in Algrest et al., eds., *The Sex of Architecture*, 11.

34. M. Christine Boyer, "Crimes in and of the City: The *Femme Fatale* as Urban Allegory," in Algrest et al., eds., *The Sex of Architecture*, 99.

35. Deutsche, "*Chinatown*, Part IV?" 197; Boyer, "Crimes in and of the City," 100; and Rosalyn Deutsche, "Men in Space," in Deutsche, *Evictions*, 197.

36. Grosz, "Women, Chora, Dwelling," 54.

37. Peter Fitting, "Recent Feminist Utopias: World Building and Strategies for Social Change," in *Mindscapes: The Geographies of Imagined Worlds*, ed. George E. Slusser and Eric S. Rabkin (Carbondale, Ill.: Southern Illinois University Press, 1989), 158.

38. For more detail on the divisions of Edo/Tokyo and how the city has changed, see Jinnai Hidenobu, *Tokyo: A Spatial Anthropology*, trans. Kimiko Nishimura (Berkeley: University of California Press, 1995).

39. Sheldon Garon, *Molding Japanese Minds: The State in Everyday Life* (Princeton, N.J.: Princeton University Press, 1997), 115.

40. Masami Ohinata, "The Mystique of Motherhood: A Key to Understanding Social Change and Family Problems in Japan," trans. Timothy John Phelan; in *Japanese Women: New Feminist Perspectives on the Past, Present, and Future*, ed. Kumiko Fujimura-Fanselow and Atsuko Kameda (New York: Feminist Press at the City University of New York, 1995), 204.

41. Yoshiko Miyake, "Doubling Expectations: Motherhood and Women's Factory Work under State Management in Japan in the 1930s and 1940s," in Bernstein, ed., *Recreating Japanese Women*, 268.

42. Uno, "Death of 'Good Wife, Wise Mother,'" 300.

43. Ibid., 303.

44. Quoted in Arioka Jiro, "Fewer Babies: A Private Matter?" *Japan Quarterly* 36, no. 1 (January–March 1991): 51.

45. David E. Sanger, "Tokyo Official Ties Birth Decline to Education," *New York Times*, 14 June 1990, A9. This incident received more coverage in Sanger's "Babies, Rice Farms, and Diplomas," *New York Times*, 20 June 1990, A24.

46. For more on the royal wedding, see Amanda Seaman, "Modeling Masako: Commodities and the Construction of a Modern Princess," *Chicago Anthropology Exchange* 21 (spring 1995): 35–70.

47. The *Japan Times* help-wanted sections every Monday are full of advertisements looking for women to work in foreign companies. The interpreting schools in Tokyo, moreover, are filled with young women looking for ways to start new careers.

48. Muriel Jolivet, *Japan: The Childless Society,* trans. Anne-Marie Glasheen (New York: Routledge, 1997), 42–43.

49. Ibid., 50.

50. Ibid., 77.

51. Ibid., 80–81.

52. Ibid., 82.

53. Ibid., 85.

54. Funabashi Keiko, "Reassessing the Value of Children, " *Japan Echo* 26, no. 1 (February 1999): 34.

55. Currently, the Tokyo metropolitan government requires that all women residents register their pregnancies with their ward offices. When a resident becomes pregnant, she must take an official pregnancy test and register her pregnancy with the Koseki Juminka, or the Family Register Section, whereupon she will receive the *boshi kenko techō* (mother-child health handbook), provided for "recording health exams prior to childbirth, the condition of the mother and child after birth, and the growth of the child. This handbook is required when receiving health check-ups and vaccines." From Bunkyo-ku Kuyakusho, *Bunkyo-ku e yōkōso.*

56. Funabashi, "Reassessing the Value of Children," 34.

57. Kawamura Kunimitsu, *Sekushuaritei no kindai* (Sexuality's modernity) (Tokyo: Kodansha, 1996), 20.

58. My thanks to Julie Christ for sharing her unpublished 1998 paper, "Conquering but Not Controlling: Yanagi Sōetsu and His Creation of the *Mingei* Discourse."

59. This is the concept of *tentō,* or inversion, employed by Karatani Kojin in his *Origins of Modern Japanese Literature.*

60. This physical separation of a pregnant woman from the rest of society was seen as total. "Then by the edge of the beach, a parturition hut was built, thatched with cormorant feathers. But before the parturition hut had been completely thatched, the urgency of her womb became unendurable, and she entered into the parturition hut." *Kojiki,* ed. and trans. Donald L. Phillipi (Tokyo: University of Tokyo Press, 1968), I.45.3–4.

61. The practice was followed from the Heian (794–1185) through the Kamakura (1185–1333) eras, after which it waned among the upper classes. Iinuma Kenji, "Chūsei zenki no josei no shōgai—Jinsei no shodankai no kentō o tojite" (The lives of women in the late middle ages: An examination of the phases of a person's life), in *Nihon josei seikatsushi* (The history of women's lives), ed. Josei Sōgō Kenkyukai (Tokyo: Tokyo daigaku shuppansha, 1990), 40.

62. *Kojiki,* 66n. 15.

63. In the later Heian period (794–1185), *kegare,* or the imbalance between man and nature brought about by the presence of pollution from processes of childbirth and death, became a pressing concern of the Kyoto nobility, leading to the creation of special bounded spaces for the containment of pollution. Amino Yoshihiko, *Nihon*

no rekishi o yominaosu (Rereading Japanese history) (Tokyo: Chikuma primaa bukkusu 50, 1991), 90–91. Mary Douglas has suggested that such preoccupations with the boundaries of the body stem from concerns over challenges to community boundaries. See her *Purity and Danger: An Analysis of Concepts of Pollution and Taboo* (London: Routledge, 1966).

64. Nishiyama Yayoi, "The Hidden World of the Parturition Hut," *Feminist International* 2 (1980): 66.

65. See in particular Mandel, *Delightful Murder.*

66. Interestingly, Matsuo's work has become popular among people who read maternity magazines for its depiction of *ninpu bunka* (the culture of pregnancy). Kotani Mari, "Moshimo. . . to iu jikkenba de josei SF sakka ni totte no haha" (What if . . . women SF writers experiment with writing mothers), in *Bosei fuashisumu: Haha naru jizen no yuwaku* (Maternal fascism: the temptation of natural motherhood), ed. Kano Mikiyo (Tokyo: Gakuya, 1995), 187.

67. Crawford, "Investigating the City," 125; Klein, *The Woman Detective,* 173–174.

68. Munt, *Murder By the Book?* 194.

Afterword

1. Mason, "Nancy Drew," 79.

2. Kirino Natsuo, "Rōzu gaaden," in Kirino, *Rōzu gaaden* (Rose garden) (Tokyo: Kodansha, 2000), 5–78.

3. While the Japanese media focused on the shocking aspects of Kirino's novel, it is worth noting that in two long interviews with the author neither interviewer asked her about the book's final rape scene, focusing instead upon the idea of housewives dismembering corpses for money. See Saito Yukari, "Kirino Natsuo: Rongu intabyu" (Kirino Natsuo: Long interview), *In Pocket,* June–July 2002, 3–23, and Kogura Chūtaro, "Onna tachi no kodoku na tataki" (Women's solitary struggle), *Yurika,* December 1999, 60–69.

4. Matsuo Yumi, "Murder in Balloon Town," trans. Amanda Seaman in *New Japanese Fiction,* ed. Gordon and McCaffrey, 91–110.

5. Miyabe Miyuki, *Mohohan* (The copycat) (Tokyo: Shogakkan, 2001).

6. On the phenomenon of niche marketing in Japan more generally, see Ivy, "Formations of Mass Culture." As in other industries, the recent rise of the Internet has allowed publishing houses like Shinchosha to supplement older gauges of interest, such as reader response cards *(aidokusho)* and readers' clubs, with more effective and instantaneous avenues for consumer feedback.

7. Howard W. French, "Hot New Marketing Concept: Mall as Memory Lane," *New York Times* (online edition), 7 January 2003.

Bibliography

Japanese Sources

Akagawa Manabu. "AV no shakai shi" (The social history of adult video). In Ueno Chizuko, ed., *Iro to yoku*, Ueno Chizuko, 167–190.

Akagi Kanko. "Atto iwaseru Matsuo Yumi no monogatari settei" (Of course! Matsuo Yumi's story settings). *Hayakawa Mystery Magazine* 489 (December 1996): 226–230.

Amino Yoshihiko. *Nihon no rekishi no yominaosu* (Rereading Japanese history). Tokyo: Chikuma primaa bukkusu 50, 1991.

Aoki Chie. "Kogoeru kiba" (Frozen fangs). In Ikegami Fuyuki, ed., *Misuteri besuto 201 Nihonban*, 216.

Arai Noriko. "Nonami Asa: Kono hito no ikikata ga suteki 42" (Nonami Asa: great lives, no. 42). *Oggi (Japan)*, March 1997, 154–159.

Bessatsu Takarajima Henshubuhen, ed. *Kono misuterii ga sugoi! Kessakusen* (This mystery is great! A selection of masterpieces). Tokyo: Takarajimasha, 1997.

Bunkyō-ku Kuyakusho. *Bunkyō-ku e yōkōso* (Welcome to Bunkyo Ward). Tokyo: Bunkyō-ku Kuyakusho, December 1995.

Edogawa Ranpo. *Edogawa Rampo: Tales of Mystery and Imagination*. Trans. James B. Harris. Rutland, Vt.: Charles E. Tuttle, 1956.

_____. *Kuro Tokage* (Black Lizard). In *Edogawa Ranpo chōhen zenshū* (Collected works of Edogawa Rampo), 10: 2–142. Tokyo: Shunyōdo, 1972.

_____. *Tantei shōsetsu yonjūnen* (Forty years of detective fiction). Tokyo: Chūsekisha, 1989.

_____. "Yaneura no sanpōsha" (A stroller in the attic). In *Edogawa Ranpo meisakushū* (Best-known works of Edogawa Rampo), 3: 143–185. Tokyo: Shunyōdo, 1959.

Enchi Fumiko. *Onnamen* (Masks). Trans. Juliet Winters Carpenter. New York: Vintage, 1983.

Fujimoto Yukari. "Onna no yokubo no katachi: Redeisu komikkusu ni miru onna no sei gensho" (The structure of women's desire: The sexual phenomenon as seen in ladies' comics). In Shirafuji Kayako, ed., *Porunogurafuii*, 70–90.

Hamano Takuya. *Tokyo Suitengu monogatari* (The story of Tokyo's Suitengu Shrine). Tokyo: Kodansha, 1985.

Hayami Yukiko. "Akutagawa-sho wa tsumaranai" (The Akutagawa Prize is boring). *Aera*, 1 January 1996, 46–52.

Hayashi Eriko. *Onna tantei monogatari: Serisawa Masako jikenbo* (A tale of a woman detective: The record of Serisawa Masako). Tokyo: Rokufun shuppan, 1990.

Hirabayashi Hatsunosuke. "Nihon no kindaiteki tantei shōsetsu—toku ni Edogawa Rampo ni oite" (Japan's modern detective fiction—in particular, Edogawa Rampo). In *Bungei hiron zenshū*, 3: 220–227. Tokyo: Bunseido shoten, 1976.

Hirabayashi Taiko. "Irezumi jiken no shinsō" (The truth about the tattoo affair). In *Hirabayashi Taiko zenshū* (The collected works of Hirabayashi Taiko), 1: 32–39. Tokyo: Asahi shuppansha, 1979.

———. "Supai jiken" (The spy incident). In *Hirabayashi Taiko zenshū*, 1: 14–19. Tokyo: Asahi shuppansha, 1979.

———. "Tantei shōsetsu mandan" (A chat about detective fiction). In *Hirabayashi Taiko zenshū*, 10: 308–310. Tokyo: Asahi shuppansha, 1979.

Hirano Ken, Itō Sei, and Yamamoto Kenkichi. "Junbungaku to taishūbungaku" (Pure and popular literature). *Gunzo*, October 1961, 154–172.

Ienaga Saburo. *The Pacific War, 1931–1945.* Trans. Frank Baldwin. New York: Pantheon Books, 1978.

Iinuma Kenji. "Chūsei zenki no josei no shōgai: Jinsei no shodankai no kentō o tojite" (The lives of women in the late Middle Ages: An examination of the phases of a person's life). In *Nihon josei seikatsushi* (The history of women's lives), ed. Josei Sōgō Kenkyukai, 31–74. Tokyo: Tokyo daigaku shuppansha, 1990.

Ikegami Fuyuki, ed. *Misuteri besuto 201 Nihonban* (201 best Japanese mysteries). Tokyo: Shinshokan, 1997.

Ikeshita Ikuko and Kirino Natsuo. "Yonjūdai wa onna no yūjō no migakidoki" (The forties are a time for polishing women's friendships). *Fujin kōron*, March 1996, 117–122.

Inoue Ken. "Honyaku sareta gunshū: 'Gunshū no hito' no keifu to kindai Nihon" (Translated crowd: The geneology of "The Man in the Crowd" and modern Japan). *Hiten bungaku kenkyū* 69 (December 1996): 37–66.

Itō Hideo. *Showa no tantei shōsetsu* (Showa-era detective fiction). Tokyo: San'ichi shobo, 1993.

———. *Taisho no tantei shōsetsu* (Taisho-era detective fiction). Tokyo: San'ichi shobo, 1991.

Itō Hiromi. *Ii oppai, warui oppai* (Good breasts, bad breasts). Tokyo: Shueisha bunko, 1992.

Itō Sei. "'Jun' bungaku wa sonzai shiuru ka?" (Does "pure" literature exist?). *Gunzo*, November 1961, 180–187.

Iwabuchi Hiroko. "Rezubianizumu no yuragi—Miyamoto Yuriko 'Ippon no hana'" (The tremor of lesbianism in Miyamoto Yuriko's "One Flower"). In Iwabuchi Hiroko et al., eds., *Hueminizumu no hihyō e no shōtai*, 149–174.

Iwabuchi Hiroko, Kitada Sachie, and Koura Rumiko, eds. *Hueminizumu no hihyō e no shōtai: Kindai josei bungaku o yomu* (An introduction to feminist criticism: Reading modern women's literature). Tokyo: Bungei shorin, 1994.

Jinnai Hidenobu. *Tokyo: A Spatial Anthropology.* Trans. Kimiko Nishimura. Berkeley: University of California Press, 1995.

"Kao ni furikakaru ame, Kirino Natsuo" (Her face, veiled in rain, Kirino Natsuo) *Hōseki,* December 1993, 295.

Karatani Kojin. *Origins of Modern Japanese Literature.* Trans. Brett de Bary et al. Durham, N.C.: Duke University Press, 1993.

Kasai Kiyoshi. "Tantei shōsetsu no chisōgaku" (Excavating mysteries). In Kasai Kiyoshi, ed., *Honkaku misuteri no genzai,* 5–21.

_____. "Tantei shōsetsu to keishiki" (Detective fiction and its form). In *Nyū weibu misuteri dokuhon* (Reading new wave mysteries), ed. Yamaguchi Masaya, 222–227. Tokyo: Hara shobo, 1997.

_____, ed. *Honkaku misuteri no genzai* (The new wave of Japanese mystery). Tokyo: Kokusho kankōkai, 1997.

Kataoka, Teppei. "Josei fuan to dōseiai" (Women's discontent and homosexuality). *Kaizō,* March 1934, 78–84.

Kawamura Kunimitsu. *Sekushuaritei no kindai* (Sexuality's modernity). Tokyo: Kodansha, 1996.

Kirino Natsuo. *Fuaiabooru burusu* (Fireball blues). Tokyo: Bunshun bunko, 1998.

_____. *Kao ni furikakaru ame* (Her face, veiled in rain). Tokyo: Kodansha, 1993.

_____. *Out.* Tokyo: Kodansha, 1997.

_____. *Rōzu gaaden* (Rose garden). Tokyo: Kodansha, 2000.

_____. *Tenshi ni misuterareta yoru* (Night abandoned by angels). Tokyo: Kodansha, 1994.

Kogura Chūtaro. "Onnatachi no kodoku na tatakai" (Women's solitary struggle). *Yurika,* December 1999, 60–69.

Kojiki. Ed. and trans. Donald L. Phillipi. Tokyo: University of Tokyo Press, 1968.

Kotani Mari. "Moshimo . . . to iu jikkenba de josei SF sakka ni totte no haha" (What if . . . women SF writers experiment with writing mothers). In *Bosei fuashisumu: Haha naru jizen no yuwaku* (Maternal fascism: The temptation of natural motherhood), ed. Kano Mikiyo, 186–193. Tokyo: Gakuya shobo, 1995.

Maeda Ai. "Yamanote no oku" (In the recesses of the high city). In *Toshi kūkan no naka no bungaku* (Literature in the context of the city). Tokyo: Chikuma shobo, 1989.

Matsumoto Kenichi. "Modanismu kara fuashizumu e: *Shinseinen* to Ranpo/Kyūsaku" (From modernism to fascism: *Shinseinen* and Rampo/Kyūsaku). *Kokubungaku* 36, no. 3 (March 1991): 20–28.

Matsumoto Seichō. "The Face" (Kao). In *The Voice and Other Stories.* Trans. Adam Kabat, 27–62. New York: Kodansha, 1989.

_____. *Points and Lines (Ten to sen).* Trans. Makiko Yamamoto and Paul C. Blum. Tokyo: Kodansha, 1986.

Matsuo Yumi. *Baruun Taun no satsujin* (Murder in Balloon Town). Tokyo: Hayakawa, 1994.

_____. *Baruun Taun no tejinashi* (The sorcerer of Balloon Town). Tokyo: Bungei shunjū, 2000.

_____. *Baruun Taun no temari uta* (Handball songs of Balloon Town). Tokyo: Bungei shunjū, 2002.

————. "Baruun Taun no ura mado" (Balloon Town's rear window). *Shōsetsu tripper,* winter 1997, 66–80.

Matsuyama Iwao. *Ranpo to Tokyo: Toshi no kao* (Rampo and Tokyo: The face of the city). Tokyo: Chikuma gakugei bunko, 1994.

McCaffrey, Larry, Tatsumi Takayuki, and Sinda Gordon, eds. *New Japanese Fiction. Review of Contemporary Fiction* 22, no. 2 (2002).

"Misuterii no haba hirogaru." (Interview with Miyabe Miyuki). *Yomiuri shinbun,* 12 October 1994, 8.

Miyabe Miyuki. *Heisei otaho nikki* (The Heisei traveler's diary). Tokyo: Shinchosha, 1998.

————. Interview. Tokyo, 7 February 1997.

————. *Kasha.* Tokyo: Futabasha, 1992. Translated by Alfred Birnbaum as *All She Was Worth.* New York and Tokyo: Kodansha International, 1996.

————. "Mienakute kowai totsukuni" (An unseen foreign land). *Asahi shinbun,* 27 June 1994, 25.

————. *Mohohan* (The copycat), vols. 1 and 2. Tokyo: Shogakkan, 2001.

————. *Riyū* (The reason). Tokyo: Asahi shinbun shuppansha, 1998.

————. *Sabishii karyūdo* (The lonely hunter). Tokyo: Shinchosha, 1993.

————. *Tokyo shitamachi satsujin bōshōku* (Murders in downtown Tokyo). Tokyo: Kobunsha bunko, 1994.

Miyadai Shinji. "'Terekura' no minzokushi" (The folklore of *terekura*). In Ueno Chizuko, ed., *Iro to yoku,* 123–166.

Miyazawa Setsuo. *Policing In Japan: A Study on Making Crime.* Trans. Frank G. Bennett Jr. and John O. Haley. Albany: State University of New York Press, 1992.

Namioka Hisako. "Katari to tomoshibi" (Tales and lanterns). In Kasai Kiyoshi, ed., *Honkaku misuteri no genzai,* 255–279.

"Naoki-sho jushō wa watashi no jinsei no misuterii" (The Naoki Prize is my life's mystery). *Gendai,* September 1993, 103–105.

Narita Akemi. Interview. Tokyo, 28 January 1998.

Narita Ryuichi. "The Overflourishing of Sexuality in 1920s Japan." Trans. Sarah Teasley. In *Gender and Japanese History,* vol. 1, ed. Wakita Haruko, Anne Bouchy, and Ueno Chizuko, 345–370. Osaka: Osaka University Press, 1999.

Nonami Asa. *Hana chiru goro no satsujin* (Murders when the petals scatter). Tokyo: Shincho bunko, 1999.

————. *Kogoeru kiba* (Frozen fangs). Tokyo: Shinchosha, 1996.

————. *Kusari* (Chains). Tokyo: Shinchosha, 2000.

————. *Miren* (Attachment). Tokyo: Shinchosha, 2001.

Nonoyama Yoshitaka. "Sakka no 'gimu' wa shōsetsu o koete" (An author's "duty" goes beyond the novel). *Gendai,* December 1995, 65–69.

Ohba Minako. "The Smile of the Mountain Witch" *(Yamauba no bisho).* In *Japanese Women Writers.* Trans. and ed. Noriko Mizuta Lippit and Kyoko Iriye Selden, 194–206. Armonk, N.Y: M. E. Sharpe, 1991.

Okamoto Kidō. "Umoregi" (Buried tree). *Shufu no tomo,* August 1924, 5.

Omori Nozomi. "Miyabe Miyuki." *Marco Polo* 3, no. 8 (August 1993): 22–27.

"Onna to Jieitai" (Women in the Self-Defense Forces). *Uno!*, February 1997, 164–165.

Saito Yukari. "Kirino Natsuo: Rongu intabyu" (Kirino Natsuo: Long interview). *In Pocket*, June–July 2002, 3–23.

Sakata Makoto. *Sengo o yomu: Gojussatsu no fikushon* (Reading the postwar: Fifty works of fiction). Tokyo: Iwanami shisho, 1995.

Sato Shinichiro. Interview. December 1996.

_____. Interview. July 2002.

Sengai Akiyuki. "Kaisetsu" (Analysis). In Shibata Yoshiki, *Riko—Viinasu no eien*, 390–396.

Shibata Yoshiki. *Daiana no asaki yume* (Diana's daydream). Tokyo: Kadokawa shoten, 1998.

_____. *Riko—Viinasu no eien* (Riko—Forever Venus). Tokyo: Kadokawa bunko, 1995.

_____. *Seibo no fukaki fuchi* (Madonna's abyss). Tokyo: Kadokawa shoten, 1996.

Shinseinen Kenkyukai, ed. *Shinseinen yomihon* (A *Shinseinen* reader). Tokyo: Sakuhinsha, 1988.

Shirafuji Kayako and Saito Ayako. "*Osama no monogatari* o dō yomu ka" (How to read *The Story of O*). In Shirafuji Kayako, ed., *Porunogurafuii*, 22–34.

Shirafuji Kayako and Yamaguchi Bunken. "Ren'ai to poruno no aida fukai dobu" (The chasm separating love and porn). In Shirafuji Kayako, ed., *Porunogurafuii*, 6–21.

Shirafuji Kayako, ed. *Porunogurafuii: Yureru shisen no seijigaku* (Pornography: The blurred line of political science). Tokyo: Gakuyo shobo, 1992.

Sugiyama Tamae. "Aru katei ni okotta futatsu no tantei hiwa" (Two secret investigations in a certain household). *Shufu no tomo*, April 1924, 236–242.

Takamura Kaoru. "Sakakibara seito wa jidai no ko ka ijōsha ka." *Bungei shunjū*, August 1997, 150–158. Translated into English as "Japanese Society and the Psychopath." *Japan Echo* (online edition) 24, no. 4 (October 1999).

"Takamura Kaoru to Miyabe Miyuki supeshiaru taidan" (A conversation between Takamura Kaoru and Miyabe Miyuki). *Shūkan Asahi*, 30 July 1993, 128–132.

Tanaka Yasuo. *Nantonaku, kurisutaru* (Somehow, crystal). Tokyo: Shinchosha, 1980.

Tanizaki Junichiro. "The Incident at the Willow Bathhouse" (Yanagi-yu jiken). Trans. Phyllis I. Lyons. In *Studies in Modern Japanese Literature: Essays and Translation in Honor of Edwin McClellan*, ed. Dennis Washburn and Alan Tansman, 321–339. Ann Arbor: University of Michigan Center for Japanese Studies, 1997.

_____. *Quicksand (Manji)*. Trans. Howard Hibbett. New York: Alfred A. Knopf, 1994.

_____. "The Secret" (Himitsu). Trans. Anthony Hood Chambers. In *New Leaves: Studies and Translation of Japanese Literature in Honor of Edward Seidensticker*, ed. Aileen Gatten and Anthony Hood Chambers, 157–173. Ann Arbor: University of Michigan Center for Japanese Studies, 1993.

Tomita Hitoshi. *Ranpo Tokyo chizu* (The Rampo Tokyo criminology map). Tokyo: Sakuhinsha, 1997.

Ueda Akinari. *Tales of Moonlight and Rain (Ugetsu monogatari)*. Trans. Kenji Hamada. New York: Columbia University Press, 1972.

Ueno Chizuko, ed. *Iro to yoku* (Desire and sex). Tokyo: Shogakkan, 1996.

Yamamae Yuzuru. "Kirino Natsuo." In Yamamae, ed., *Shiro no misuterii*.

_____. "Nihon no josei suiri sakka: Taktōki kara seijukuki e" (Japanese women mystery writers: From prominence to maturity). In Yamamae, ed., *Aka no misuterii*.

_____. "Nihon no josei suiri sakka: Zensei jikai no tōrai" (Japanese women mystery writers: The arrival of the golden age). In Yamamae, ed., *Aka no misuterii*.

_____. "Shibata Yoshiki." In Yamamae, ed., *Shiro no misuterii*.

_____, ed. *Aka no misuterii: Josei no misuterii sakka kessaku* (Red mystery: A collection of women's mysteries). Tokyo: Eibunsha, 1997.

_____, ed. *Shiro no misuterii: Josei misuterii sakka kessaku* (White mystery: A collection of women's mysteries). Tokyo: Eibunsha, 1997.

Yamashita Takeshi. "Joryū tantei sakka daiichigo: Ogura Teruko" (The first woman mystery writer: Ogura Teruko). In *"Shinseinen" o meguru sakkatachi* (Authors of *Shinseinen*). Tokyo: Chikuma shobo, 1996.

Yoshimoto Banana. *Kichin*. Tokyo: Fukutaku shoten, 1991. Translated by Megan Backus as *Kitchen*. New York: Washington Square Press, 1993.

English Sources

Abrams, M. H. *A Glossary of Literary Terms*. New York: Harcourt, Brace, and Jovanovich, 1993.

Algrest, Diana, Patricia Conway, and Leslie Kanes Weisman, eds. *The Sex of Architecture*. New York: Harry Abrams, 1996.

Allison, Anne. *Nightwork: Sexuality, Pleasure, and Corporate Masculinity in a Tokyo Hostess Club*. Chicago: University of Chicago Press, 1994.

_____. *Permitted and Prohibited Desires: Mothers, Comics and Censorship in Japan*. Boulder, Colo.: Westview Press, 1996.

AMPO-Japan Asia Quarterly Review, ed. *Voices of the Japanese Women's Movement*. Armonk, N.Y.: M. E. Sharpe, 1996.

Appier, Janis. *Policing Women: The Sexual Politics of Law Enforcement and the LAPD*. Philadelphia: Temple University Press, 1998.

Arioka, Jiro. "Fewer Babies: A Private Matter?" *Japan Quarterly* 36, no. 1 (January–March 1991): 50–56.

Aso, Noriko. "Tradition and Modernity in Pre-War Japanese Department Stores." Paper presented at the annual meeting of the Association for Asian Studies, Washington, D.C., 26–28 March 1998.

Babener, Liahna. "Uncloseting Ideology in the Novels of Barbara Wilson." In Klein, ed., *Women Times Three*, 143–161.

Bachelard, Gaston. *The Poetics of Space*. Trans. Maria Jolas. Boston: Beacon Press, 1964.

Benjamin, Walter. *Charles Baudelaire: A Lyric Poet in the Era of High Capitalism*. Trans. Harry Zohn. London: Verso, 1973.

Bernstein, Gail Lee, ed. *Recreating Japanese Women, 1600–1945*. Berkeley: University of California Press, 1991.

Bestor, Theodore. *Neighborhood Tokyo*. Stanford, Calif.: Stanford University Press, 1989.

Betz, Phyllis. "Playing the Boys' Game." In Gosselin, ed., *Multicultural Detective Fiction*, 85–103.

Bourdieu, Pierre. *Distinction: A Social Critique of the Judgement of Taste*. Trans. Richard Nice. Cambridge, Mass.: Harvard University Press, 1984.

Boyer, M. Christine. "Crimes in and of the City: The *Femme Fatale* as Urban Allegory." In Algrest et al., eds., *The Sex of Architecture*, 97–118.

Buckley, Sandra. "The Foreign Devil Returns: Packaging Sexual Practice and Risk in Contemporary Japan." In *Sites of Desire, Economies of Pleasure: Sexualities in Asia and the Pacific.*, ed. Lenore Manderson and Margaret Jolly, 262–291. Chicago: University of Chicago Press, 1997.

Butler, Judith. "Merely Cultural." *Social Text* 52/53 (fall/winter 1997): 265–277.

Cawelti, John G. *Adventure, Mystery, and Romance: Formula Stories as Art and Popular Culture*. Chicago: University of Chicago Press, 1976.

Christ, Julie. "Conquering but Not Controlling: Yanagi Sōetsu and His Creation of the *Mingei* Discourse." Unpublished paper, March 1998.

Clammer, John. *Contemporary Urban Japan: A Sociology of Consumption*. Oxford: Blackwell, 1997.

Colomina, Beatriz, ed. *Sexuality and Space*. Princeton, N.J.: Princeton University Press, 1992.

Coward, Rosalind. *Patriarchal Precedents: Sexuality and Social Relations*. London: Routledge, 1983.

Coward, Rosalind, and Linda Semple. "Tracking Down the Past: Women and Detective Fiction." In *Genre and Women's Fiction in the Postmodern World*, ed. Helen Carr, 39–57. London: Pandora, 1989.

Crawford, Margaret. "Investigating the City—Detective Fiction as Urban Interpretation: A Reply to M. Christine Boyer." In Algrest et al., eds., *The Sex of Architecture*, 119–126.

Deutsche, Rosalyn. "*Chinatown*, Part IV? What Jake Forgets about Downtown." In Deutsche, *Evictions*, 245–253.

————. *Evictions: Art and Spatial Politics*. Cambridge, Mass.: MIT Press, 1997.

————. "Men in Space." In Deutsche, *Evictions*, 195–202.

Dilley, Kimberly J. *Busybodies, Meddlers, and Snoops: The Female Hero in Contemporary Women's Mysteries*. Westport, Conn.: Greenwood Press, 1998.

Douglas, Mary. *Purity and Danger: An Analysis of Concepts of Pollution and Taboo*. London: Routledge, 1966.

Dworkin, Andrea. *Intercourse*. New York: Free Press, 1987.

————. *Pornography: Men Possessing Women*. New York: Perigree Books, 1979.

"Experts Sought to Halt Loan Words." *Japan Times Online*, 26 June 2002 (http://www.japantimes.com).

Field, Norma. "Somehow: The Postmodern as Atmosphere." In Miyoshi and Harootunian, eds., *Postmodernism and Japan,* 169–188.

Firestone, Shulamith. *The Dialectic of Sex: The Case for Feminist Revolution.* New York: William Morrow, 1970.

Fitting, Peter. "Recent Feminist Utopias: World Building and Strategies for Social Changes." In *Mindscapes: The Geographies of Imagined Worlds,* ed. George E. Slusser and Eric S. Rabkin, 155–163. Carbondale, Ill.: Southern Illinois University Press, 1989.

Fowler, Edward. *San'ya Blues: Laboring Life in Contemporary Tokyo.* Ithaca, N.Y.: Cornell University Press, 1996.

Fraser, Nancy. "Rethinking the Public Sphere: A Contribution to the Critique of Actually Existing Democracy." In *Postmodernism and the Re-reading of Modernity,* ed. Francis Barker, Peter Hulme, and Margaret Iverson, 197–231. Manchester: Manchester University Press, 1992.

French, Howard A. "Hot New Marketing Concept: Mall as Memory Lane." *New York Times* (online edition), 7 January 2003.

———. "To Grandparents, English Word Trend Isn't 'Naisu.'" *New York Times* (online edition), 23 October 2002.

———. "A Resignation Is Cheered by Feminists around Japan." *New York Times,* 22 December 1999, A6.

Frühstück, Sabine. "Managing the Truth of Sex in Imperial Japan." *Journal of Asian Studies* 59, no. 2 (May 2000): 332–358.

Funabashi, Keiko. "Reassessing the Value of Children." *Japan Echo* 26, no. 1 (February 1999): 32–35.

Gallo, Gina. *Armed and Dangerous: Memoirs of a Chicago Policewoman.* New York: Forge, 2001.

Gaouette, Nicole. "Japan Abuzz over Sexual Harassment." *Christian Science Monitor* (online edition), 14 April 1998.

Garon, Sheldon. *Molding Japanese Minds: The State in Everyday Life.* Princeton, N.J.: Princeton University Press, 1997.

Glover, David. "The Stuff That Dreams Are Made Of: Masculinity, Femininity and the Thriller." In *Gender, Genre, and Narrative Pleasure,* ed. Derek Longhurst, 67–83. London: Unwin Hyman, 1989.

Gordon, Andrew, ed. *Postwar Japan as History.* Berkeley: University of California Press, 1993.

Gosselin, Adrienne Johnson, ed. *Multicultural Detective Fiction: Murder from the "Other" Side.* New York: Garland Press, 1999.

Gould, Carol C., ed. *Gender.* Atlantic Highlands, N.J.: Humanities Press, 1997.

Grafton, Sue, and Bruce Taylor. "G is for (Sue) Grafton: An Interview with the Creator of the Kinsey Millhone Private Eye Series." *Armchair Detective* 22, no. 1 (1989): 4–13.

Grosz, Elizabeth. "Bodies/Cities." In Colomina, ed., *Sexuality and Space,* 241–254.

———. "Women, Chora, Dwelling." In *Postmodern Cities and Spaces,* ed. Sophie Watson and Katherine Gibson, 47–58. Oxford: Blackwell, 1995.

Gunning, Tom. "Tracing the Individual Body: Photography, Detectives and Early Cinema." In *Cinema and the Invention of Modern Life,* ed. Leo Charney and Vanessa L. Schwartz, 15–45. Berkeley: University of California Press, 1995.

Hammett, Dashiell. *Red Harvest.* New York: Vintage, 1972.

Hara, Minako. "Lesbians and Sexual Self-Determination." In AMPO-*Japan Asia Quarterly Review,* ed., *Voices from the Japanese Women's Movement,* 129–132.

Harvey, David. *Justice, Nature, and the Geography of Difference.* Cambridge, Mass: Blackwell, 1996.

Hochschild, Arlie Russell. *The Time Bind: When Work Becomes Home and Home Becomes Work.* New York: Metropolitan Books, 1997.

Humm, Maggie. "Legal Aliens: Feminist Detective Fiction." In *Border Traffic: Strategies of Contemporary Women Writers,* 185–211. Manchester: Manchester University Press, 1991.

Igarashi, Akio. "'Inhabitant' or 'Resident': Japan's Metropolises at a Crossroads." Paper presented at the "Fora on Cities," Seoul, Korea, 10–13 December 1996.

Igarashi, Yoshikuni. "Edogawa Rampo and the Excess of Vision." Paper presented at the annual meeting of the Organization for Asian Research, Chicago, 29 March 2001.

Irigaray, Luce. *This Sex Which Is Not One.* Trans. Catherine Porter and Carolyn Burke. Ithaca, N.Y.: Cornell University Press, 1985.

Irons, Glenwood, ed. *Feminism in Women's Detective Fiction.* Toronto: University of Toronto Press, 1992.

Itoh, Kyoko. "Women Ask, 'What's in a Name?'" *Japan Times,* 6 March 1997, 14.

Ivy, Marilyn. *Discourses of the Vanishing: Modernity, Phantasm, Japan.* Chicago: University of Chicago Press, 1995.

————. "Formations of Mass Culture." In Gordon, ed. *Postwar Japan as History,* 239–258.

Iwao, Sumiko. *The Japanese Woman: Traditional Image and Changing Reality.* Cambridge, Mass.: Harvard University Press, 1993.

Jolivet, Muriel. *Japan: The Childless Society.* Trans. Anne-Marie Glasheen. New York: Routledge, 1997.

Kamada, Mamie. "The Awkward Writer: Opinions about and Influence of Matsumoto Seichō." *Japan Interpreter* 8, no. 2 (spring 1978): 149–170.

Karube, Keiko. "Sexual Harrassment at Japanese Colleges and Universities: Causes, Patterns and Some Countermeasures." Paper presented at the annual meeting of the Association for Asian Studies, Boston, 13 March 1999.

Kato, Hidetoshi. "Some Thoughts on Japanese Popular Culture." In Powers and Kato, eds., *Handbook of Japanese Popular Culture,* xvii–xviii.

Kelly, R. Gordon. *Mystery Fiction and Modern Life.* Jackson, Miss.: University of Mississippi Press, 1998.

Kelly, William. "Finding a Place in Metropolitan Japan: Ideologies, Institutions and Daily Life." In Gordon, ed., *Postwar Japan as History,* 189–238.

Kipnis, Laura. "(Male) Desire and (Female) Disgust: Reading *Hustler.*" In *Cultural Studies,* ed. Lawrence Grossberg, Cary Nelson, and Paula Treichler, 373–404. New York: Routledge, 1992.

Kittay, Eva Feder. "Pornography and the Erotics of Domination." In Gould, ed., *Gender,* 424–433.

Klein, Kathleen Gregory. *The Woman Detective: Gender and Genre.* Urbana: University of Illinois Press, 1988.

————, ed. *Women Times Three: Writers, Detectives, Readers.* Bowling Green, Ohio: Bowling Green State University Popular Press, 1995.

Lakoff, George, and Mark Johnson. *Metaphors We Live By.* Chicago: University of Chicago Press, 1980.

McCormack, Gavan. *The Emptiness of Japanese Affluence.* Armonk, N.Y.: M. E. Sharpe, 1996.

MacKinnon, Catharine A. "Feminism, Marxism, and Method of the State: An Agenda for Theory." *Signs* 7, no. 3 (spring 1982): 515–544.

————. "Only Words." In Gould, ed. *Gender,* 434–446.

Mandel, Ernst. *Delightful Murder: A Social History of the Crime Story.* Minneapolis: University of Minnesota Press, 1984.

Mason, Bobby Ann. "Nancy Drew: The Once and Future Prom Queen." In Irons, ed., *Feminism in Women's Detective Fiction,* 73–93.

Massey, Doreen. *Space, Place, and Gender.* Minneapolis: University of Minnesota Press, 1994.

Miyake, Yoshiko. "Doubling Expectations: Motherhood and Women's Factory Work under State Management in Japan in the 1930s and 1940s." In Bernstein, ed., *Recreating Japanese Women,* 267–295.

Miyoshi, Masao. *Offcenter: Power and Culture Relations between Japan and the United States.* Cambridge, Mass.: Harvard University Press, 1991.

Miyoshi, Masao, and H. D. Harootunian, eds. *Postmodernism and Japan.* Durham, N.C.: Duke University Press, 1991.

Moretti, Franco. "Clues." In *Signs Taken for Wonders: Essays in the Sociology of Literary Forms.* Trans. Susan Fischer, David Foryacs, and David Miller, 130–156. London: Verso, 1988.

Mulhern, Chieko Irie. "Japanese Harlequin Romances as Transcultural Woman's Fiction." *Journal of Japanese Studies* 48, no. 1 (February 1989): 50–70.

Munt, Sally R. *Murder by the Book? Feminism and the Crime Novel.* New York: Routledge, 1994.

Nickerson, Catherine Ross. *The Web of Iniquity: Early Detective Fiction by American Women.* Durham, N.C.: Duke University Press, 1998.

Nishiyama, Yayoi. "The Hidden World of the Parturition Hut." *Feminist International* 2 (1980): 64–66.

Nolte, Sharon, and Sally Ann Hastings. "The Meiji State's Policy toward Women." In Bernstein, ed., *Recreating Japanese Women,* 151–174.

Oe Kenzaburo. "Japan's Dual Identity: A Writer's Dilemma." In Miyoshi and Harootunian, eds., *Postmodernism and Japan,* 189–213.

Ogasawara, Yuko. *Office Ladies and Salaried Men: Power, Gender, and Work in Japanese Companies.* Berkeley: University of California Press, 1998.

Ohinata, Masami. "The Mystique of Motherhood: A Key to Understanding Social Change and Family Problems in Japan." Trans. Timothy John Phelan. In

Japanese Women: New Feminist Perspectives on the Past, Present, and Future, ed. Kumiko Fujimura-Fanselow and Atsuko Kameda, 199–211. New York: Feminist Press at the City University of New York, 1995.

Ortner, Sherry B. "Is Female to Nature as Male Is to Culture?" In *Making Gender: The Politics and Erotics of Culture,* 21–42. Boston: Beacon Press, 1996.

Pateman, Carole. "Feminist Critiques of the Public/Private Dichotomy." In *The Disorder of Women: Democracy, Feminism, and Political Theory,* 118–140. Stanford, Calif.: Stanford University Press, 1989.

Pederson-Krag, Geraldine. "Detective Stories and the Primal Scene." In *Poetics of Murder: Detective Fiction and Literary Theory,* ed. Glenn W. Most and William W. Stowe, 13–20. New York: Harcourt, Brace, and Jovanovich, 1983.

Pflugfelder, Gregory M. *Cartographies of Desire: Male-Male Sexuality in Japanese Discourse, 1600–1950.* Berkeley: University of California Press, 1999.

Porter, Dennis. *The Pursuit of Crime: Art and Ideology in Detective Fiction.* New Haven, Conn.: Yale University Press, 1981.

Powers, Richard Gid, and Hidetoshi Kato, eds. *Handbook of Japanese Popular Culture.* New York: Greenwood Press, 1989.

Prindle, Tamae K., trans. and ed. *Made in Japan and Other Japanese "Business Novels."* Armonk, N.Y.: M. E. Sharpe, 1989.

Reddy, Maureen. *Sisters in Crime: Feminism and the Crime Novel.* New York: Continuum, 1988.

Reekie, Gail. "Changes in the Adamless Eden: The Spatial and Sexual Transformation of a Brisbane Department Store, 1930–1990." In *Lifestyle Shopping: The Subject of Consumption,* ed. Rob Shields, 170–194. London: Routledge, 1992.

Reitman, Valerie. "Japan's New Growth Industry: Schoolgirl Prostitution." *Wall Street Journal,* 2 October 1996, A8.

Robertson, Jennifer. "Dying to Tell: Sexuality and Suicide in Imperial Japan." *Signs* 25, no. 1 (autumn 1999): 1–35.

———. *Native and Newcomer: Making and Remaking a Japanese City.* Berkeley: University of California Press, 1991.

———. *Takarazuka: Sexual Politics and Popular Culture in Modern Japan.* Berkeley: University of California Press, 1998.

———. "Yoshiya Nobuko: Out and Outspoken in Practice and Prose." In *The Human Tradition in Modern Japan,* ed. Anne Walthall, 155–174. Wilmington, Del.: SR Books, 2002.

Roden, Donald. "Taisho Culture and the Problem of Gender Ambivalence." In *Culture and Identity: Japanese Intellectuals during the Interwar Years,* ed. J. Thomas Rimer, 37–55. Princeton, N.J.: Princeton University Press, 1990.

Rose, Gillian. "Place and Identity: A Sense of Place." In *A Place in the World?* ed. Doreen Massey and Pat Jess, 87–132. London: Open University Press, 1995.

Rose, Margaret A. *Parody: Ancient, Modern and Postmodern.* Cambridge: Cambridge University Press, 1993.

Ross, Kristin. *Fast Cars, Clean Bodies.* Cambridge, Mass.: MIT Press, 1995.

Roth, Marty. *Fair and Foul Play: Reading Genre in Classic Detective Fiction.* Athens, Ga.: University of Georgia Press, 1995.

Rutherford, Jonathan. "A Place Called Home: Identity and the Cultural Politics of Difference." In *Identity: Community, Culture, Difference,* ed. Jonathan Rutherford, 18–35. London: Lawrence and Wishart, 1990.

Sanger, David E. "Babies, Rice Farms, and Diplomas." *New York Times,* 20 June 1990, A24.

———. "Tokyo Official Ties Birth Decline to Education." *New York Times,* 14 June 1990, A9.

Schreiber, Mark. *Shocking Crimes of Postwar Japan.* Tokyo: Yenbooks, 1996.

Seaman, Amanda. "Modeling Masako: Commodities and the Construction of a Modern Princess." *Chicago Anthropology Exchange* 21 (spring 1995): 35–70.

Seidensticker, Edward. *Low City, High City: Tokyo from Edo to the Earthquake.* New York: Knopf, 1983.

———. "The 'Pure' and the 'In-Between' in Modern Japanese Theories of the Novel." *Harvard Journal of Asian Studies* 16 (1966): 174–186.

Shinpo, Hirohisa. "Parallel Lives of Japan's Master Detectives." *Japan Quarterly* 47, no. 4 (October–December 2000): 52–57.

Sievers, Sharon. *Flowers in Salt: The Beginnings of Feminist Consciousness in Modern Japan.* Stanford, Calif.: Stanford University Press, 1983.

Silver, Mark. "Crime and Mystery Writing in Japan." In *The Oxford Companion to Crime and Mystery Writing,* ed. Rosemary Herbert, 241–243. Oxford: Oxford University Press, 1999.

———. "Purloined Letters: Cultural Borrowing and Japanese Crime Literature." Ph.D. dissertation, Yale University, 1999.

Skov, Lise. "Fashion Trends, Japonisme and Postmodernism." In Treat, ed., *Contemporary Japan and Popular Culture,* 137–168.

Steinberg, Jessica. "The Homeowner's Land." *New York Times,* 5 August 1998, C1.

Stewart, Kathleen. "Nostalgia, a Polemic." *Cultural Anthropology* 3, no. 3 (1988): 227–241.

Stewart, Susan. *On Longing: Narratives of the Miniature, the Gigantic, the Souvenir, the Collection.* Durham, N.C.: Duke University Press, 1993.

Strecher, Matthew. "Purely Mass or Massively Pure?" *Monumenta Nipponica* 51, no. 3 (autumn 1996): 357–374.

Taira, Koji. "The Dialectics of Economic Growth, National Power and Distributive Struggles." In Gordon, ed., *Postwar Japan as History,* 167–189.

Tanaka, Yukiko. "Hirabayashi Taiko." In *To Live and Write: Selections by Japanese Women Writers, 1913-1938,* ed. Yukiko Tanaka, 65–73. Seattle: Seal Press, 1987.

Todorov, Tzvetan. *Poetics of Prose.* Trans. Richard Howard. Ithaca, N.Y.: Cornell University Press, 1977.

Thompson, Jon. *Fiction, Crime, and Empire: Clues to Modernity and Postmodernity.* Urbana: University of Illinois Press, 1993.

Tomc, Sandra. "Questing Women: The Feminist Mystery after Feminism." In Irons, ed., *Feminism in Women's Detective Fiction,* 46–63.

Treat, John Whittier. *Great Mirrors Shattered: Homosexuality, Orientalism, and Japan.* New York: Oxford University Press, 1999.

_____. "Yoshimoto Banana's *Kitchen*, or the Cultural Logic of Japanese Consumerism." In *Women, Media, and Consumption in Japan*, ed. Lise Skov and Brian Moeran, 274–298. Honolulu: University of Hawai'i Press, 1996.

_____. "Yoshimoto Banana Writes Home: The *Shōjo* in Japanese Popular Culture." In Treat. ed., *Contemporary Japan and Popular Culture*, 275–308.

_____, ed. *Contemporary Japan and Popular Culture*. Honolulu: University of Hawai'i Press, 1996.

Tsunoda Yukiko. "Sexual Harassment in Japan: Recent Legal Decisions." Trans. Yokokawa Muro Mariko. *U.S.-Japan Women's Journal*, English Supplement, no. 5 (1993): 52–68.

Tsurumi, E. Patricia. *Factory Girls: Women in the Thread Mills of Meiji Japan*. Princeton, N.J.: Princeton University Press, 1990.

Uno, Kathleen S. "Death of 'Good Wife, Wise Mother.'" In Gordon, ed., *Postwar Japan as History*, 293–322.

_____. "Women and Changes in the Household Division of Labor." In Bernstein, ed., *Recreating Japanese Women*, 17–41.

Vanacker, Sabine. "V. I. Warshawski, Kinsey Millhone, and Kay Scarpetta: Creating a Feminist Detective Hero." In *Criminal Proceedings: The American Crime Novel*, ed. Peter Messent, 62–86. London: Pluto Press, 1997.

Vogel, Ezra F. *Japan's New Middle Class*. 2d ed. Berkeley: University of California Press, 1971.

Walder, Dennis, ed. *The Realist Novel*. London: Routledge, 1995.

Walkowitz, Judith. *City of Dreadful Delight: Narrative of Sexual Danger in Late-Victorian London*. Chicago: University of Chicago Press, 1992.

Walton, Priscilla L. "Identity Politics: April Smith's *North of Montana* and Rochelle Majer Krich's *Angel of Death*." In *Detective Fiction and Diversity*, ed. Kathleen Gregory Klein, 130–143. Bowling Green, Ohio: Bowling Green State University Popular Press, 1999.

Walton, Priscilla L., and Manina Jones. *Detective Agency: Women Rewriting the Hard-Boiled Tradition*. Berkeley: University of California Press, 1999.

van der Wetering, Janwillem. *The Hollow-Eyed Angel*. New York: Soho, 1996.

Wigley, Mark. "Untitled: The Unhousing of Gender." In Colomina, ed., *Sexuality and Space*, 327–389.

Williams, Linda. *Hard Core: Power, Pleasure and the "Frenzy of the Visible."* Berkeley: University of California Press, 1999.

Wilson, Ann. "The Female Dick and the Crisis of Heterosexuality." In Irons, ed., *Feminism in Women's Detective Fiction*, 148–156.

Winston, Robert P., and Nancy C. Mellerski. *The Public Eye: Ideology and the Police Procedural*. New York: St. Martin's Press, 1992.

Woods, Paula L. *Inner City Blues*. New York: Ballantine, 1999.

Yoshida, Kazuo. "Japanese Mystery Literature." In Powers and Kato, eds., *Handbook of Japanese Popular Culture*, 275–299.

Yunomae, Tomoko. "Commodified Sex (Sexism): Japan's Pornographic Culture." In *AMPO-Japan Asia Quarterly Review*, ed., *Voices of the Japanese Women's Movement*, 101–110.

Index

88–90, 91, 112, 114–115; social
critique and, 2, 8, 25, 61, 141, 145;
and space, 120–122. *See also* hard-
boiled detective fiction; *honkaku-ha*
mysteries; mystery; *noir*; police
procedural; *shakai-ha* mysteries;
women's detective fiction
Deutsche, Rosalyn, 23, 134
Doyle, Arthur Conan, 3, 4, 120
dystopia, 135–136, 137, 147

Edogawa Rampo, 4, 6, 8, 9, 10,
114–115, 120, 153n. 38; and
ero-guro-nansensu, 114–115; works:
"Imomushi" (The caterpillar), 8;
Kuro Tokage (Black Lizard), 115;
"Ni-sen dōka" (The two-sen copper
coin), 4; "Yaneura no sanposha"
(The stroller in the attic), 7
Enchi Fumiko, 105, 170n. 43
enjo kōsai, 46, 170n. 44
Equal Employment Opportunity Law,
62, 63, 124
Eto Jun, 50

family, 29, 119, 137, 147; and
community, 41, 54, 74, 122, 137,
139; and identity, 50–52; problems
with, 36, 69–71; role in detective
fiction, 24, 69, 89
femme fatale, 23, 25, 88, 91, 104, 113,
117; and *homme fatal*, 100, 117
Field, Norma, 50, 51, 99
Fowler, Edward, 55
Freeman, Austin, 3
furusato, 34, 48, 50

Gaboriau, Émile, 3
Garon, Sheldon, 137
gaze, 24, 91–92, 97, 100
gender, 29, 44, 57, 74, 116, 134, 146;
in detective fiction, 23, 49, 122;
divisions, 18, 64–66; and space,
122–124, 129

Grafton, Sue, 13, 22, 25, 66, 88, 92,
117–118
Green, Anna Katharine, 3
Grosz, Elizabeth, 122–123, 133

hara obi, 129; photograph of, 132
hard-boiled detective fiction, 8, 9, 22,
25, 88; female detectives in, 86, 89;
lesbian detectives in, 102; use of
first person in, 91; women in early
works, 23–24
Harvey, David, 55
Hirabayashi Hatsunosuke, 3
Hirabayashi Taiko, 5
Hirano Ken, 10–11
Hiratsuka Raichō, 5
Hochschild, Arlie Russell, 69
home, 37, 39, 49, 69, 138; and the
butsudan, 37; as domestic sphere,
123, 172n. 16; isolation in, 69–71;
as source of identity, 47, 48, 76
homosexuality, 115–117, 146. *See also*
lesbianism
honkaku-ha mysteries, 8, 9, 12, 27,
153n. 38

Ichijō Eiko, 5
identity, 2, 13, 43, 50–53, 145; and
community, 34, 54–55, 70; and
consumption, 34, 36–37, 43, 46, 71;
and the home, 29, 36, 47, 48; and
sexuality, 105, 111; theft of, 28–30,
36–37, 39, 47
Imamura Aya, 21
Irigaray, Luce, 112
Itō Sei, 10–11
Ivy, Marilyn, 45, 50

Jolivet, Muriel, 139–140
junbungaku, 11, 12, 27, 81, 155n. 56;
and detective fiction, 10–11

Karatani Kōjin, 3
Kasai Kiyoshi, 12, 147, 153n. 38

About the Author

Amanda Seaman received her Ph.D. from the University of Chicago. She is presently assistant professor of Japanese literature at the University of Massachusetts, Amherst.

Production Notes for
Seaman/BODIES OF EVIDENCE

Cover and interior design and composition
by Janette Thompson (Jansom)

Set in Sabon, with display type in Dax

Printing and binding by The Maple-Vail
Book Manufacturing Group

Printed on 60# Text White Opaque, 426 ppi